YOUR
SECONDARY
SCHOOL DIRECT
TOOLKIT

YOUR
SECONDARY
SCHOOL DIRECT
TOOLKIT

JOHN KEENAN & ANDY HIND

Los Angeles | London | New Delhi
Singapore | Washington DC | Melbourne

Los Angeles I London I New Delhi
Singapore I Washington DC I Melbourne

SAGE Publications Ltd
1 Oliver's Yard
55 City Road
London EC1Y 1SP

SAGE Publications Inc.
2455 Teller Road
Thousand Oaks, California 91320

SAGE Publications India Pvt Ltd
Unit No 323-333, Third Floor, F-Block
International Trade Tower, Nehru Place
New Delhi 110 019

SAGE Publications Asia-Pacific Pte Ltd
3 Church Street
#10-04 Samsung Hub
Singapore 049483

Editor: James Clark
Assistant Editor: Diana Alves
Production Editor: Neelu Sahu
Copyeditor: Diana Chambers
Proofreader: Rosemary Campbell
Indexer: Michael Allerton
Marketing Manager: Lorna Patkai
Cover Design: Naomi Robinson
Typeset by KnowledgeWorks Global Ltd
Printed in the UK

Library of Congress Control Number: 2022943380

British Library Cataloguing in Publication data

A catalogue record for this book is available from the British Library

ISBN 978-1-5297-8139-7

ISBN 978-1-5297-8138-0 (pbk)

At SAGE we take sustainability seriously. Most of our products are printed in the UK using responsibly sourced papers and boards. When we print overseas we ensure sustainable papers are used as measured by the PREPS grading system. We undertake an annual audit to monitor our sustainability.

CONTENTS

ABOUT THE AUTHORS

John Keenan taught English in secondary schools, sixth form and Further Education before moving to Higher Education. He taught at Leicester University, Coventry University, Worcester University and now Newman University, where he is Senior Lecturer in education. Previous roles included lead tutor of Teach First English for the West Midlands, co-ordinator of an Advertising and Media degree and lead tutor of PGCE English. John has a research focus on teacher education and Further Education and supervises doctoral students researching these areas. He has published journal articles and book chapters in the field of education and has co-edited a book on College-based Higher Education.

Andy Hind worked as a science teacher in Leeds and Bradford before moving to the University of Leeds as a researcher of science education. Andy then returned to secondary teaching as Head of Science in a secondary school in Leeds. He moved on to work in Initial Teacher Education as a science tutor for both the Open University and Manchester University. Andy moved to Newman University in 2010 where he taught on both undergraduate and postgraduate programmes before his current role as Head of Secondary Teacher Education at Warwick University. He is also a member of the Universities' Council for the Education of Teachers and sits on national steering committees, helping to define the future direction of teacher training.

ACKNOWLEDGEMENTS

Thank you, Rebecca and Blossom, for your love and encouragement – John.

Thank you, Sarah, Rebecca and Rory, for your unfailing support and kindness, especially in the run-up to deadlines – Andy.

We would like to thank the following contributors for allowing us to publish their work, produced during their teacher training year: Aisha Ahmed, Luke Amos, Arte Artemiou, Sidra Bi, Dan Bevan, Dale Booton, Joel Collins, Gemma Durnford, Flick Ellis, Barwago Ismail, Ellen Jones, Sam McDonagh, Leaon McDonald. Our thanks are extended to all our students, past and present, because this book contains their experiences, and we learned so much from being part of their lives during a year of ups, downs, and a deep desire to just get more sleep. We also thank our editor, Diana Alves, for her ever-positive support and enthusiasm.

INTRODUCTION

The American psychologist Abraham Maslow wrote:

I suppose it is tempting, if the only tool you have is a hammer, to treat everything as if it were a nail. (1966: 16)

This book is about making sure you go into the classroom with more than a metaphorical hammer in your hands. As DIY unenthusiasts, we can testify to the dangers of approaching any job around the home without appropriate tools and training to use them. For example, one of us, having discovered a faulty toilet cistern, attempted to fix it, fuelled only by self-belief; this resulted in standing in a foot of water, hand on a gushing part (the name of which is still unknown) of the cistern while realising that the tap to turn the house water off was located somewhere downstairs. If knowing how to fix a simple toilet cistern poses such a challenge, how much more do we need to know about the ultra-complex world of teaching?

The problem with the metaphor of tools and toolkits is that it just seems too easy – have this, and this will result. When dealing with people, this is never the case. A screwdriver will probably not slip out of the room when you need it, but a child in your class may do so: we need to think of this toolkit as containing living, breathing, changing and moving tools. To rigidly fix in place a strategy for dealing with a situation is to take the right approach in what may well be the wrong circumstances. Raising your hand and counting down to silence may work well with top set Year 7, but with bottom set Year 10, you could end up looking like the man in Stevie Smith's (1957) poem, 'Not Waving but Drowning' – a bit lost in all the noise with your hand in the air.

We will introduce you to our experience as long-standing teachers and teacher-trainers with over 50 years of experience of schools to share. We will share the experience of having delivered School Direct (SD) training in five universities and, through connections via external examining and informal links, many more. We will also select the best of what we have witnessed from the evidence-base – the writing on, about or around education. Our approach is conversational in style (albeit, in the circumstances, a little one-way); questioning and open to being – hoping to be – questioned is our approach. This might be frustrating, as while it is a 'how-to-do' book, neither of us thinks that we can give you a straightforward recipe for success. It is very easy to write with certainty – much in the style of a *How to Get Rich in Three Easy Stages* book which starts with the advice on how to write a *How to Get Rich in Three Easy Stages* book. There is no certainty in teaching and the answer to most questions about whether this or that approach will work is, 'it depends'. Should you be strict at the start? It depends – on the class, on who you are, the school, the time of day, the needs of the pupils in the room.

This book acts as a catch-all, all-you-need volume – a **PGCE** course in itself. You can skip the philosophy and even the attempts at humour if you like, and move to the bullet points as these will contain the 'what-to-do'. We hope you won't, though. SD training teachers do not always get the same level of theoretical and philosophical (or pedagogical) teaching and time that those on some other routes do. Due to the nature of being sent 'directly to school', there is going to be a practice-first expectation. Practical experience is a strength of the SD routes, but there is a need to balance 'doing' with 'informed thinking'. You may even have a suspicion of educational theory – we hope not (and because you are reading this, we suspect not). We find that some SD training teachers do, such as the one who habitually sits at the back of our class playing on their phone. In an attempt to refocus this individual, we asked a question about educational theory and were faced with a 'Well, what I did last week …' response, before returning to their phone as if they did not need to know and, furthermore, as if those who just talk about teaching could take the answer, put it in their pipes and smoke it. To counter the possibility of this type of response, we have tried to make sure this book is useful, functional and focused on what can genuinely improve your practice. It is 'practice-informing research and theory' (Goodson, 2003: 123). For some, even this type of theory is seen as a luxury that training teachers cannot afford. If this is the case, it is to their detriment, as they become trained in the system as it is, without the understanding that it was not always so and will not always be so. It is not future-proofing to replicate current practice, and it is even more dangerous, we feel, to keep changing practice, responding to the pressures from school and government policy without thinking, judging and negotiating.

This book gives you space and permission to question what happens in school, and the theoretical tools to do so from an informed position. We care that you care enough to want to engage with your chosen profession. From our experience, most SD training teachers want this very much because they do care, and will take all the help they can get. This book has been written to allow this to happen and to make the SD experience more fulfilling by enriching your practice with theory to help make sense of your experience. You are neither the first nor the last to go through a training year, but are entering into a 'well-trodden path'. It may not seem like it when you are faced with the prospect of engaging 9Y on a wet Wednesday afternoon, but in fact, this set-up has been experienced millions of times. To realise that your experience has long been shared, you need only to read 'Last Lesson of the Afternoon' written in 1913 by former teacher D.H. Lawrence, who wearily resolves to endure the the last minutes of the lesson until he will be saved by the bell. Nonetheless, your position as teacher and the nature of the pupils are both unique to the moment, because never before have you been in the room at that time and never before have those individual children. You are new to this situation and the 'tools' presented are here to help you in that space and that time with those children.

While we very much hope that the contents of this book are applicable to all those training to teach in school and interested in education, it is directly aimed at secondary SD training teachers in England. The UK is a devolved country, meaning that each part has its own education system and rules. England, Scotland, Wales and Northern Ireland act differently and have differing curricula. If you live in Scotland, for example, you get the benefit of a free PGCE course and, if you qualify, even a **maintenance loan** (Teach in Scotland, 2022). There are different rules for teaching in Scotland (GTCS, 2022), besides which, Scotland does not offer an SD route. Similarly in Northern Ireland, there is no SD route and training is university-led only, either on a four-year B.Ed. or one-year PGCE (UCAS, 2022). The Welsh government, likewise, acts independently and has updated its teaching professional standards and curriculum (GOV.WALES, 2022), including such forward-thinking ideas as **sustainable development** alongside learning Welsh language and culture.

Education theory is chock-full of Dead White Males (DWMs) and this book has been produced by two non-dead ones (at the time of writing). The attribution of what are often common-sense ideas to males who were given their status by a patriarchal power system is something we both challenge and yet are forced to replicate. The challenge is to recognise the biases and promote equality. The replication is through use as, for example, Bruner (Jerome), Sweller (John) and Rosenshine (Barak) dominate the thinking in school about memory and retention. Often, their contributions are merely metaphors or visualisations – as 'toolkit' is – easy ways to explain complex ideas. All these men-with-power did is provide us with a way of more easily understanding something complex – which pretty much explains what this book is about.

For all the tried-and-tested educational approaches and theories presented, we recognise that neither we (the currently undead males) nor they (the DWMs) have the answer. You do. We present the 'kit' (this book) with the 'tools' (approaches to education, information about the system and advice about how to make sense of it) and invite you to make something purposeful, extraordinary and life-changing. With these tools, in this kit, are you a craftsperson? An artisan? A bodger of the job? At times, we all are 'bodgers' and part of this book's tone and approach is to tell you that this is okay. You are more than allowed to make mistakes: you must. The bumper sticker 'I have learned so much from my mistakes, I am thinking of making a few more' should be firmly stuck on the front of this book. There is an ancient story of men without sight who came across an elephant, each grabbing hold of part of it. The one with the leg was convinced that he had found a trunk of a tree; the one with the tusk was convinced that he had found a spear, and the one with the tail was convinced that it was a rope. As the poet John Godfrey Saxe (1872) retold the story, 'Though each was partly in the right/ They all were in the wrong!' It is like this with education theory – someone gets hold of part of it, finds an approach or a theory, but does not see the whole system or circumstances, so their insight is only relevant in some cases. The ideas we present will both be right and wrong: they will work in some circumstances and not in others; they will work for another teacher but not for you. As training teachers, you are trying to make sense of what is new and we hope to widen your experience to let you see more of the whole elephant – if this is not too strange an idea.

The book tries to address key issues which will face you while you are training to be a teacher.

- Chapter 1 focuses on the history of your chosen SD route, how it differs from other courses and the particular experiences, needs and challenges it brings.
- Chapter 2 is about well-being, and includes a 'heavy steer' towards encouraging you to be a reflective practitioner.
- One question we ask when interviewing prospective training teachers is: 'What do teachers do apart from teach?' Chapter 3 gives you such details. We review how to manage the workload of administration, meetings, contacting parents/carers, checking the virtual learning environment, assembly, form, bus duty, playground duty, detentions, after-school clubs, holiday revision sessions, continuing professional development, and more.
- Going into a school without an understanding of the general and specific laws which governs your practice is not a good idea, so Chapter 4 is about the regulatory framework of teaching.
- Chapter 5 addresses lesson planning and implementation.
- Chapter 6 gives strategies for managing behaviour in the classroom.
- Chapter 7 explores how to adapt your teaching to the pupils in the room.
- Chapter 8 focuses on how to assess learning.
- Literacy and **numeracy** are the focuses of Chapter 9, with a message that you are a teacher of both, alongside your subject specialism.
- Parents and carers are crucial to the process of learning for each child is the message of Chapter 10, which gives advice about bringing them into the learning process.
- Chapters 11 and 12 on curriculum and extracurricular activities guide you regarding the nature of secondary teaching. They explore what it means to be a subject specialist, and consider ways in which your role can extend beyond this to offer service to the life of the school.
- Finally, Chapter 13 concludes the book with a message about principled practice and how your moral standpoint, or ethos, can be a driving force through your career in teaching.

Throughout the book, we recognise the frustrations you may encounter on a day-to-day basis. You have limited time and worse, limited 'brain-time' when you can stop, think and take stock of what is happening. Taking some of your limited time to read this book, alongside all you have to do, will save you time in the long run. We present the experience of centuries of learning about your profession, from Socrates onwards, distilled, we hope, into a manageable form. In each chapter, we advise you on places you can go to study more on each topic, include reflection points to help you to think about what each topic means for your practice, and offer an example of someone who has done this ahead of you. In the end, teaching is this: you and a group of children in a room in a particular time and space with a curriculum to teach and learn. This book cannot protect you from this reality nor the problems you may face (unless you take it in with you and hold it in front of your body to bat away the projectiles). You are the master of your fate, which is a satisfying place to be. All the theory of the minds of all the people in the world cannot change what the psychologist William James knew about the subject he helped to create:

> You make a great, a very great mistake, if you think psychology, being the science of the mind's laws, is something from which you can deduce definite programmes and schemes and methods of instruction for immediate schoolroom use. Psychology is a science, and teaching is an art. (James, 1899: 14)

REFERENCES

Goodson, I. (2003) *Professional Knowledge, Professional Lives*. Maidenhead: Open University Press.

GOV.WALES (2022) *Curriculum for Wales*. Available from: https://hwb.gov.wales/curriculum-for-wales/summary-of-legislation

GTCS (2022) *The General Teaching Council for Scotland*. Available from: www.gtcs.org.uk

James, W. (1899) *Talks To Teachers on Psychology: And to Students on Some of Life's Ideals*. Available from: www.gutenberg.org/files/16287/16287-h/16287-h.htm

Lawrence, D.H. (2012) *Complete Poetry of D. H. Lawrence*. Hastings: Delphi Classics.

Maslow, A. (1966) *The Psychology of Science: A Reconnaissance*. New York: Harper & Row.

Rudd, T. and Goodson, I. (2014) 'Studying historical periodisation: Towards a concept of refraction', in A. Teodora and M. Guiherme (eds), *European and Latin American Higher Education Between Mirrors*. Rotterdam: Sense. pp. 137–54.

Saxe, J.G. (1872) *'The Blind Men and the Elephant'*. Available from: www.poemhunter.com/poem/the-blind-man-and-the-elephant

Smith, S. (2015) *The Collected Poems and Drawings of Stevie Smith*. London: Faber & Faber.

Spender, D. (1980) *Man Made Language*. London: Routledge & Kegan Paul.

Teach in Scotland (2022) Available from: https://teachinscotland.scot/become-a-teacher/funding-and-fees

UCAS (2022) *Train to Teach in Northern Ireland*. Available from: www.ucas.com/postgraduate/teacher-training/train-teach-northern-ireland

1
THE SCHOOL DIRECT TRAINING ROUTE

WHAT THIS CHAPTER WILL COVER:

- Political context of School Direct
- School Direct routes into teaching
- Pathways through the course
- *Teachers' Standards* (Parts One and Two)
- Core Content Framework
- Mentoring

INTRODUCTION

This chapter focuses on the route into teaching you chose to take. It explains the policy and governmental motivations to move teacher training into schools rather than at colleges or universities. There is no single SD route, so the different ways your course may be set up are explained along with the likely ways you can move to a successful conclusion. Part of this success will depend on your fulfilling the necessary criteria for **Qualified Teacher Status** – the *Teachers' Standards*. These are explained and explored. The framework for teacher training – the **Core Content Framework** – is also examined, because this will determine the kind of theory you will need to engage with alongside the expected teaching approaches. You will also need to build a positive working relationship with your mentor who will be essential to whether you succeed or not, so help in this direction concludes the chapter.

POLITICAL CONTEXT OF SCHOOL DIRECT

School Direct is, in some ways, not very different from the first attempt at formalising teacher training at Battersea Normal School in 1841. This established the first residential school for those aged 18+ who wanted to be teachers, with a pattern of training alongside school practice. Even the private funding model is not new as, in the nineteenth century, charities, churches and voluntary organisations were part of the ad hoc way that schools were run. This was changed by the 1870 **Forster Act**, the creation of a **Board of Education** in 1899, and the 1902 **Education Act** which established a national system of schooling alongside training for teachers, paid for by taxation and administered by regional governments. The **McNair Report** (1944) established the structure of schools which persists today, including the terminology of 'primary' and 'secondary', and advised the creation of more teacher training centres, many of which went on to become today's universities. This report is also a useful reminder that all government policy is – and always was – subject not only to the knowledge but also to the ignorance of the times: the maintenance grants were set at £43 for a man but £34 for a woman. It did, however, remedy a prior gender limitation: previously, when women married, they had been expected to resign as teachers – hence, perhaps, the lasting word 'Miss' for a female teacher. The McNair Report (1944) gives us a useful snapshot of an earlier era of teacher training. The system of training it describes is recognisable today, with universities training through four-year graduate courses and 83 training colleges providing two-year courses. Also, of the 6,500 teachers qualifying each year, most were women (4,500 women and 2,000 men; 60 of the 83 training colleges were for women only). This phenomenon persists today with 39 per cent of secondary training teachers being male (GOV.UK, 2021).

A major change to teacher training came from the New Labour government (1997–2010) which claimed, 'Our top priority was, is and always will be education, education, education' (Blair, 2001). Reflecting on this speech 20 years later, former Prime Minister Tony Blair considered these word to be not only a soundbite, but also 'a call to action and a re-setting of national priorities' (Blair and Adonis, 2021). The New Labour government did just this, changing many established systems, signalling 'The end of an era' (Furlong, 2005: 120). The era that New Labour ended was mainly for the universities and teacher training colleges that had dominated the sector in the latter half of the twentieth century. The reforms also revisioned the whole idea of a teacher as a 'professional' – from someone who is deemed worthy of holding a position of respect and authority with an inner core of moral and behavioural standards into someone who is 'managed' (Furlong, 2005: 120).

The position of a teacher as a free-thinking professional, who could decide what to teach and when, had been eroded by previous Conservative governments between 1979 and 1997 – in particular, by the **Education Reform Act** of 1988. This Act launched a **National Curriculum** and an organisation that would enforce government requirements with respect to schools, training providers and teachers: **Ofsted**. By the time New Labour came to power, much of the 'spadework' had been done to allow a new system to be introduced, particularly with the 1994 Education Act which established a governing body – the Teacher Training Agency – to oversee and fund training providers. Politicians use education as a battleground for power, knowing that here they can impose their ideas on a new generation through a controllable force:

> If a generation of teachers was to be raised who would support the new Conservative world, then the reform of teacher education and training was of paramount importance. (Furlong, 2005: 122)

Just as the Conservatives had done, New Labour imposed their ideas onto education with what they saw as a 'third way' (Giddens, 2000). This was individualised capitalism – each person would be allowed a route to economic success, but with a focus on social equality. While it was not advertised as such, there was the suspicion that this 'third way' was 'warmed over neoliberalism' (Giddens, 2000: 25) or, as Andrew Hindmoor called it, 'neoliberalism with a better marketing strategy' (2018: 7). **Neoliberalism** uses state power to impose 'freedom' from group or collective behaviour – by force if necessary:

> Neoliberalism is ... a theory of political economic practices that proposes that human well-being can best be advanced by liberating individual entrepreneurial freedoms and skills within an institutional framework characterized by strong private property rights, free markets, and free trade. The role of the state is to create and preserve an institutional framework appropriate to such practices. (Harvey, 2007: 22)

Whether or not New Labour was neoliberalist, it acted in this way when it 'liberated' teacher training by bringing in new providers. It controlled this 'free' market by giving these providers restrictions as to how they could behave by performance criteria to fulfil and targets to reach.

As part of this 'liberalisation' of teacher training, New Labour launched the direct forerunner to SD, the Graduate Teacher Programme (GTP), in 1998. It was aimed at mature learners who wanted to try out teaching (GTP, n.d.) as paid, **unqualified teachers**, and learn 'on the job' (TNA, n.d.). **Teach First** was also launched in the New Labour years alongside the promotion of School Centred Initial Teacher Training institution (SCITTs) where schools could bypass universities and train their teachers in-house.

The Conservative–Liberal Coalition government of 2010–15 made no secret of its desire to continue the process of private companies and schools running teacher training, in opposition to a university-led training system. The then Education Secretary, Michael Gove, baited ideological opponents with anti-university rhetoric, which resulted in 100 university lecturers in education criticising the changes in the letters page of *The Independent* newspaper. Gove then gleefully attacked what he saw as opponents to the reforms:

> Who are the guilty men and women who have deprived a generation of the knowledge they need? Who are the modern Enemies of Promise? … They are all academics who have helped run the university departments of education responsible for developing curricula and teacher training courses. (Gove, 2013)

Then, for good measure, Gove threw in an insult 'bomb', calling such university academics 'The Blob, in thrall to Sixties ideologies' (Gove, 2013). This was an expression of the underlying ideological ire that drove the Coalition government to present the Schools White Paper (DfE, 2010) introducing 'teaching schools'. Gove is often credited (or blamed) for the changes that took place in the education system, including the 2014 National Curriculum, but no single person can put through such legislation and behind his rhetoric there was little difference to what had been in place since 1979 – centralised control of education and acts aimed at limiting university autonomy or, as they would have it, 'weeding out poor **teacher training providers**' (GOV.UK, 2012a).

SD was launched in this political context:

> take the very best schools, ones that are already working to improve other schools, and put them in charge of teacher training and professional development for the whole system. (GOV.UK, 2012a)

Training for SD did not move wholly to schools. What actually happened was that SD became a close partnership between **teacher training providers** (which were mainly universities) and schools. The strengths of each sector were embraced. It became a partnership which created training teachers with a sense of belonging to both institutions and the best of both worlds. The government aimed for half of training teachers to be allocated directly to schools and this was largely realised by 2018, with 47 per cent at university-based training and the remaining 53 per cent divided between SD (35 per cent), SCITT (14 per cent), Teach First (9 per cent) and PGTA (4 per cent) (DfE, 2018).

SCHOOL DIRECT ROUTES INTO TEACHING

There are many ways into teaching. A comparison of the various ways helps to define the distinctive features of SD.

- **Core** – your course is not run solely by a university.
- SCITT – your course will have a link to another institution (usually a Higher Education provider) which will recommend an award of QTS.
- Teach First – you are not on a two-year programme and are not part of a scheme set up as a charity to support schools in a community with high economic deprivation.
- **Apprenticeship** – your course is not necessarily free and you do not have to spend 20 per cent of it studying teaching **pedagogy**.
- **Assessment Only Route** – your course does not demand that you work as an unqualified teacher for three years before joining and is not necessarily QTS only.

There are two types of SD training teachers: **salaried** and **non-salaried**. The DfE (2022a) document 'School Direct: guidance for schools' advises that those who are salaried should come with three or more years' work experience in any industry. A salaried SD course comes with no fees and employment as an unqualified teacher, with the benefits of having a contract of employment. Non-salaried SD training teachers, on the other hand, have tuition fees to pay, receive no salary (although they may receive a **bursary**), but they have a more gradual introduction into the classroom with more support from qualified colleagues. An SD training teacher might be with the school for the three years of full training as the guidance stipulates (DfE, 2022a). In practice (and most often in our experience), if the training teacher does not fit the organisation, or there are no jobs, or they decide against a position, then it is just a one-year programme for QTS.

PATHWAYS THROUGH THE COURSE

SD is normally a one-year course. Perhaps you may have personal difficulties during the training year; if so, you should be able to suspend your training and resume it later. The 'may' and 'should' nature of these statements is because you are in the hands of the lead school. For the academic aspect of the qualifications, you will probably (there goes that tentative language again) be in the hands of a Higher Education provider and may exit with a Level 6 Professional Graduate Certificate of Education or a **Level 7** Postgraduate Certificate of Education or a Postgraduate Diploma in Education. The initialism PGCE usually stays in place as Professional Graduate Certificate in Education (Level 6) or Postgraduate Certificate in Education (Level 7). Level 7 PGCEs do not bring a full **Master's degree** qualification. They can be for 60 **credits** (a third of a Master's degree), 90 credits (half of a Master's degree) or 120 credits, when the award becomes a Postgraduate Diploma in Education (PGDE). The PGDE requires only 60 more credits to achieve the full 180 credits and to be awarded a full Master's degree in education; these 60 credits are usually gained through a dissertation. Normally, courses are set up so that a training teacher can exit with a Level 6 or Level 7 qualification.

The academic qualification is not necessary to teach in England, but schools may be wary of employing a teacher without one. In UK schools (and many international schools), it is most often expected, and in Scotland, for example, it is essential, and has to be at PGDE level (Teach in Scotland, 2022).

Having written a paragraph of possibilities and maybes, it is a relief to be able to give a certainty: successful completion of the SD course will bring Qualified Teacher Status (QTS). You will need to teach in at least two different schools and be provided with the opportunity to do so for 120 days (24 weeks). The wording here means that it is the requirement of the provider to give you these days not for you to teach them, although they could argue that if you have missed too many days, you have not had the chance to fulfil the *Teachers' Standards* properly. QTS is a professional qualification award, which merely means that an online record attached to your name gets updated. When you enrol, you are given a **Teacher Regulation Agency** (TRA) number and, on completion of the course, the training provider recommends to the TRA that the award of QTS is given. Using the self-service login, with this number you and schools can check your status, which is updated as the training on the **Early Career Framework** (DfE, 2019b) starts. Before this stage is achieved, you will need to satisfy your provider that you have fulfilled the *Teachers' Standards*.

TEACHERS' STANDARDS

Before 1997, the criteria which made a 'competent teacher' were largely decided by the experience and instinctive judgement of professionals: fellow teachers, head teachers, teacher trainers, and Local Education Authority Inspectors. The formation of the Teacher Training Agency (TTA) in 1994 was a starting point for centralised control of what made a 'good' teacher. It was part of a move to make teaching something that is 'increasingly externally defined' (Furlong, 2005: 130). New Labour gave a list of professional standards in the document *Teaching: High Status, High Standards* (DfEE, 1997), making the criteria of what makes a 'good' teacher into law:

> in order successfully to complete a course of initial teacher training all trainees – both those starting training and those continuing training – must be assessed against, and achieve, all of the standards specified. (DfEE, 1997)

These were updated as the Standards Framework (DfES, 2002), which were updated again in 2007 to today's *Teachers' Standards* (DfE, 2011).

Throughout your teacher training course, you will be working towards achieving the *Teachers' Standards* set by the **Department for Education** (2011) for the award of Qualified Teacher Status (QTS). You will have to meet these Standards across the age range for which you are training, which will be 11–16-year-olds, 11–18-year-olds or 14–19-year-olds (DfE, 2022b). The Standards are in two parts:

Part One concentrates on your professional development in teaching, with eight Standards focused on delivery of your subject through effective lesson planning, delivery, assessment and behaviour management; Part Two concentrates on your personal and professional conduct.

In one lesson, you can fulfil many requirements of Part One of the Standards, but to gain QTS must have done so consistently through the year. You will need to show to those who are given the responsibility to recommend the award of QTS that you have consistently demonstrated the Standards by the end of the course. Here we present each Standard, with an explanation of what it means and how it can be fulfilled.

STANDARD 1: SET HIGH EXPECTATIONS WHICH INSPIRE, MOTIVATE AND CHALLENGE PUPILS

Standard 1 requires the following:

- establish a safe and stimulating environment for pupils, rooted in mutual respect
- set goals that **stretch and challenge** pupils of all backgrounds, abilities and dispositions
- demonstrate consistently the positive attitudes, values and behaviour which are expected of pupils.

There are three separate strands here: the classroom environment you create for pupils; the goals your lesson sets; the way you are in the classroom. The linking phrase is 'set high expectations'. You need to make sure that:

- you expect pupils to want to learn and be engaged in learning
- the aims of the lesson are pitched correctly in terms of what the curriculum demands at this age level and what will ensure the pupils progress with their learning
- you are on time, with resources planned, enthused about the lesson and respectful of all.

The key word for success is 'expectations'. What if the class does not want to learn, or a pupil does not? Your expectation is that they will, and you will take action to do all you can to ensure that they can and are engaged. This is about you and your actions rather than what the class does. Some classes will be easier than others because some come ready to learn. Some schools have most or all classes in this state and so, effectively, the job is done for you.

Tom Bennett (2018) has been 'cornering the market' in advice about setting high expectations with the 3 Rs:

- Routines
- Responses (rewards and sanctions)
- Relationships.

Bennett believes that the first two Rs will result in the final one, but accepts that this is the hardest part and advises:

> Don't bribe them; don't fawn or beg them to behave. Build a culture where they want to behave. (Bennett, 2018)

We echo this idea but do not have Bennett's certainty that $1 + 2 = 3$. If Bennett's approach works for you – and Bennett is very clear about the stages to fulfil this Standard – then it is a 'truth' for you. Try Bennett's ideas out, but if they do not work, you are going to have to negotiate and compromise: realities we witness in every school we visit. The training teacher who quietly places the bin under the nose of a chewing pupil rather than sanctioning them may do more to build relations than the one who gives a punishment. A long time ago, one of us was teaching when we overheard a (no-doubt bored) pupil whisper to their neighbour that they should spend some time 'making fun' (using an expletive instead of this phrase) of our tie. Rather than stop the lesson, upbraid the pupil for using foul language, not to mention insulting our sartorial style, the response was, 'What's wrong with my tie?' It was an in-the-moment response, but did more to build relations with these pupils and this class than any sanction could have done. Pupils are not robots and systems are there to be overturned. One of us, in our first year of teaching, was lecturing a pupil on what the rules are when the pupil replied, 'Rules are there to be broken'. We did not have a riposte then, and still do not. This brings us to what Bennett acknowledges as the hardest R of the 3 – Relationships – which are, we think, the key to successfully achieving this Standard.

STANDARD 2: PROMOTE GOOD PROGRESS AND OUTCOMES BY PUPILS

Standard 2 requires the following:

- be accountable for pupils' attainment, progress and outcomes
- be aware of pupils' capabilities and their prior knowledge, and plan teaching to build on these
- guide pupils to reflect on the progress they have made and their emerging needs
- demonstrate knowledge and understanding of how pupils learn and how this impacts on teaching
- encourage pupils to take a responsible and conscientious attitude to their own work and study.

The key word for this Standard is 'progress'. You must ensure that pupils learn what they need to, and that this learning is evidenced. There is an interesting comment in the Core Content Framework about 'misleading factors, such as how busy pupils appear' (DfE, 2019a: 23). This Standard ensures that you cannot go into a lesson and, effectively, babysit a group. Instead, you need to have a reason for teaching each and every lesson. To fulfil this Standard, you will need to:

- have a data record of prior achievement in the subject for each individual
- be able to use this data to inform how your lesson will aim the subject at each individual
- ensure that each pupil understands their level of learning of the subject and has a mechanism to take action to modify knowledge or practice
- work on the attitudes of the pupils so they want to learn and communicate this to you and the rest of the class.

No individual should be left behind in your lesson and, at the very least, you must take action for those who are struggling to either concentrate or understand the topic. It is also highly frustrating to be in a lesson 'learning' what is already known. If the pupils have not learned the subject from the lesson before, you should not be moving on as if they have. If even one pupil has not learned (perhaps they were absent in the last lesson either physically or mentally), then you should not be proceeding as if they have. There should be a voice in your head that asks these questions:

- What is the purpose of this lesson?
- What do I need the pupils to have learned by the end of it?
- How will I know they have learned?

These questions are for each pupil, not the class. 'The class' does not learn and the teacher who looks at one pupil's success as an indication that a subject has been taught forgets that this could have been learned outside the lesson. You will not be able to plan your next lesson without gauging what has been learned. Some pupils will learn more than others and you need a record of this and a strategy to allow their imaginations to be probed enough that they want to know more and have the mechanisms to do so. This is where we move to metaphors of the mind and 'fire-lighting' or 'lightbulb moments' come into play. Inspiring the pupil to want to learn is part of your job as a teacher and, if you get this part right, a lot will fall into place.

One of the bullet points in this Standard relates to your knowledge and understanding of learning:

- Show you are putting into practice the theory of teaching and learning

This is 'unpacked' in more detail in the ITT Core Content Framework (DfE, 2019a), which sets out a minimum curriculum entitlement for training teachers against the *Teachers' Standards*. This focuses strongly on a cognitivist view of learning as the formation of memory. You will be learning to incorporate the implications of cognitive science on teaching strategies to support lasting change in pupils' knowledge.

STANDARD 3: DEMONSTRATE GOOD SUBJECT AND CURRICULUM KNOWLEDGE

Standard 3 requires the following:

- have a secure knowledge of the relevant subject(s) and curriculum areas, foster and maintain pupils' interest in the subject, and address misunderstandings
- demonstrate a critical understanding of developments in the subject and curriculum areas, and promote the value of scholarship
- demonstrate an understanding of and take responsibility for promoting high standards of *literacy*, articulacy and the correct use of standard English, whatever the teacher's specialist subject

Your knowledge is the central factor in this Standard. Presuming that you are teaching the subject of your degree, you should be comfortable with this aspect. This can be complicated when schools have a shortage of subject teachers, and being heard boasting about climbing mountains might volunteer you for teaching Geography with Year 7. Because subject knowledge is essential, be careful about what you take on outside your main subject. Alongside subject knowledge, you will need to know the curriculum, so make sure you are up to date with the expectations of the subject in school, and the examination boards. Do all you can to get training in this direction, whether through courses or talks with your subject mentor, and record this, as the Standards have to be evidenced. To fulfil this Standard, you will need to:

- know the subject you are teaching
- keep up to date with the way the subject is to be taught in school
- be a teacher of literacy as well as your subject.

STANDARD 4: PLAN AND TEACH WELL-STRUCTURED LESSONS

Standard 4 requires the following:

- impart knowledge and develop understanding through effective use of lesson time
- promote a love of learning and children's intellectual curiosity

- set homework and plan other out-of-class activities to consolidate and extend the knowledge and understanding pupils have acquired
- reflect systematically on the effectiveness of lessons and approaches to teaching
- contribute to the design and provision of an engaging curriculum within the relevant subject area(s).

This Standard deals with the smooth running of the lesson. You will need to:

- plan each lesson thoughtfully so that the timing is decided in advance, and adapted as the lesson requires
- make good use of directed study time – purposeful homework and tasks to do outside the lesson.

Having 'chunked' your lesson into manageable learning stages in advance, changed the pace according to pupil responses and made sure there is extension work for all, you need to focus on yourself to fulfil the rest of this Standard:

- ensure that pupils know how much you care about your teaching subject and the content of the lesson
- be able to self-assess each lesson and satisfactorily be able to know strengths and weaknesses
- be part of the subject department by helping to develop resources and teaching schedules.

Whenever the Standards turn to you as a training teacher and how you behave, they become easier to fulfil as you are independent of the school, the pupils or other outside factors. You can fulfil these by being, acting and communicating that you are 'living and breathing' the subject as it is taught in the school. You need to be proactive (many times we have seen the lack of this quality used as a criticism of a training teacher) about your place in the school and contribution to the running of the subject. This must be tempered by not being too 'pushy' or seeming like you know it all, and by not assuming that the school needs to be 'shaken up' to new ways of doing things. In all matters, talk with your mentor first about what is appropriate when you offer to do more.

STANDARD 5: ADAPT TEACHING TO RESPOND TO THE STRENGTHS AND NEEDS OF ALL PUPILS

Standard 5 requires the following:

- know when and how to differentiate appropriately, using approaches which enable pupils to be taught effectively

- have a secure understanding of how a range of factors can inhibit pupils' ability to learn, and how best to overcome these
- demonstrate an awareness of the physical, social and intellectual development of children, and know how to adapt teaching to support pupils' education at different stages of development
- have a clear understanding of the needs of all pupils, including those with special educational needs; those of high ability; those with **English as an additional language**; those with disabilities; and be able to use and evaluate distinctive teaching approaches to engage and support them.

The key word here is 'adapt'. You need to:

- give a different lesson to each pupil as needed
- know strategies to support those with specific learning needs
- understand the stages of child development and the expectations of learning at different ages
- target, specifically, those whose learning is more advanced, those for whom English is not their first language, those who have learning and/or physical disabilities.

A key to fulfilling this Standard is in your knowledge of what learning difficulties are and putting provision in place. True adaptation starts with knowing the pupils and realising what each individual needs to help them achieve. The way in which this Standard is presented in training has moved away from '**differentiation**' as an approach to adaptive teaching that maintains high expectations for all pupils.

STANDARD 6: MAKE ACCURATE AND PRODUCTIVE USE OF ASSESSMENT

Standard 6 requires the following:

- know and understand how to assess the relevant subject and curriculum areas, including **statutory** assessment requirements
- make use of formative and **summative assessment** to secure pupils' progress
- use relevant data to monitor progress, set targets and plan subsequent lessons
- give pupils regular feedback, both orally and through accurate marking, and encourage pupils to respond to the feedback.

Successful assessment – diagnostic, formative and summative – are the keys to fulfilling this Standard. This starts with knowledge gained from reading about teaching, the advice from your mentors and other professionals and training courses, applied with **reflexivity** and sensitivity, in the classroom. To fulfil this Standard you will need to:

- understand both the school's and the government's ways of assessing pupils in a summative manner
- successfully use in-class checks on learning and examinations
- be clear about the purpose of any assessment and ensure that judgements about learning are founded on valid assessments
- use pupil data to plan lessons to cater for each individual pupil in the room
- correctly and supportively give feedback to pupils.

STANDARD 7: MANAGE BEHAVIOUR EFFECTIVELY TO ENSURE A GOOD AND SAFE LEARNING ENVIRONMENT

Standard 7 requires the following:

- have clear rules and routines for behaviour in classrooms, and take responsibility for promoting good and courteous behaviour both in classrooms and around the school, in accordance with the school's behaviour policy
- have high expectations of behaviour, and establish a framework for discipline with a range of strategies, using praise, sanctions and rewards consistently and fairly
- manage classes effectively, using approaches which are appropriate to pupils' needs in order to involve and motivate them
- maintain good relationships with pupils, exercise appropriate authority, and act decisively when necessary

This Standard is about what you do and is centred around the word 'manage'. To fulfil this Standard, you will need to:

- establish in your lesson the school's rules, and exercise sanctions and praise to ensure they are adhered to
- be able to motivate pupils to learn
- be a figure of control who the pupils can relate to.

You are not 'the law' in a school, but the upholder and enforcer of it. The school has its own policy for behaviour management, and it is your job to know it and make sure that any breaches of it by children means they are suitably recognised and, if needs be, sanctioned. We interview would-be teachers and get a sense of who can 'hold a room' and who cannot. We have also worked with teacher trainers who are very suspicious of charisma – the personally attractive qualities behind which some teachers may hide their lack of preparation. If you cannot hold a class's attention through the power of your personality (and most cannot), you need to develop a 'teacher persona'. Can you be yourself in the classroom? Yes, if 'yourself' has the ability to engage children in learning. If not, a 'professional self' needs to be developed. In teaching, you will have to be the following – just add the suffix 'er' or 'or' (which means it is something you do) to these:

- Organis
- Lead
- Evaluat
- Counsell
- Protect
- Disciplin
- Provid
- Explain
- Arbit

One of these is 'protector' and you have to make sure that there is a strong enough authority in the room to stop those who want to damage others being able to do so in the 'safe space', which a lesson must be. You will also need to give sanctions at times, as children are still learning social and institutional boundaries and may need to transgress them to find out where they are. Children, we have found, need and want to know the limits of their actions, as freedom to do whatever they want is scary. Your lesson needs to be a place – an oasis – where they know what they can and cannot do, and when.

STANDARD 8: FULFIL WIDER PROFESSIONAL RESPONSIBILITIES

Standard 8 requires the following:

- make a positive contribution to the wider life and ethos of the school
- develop effective professional relationships with colleagues, knowing how and when to draw on advice and specialist support
- deploy support staff effectively
- take responsibility for improving teaching through appropriate professional development, responding to advice and feedback from colleagues
- communicate effectively with parents with regard to pupils' achievements and well-being.

By the time you get to Standard 8, you may be thinking, 'I'm exhausted'.

Teaching can be an exhausting job, as well as invigorating, energising, stimulating and other energy-sapping positive verbs. They are to be fulfilled over the course of the training period and not in one go, although each lesson is a chance to do them all. In order to fulfil this Standard, you will need to:

- help the school and pupils beyond what you do in the classroom
- understand and consult other professionals in the school, including those with specialist responsibilities
- be able to purposefully direct anyone who is supporting your lesson
- act on professional advice in a positive and constructive manner
- be in regular contact with parents.

You are to become part of the life of the school and are not allowed to hide until lesson time. The school needs to be a place of more than subject education, as it has the moral, spiritual, cultural, mental and physical development of the pupils (DfE, 2014) at heart, and that applies to all teachers at all times. Offer, but do not impose your ideas. Your mentor is there as a guide and is the 'insider' who can ensure that you stay within the expectations of the school and have avenues to support it.

TEACHERS' STANDARDS: PART TWO

Part Two of the Standards governs the minimum expected behaviour of a teacher inside and outside school, including the following:

- Treating pupils with dignity, building relationships rooted in mutual respect and at all times observing proper boundaries appropriate to a teacher's professional position
- Having regard for the need to safeguard pupils' well-being, in accordance with statutory provisions
- Showing tolerance of and respect for the rights of others
- Not undermining fundamental **British values**, including democracy, the rule of law, individual liberty and mutual respect, and tolerance of those with different faiths and beliefs
- Ensuring that personal beliefs are not expressed in ways that exploit pupils' vulnerability or might lead them to break the law
- Teachers must have proper and professional regard for the ethos, policies and practices of the school in which they teach, and maintain high standards in their own attendance and punctuality
- Teachers must have an understanding of, and always act within, the statutory frameworks that set out their professional duties and responsibilities.

The *Teachers' Standards* have legal power (although there is the caveat, 'unless there is a good reason not to'). Always a minimum requirement, they give schools legal power to cease employment if they are not fulfilled. The 'must' on the *Teachers' Standards* allows schools to break a contract if any are proven to be transgressed. If, for example, you express intolerance of a faith on social media, you have broken the code and therefore broken the law. You would then be judged separately on criminal grounds as to whether you should be prosecuted in a court of law.

The legal and **regulatory** framework controls who gets into the profession and whether they can stay. As with many other professions which come with additional legal requirements (such as the armed forces or the emergency services), there is an internal process of investigation and punishment. The Teaching Regulation Agency (TRA) intervenes when there is concern over a teacher's behaviour. The TRA is controlled by the Department for Education, which, in turn, is controlled by the **Secretary of State for Education**. Before it gets to the person in this role, there is a lengthy process of review by an independent panel which has a legal adviser who will determine whether, 'the behaviour of the person concerned has been fundamentally incompatible with being a teacher' (TRA, 2022). If this is the case, the person is 'prohibited' or barred from teaching in schools, sixth form colleges and any youth institution.

CORE CONTENT FRAMEWORK

The Core Content Framework (CCF) was written in consultation with leaders of teacher training departments and schemes, such as Sam Twistleton of the Sheffield Institute of Education and Reuben Moore of Teach First and the Education Endowment Foundation (EEF). The EEF advertises itself as an 'independent charity' (EEF, 2022) but is heavily funded (GOV.UK, 2012b) by the government. The aim of the EEF is to 'break … the link between family income and educational achievement' (EEF, 2022), or what is popularly known as 'levelling-up'. This ambition to give those whose parents are on a low income as good an education as those who are on a high income is the moral imperative behind the organisation and the driving force to bring in reforms of education. This has been the explicit political rhetoric since the Conservatives returned to power after New Labour in 2010 – those who are underachieving generally are those who are disadvantaged economically (true), so a centralised curriculum needs to change to redress this failure (not necessarily true). Those critical of government may see this as a cynical attempt to use a moral argument to impose control on teaching. Those tired of the underachievement of economically disadvantaged children will welcome a 'shake-up' of the teaching establishment no matter what the outcome, as at least it might do something to change matters.

The CCF is a detailed document that states the minimum requirement of the teaching content for training providers. It recognises that individual training providers will still need to design their own curriculum. In one way, it makes sense that all teacher trainers across the country tell training teachers what makes successful teaching in order for them to replicate it in schools. The CCF contains a selection of 'evidence-based' education theory and insists that this is included on teacher training courses. As the CCF is a document designed for training providers, it is not directly aimed at training teachers; nevertheless, it would be empowering for you to draw on the 'Learn How To …' sections to inform mentoring conversations in schools. It is also important to note that you do not need to evidence the CCF but the *Teachers' Standards* (DfE, 2011).

There is a danger that training providers interpret the CCF as a recipe for formulaic lessons and see such measures as part of what Stephen Ball called a 'terror' caused by performativity:

> Policy technologies involve the calculated deployment of techniques and artefacts to organize human forces and capabilities into functioning networks of power. (2003: 216)

We see hope in the training teachers we visit who, of course, fulfil the CCF's requirements but see them as they are supposed to be seen: a minimum requirement. The methods advocated by the CCF are focused on direct teaching, recapping, modelling and revision, which reduces time for creativity, lateral thinking, finding out for yourself and the 'lighting of fires' in the imagination, but it does not prevent them. It is mind-numbing to go from one lesson to another with what is essentially the same lesson being differentiated only by content. Sam Twistleton, Reuben Moore and the EEF would not want you to be performing anything that was detrimental to you, your pupils, their learning or anyone's mental health. Good schools and good training providers, we have found, know how to give the individual training teacher the chance to create a lesson, and know that pupils need a varied day and a range of activities. Learning is an in-the-moment event. The CCF should not be used as an excuse for unthinking and formulaic lessons: no-one wants this. The *Teachers' Standards* are quite specific about the need to 'stimulate' the pupils, and this happens from a combination of your passion and the creative lesson ideas that will make it theirs too.

MENTORING

In Homer's *Odyssey*, Mentor's attempts to look after Telemachus's education were interrupted when he was replaced by the goddess Athena, showing that from the beginning, the concept of mentoring was never a simple process. For some, mentoring is giving 'general advice and motivation regarding one's career and life' (Yost and Plunkett, 2009: 110). For others, it is the rather scary-sounding 'intense interpersonal exchange' (Russell and Adams, 1997: 2). This relationship 'provides emotional and psychological support, assists with professional development, and offers role modelling' (Barker and Pitts, 1997: 222).

There are many forms of mentoring (including good, bad and indifferent), but it always involves a 'mentor' and 'mentee', and the former should help and support the latter to develop professionally. Klasen and Clutterbuck (2002) noted all the things a mentor might be, from a facilitator who makes sure you can do your job, to a counsellor who guides you emotionally, to a caretaker who watches out for you. This in-person support is designed:

> To help and support people to manage their own learning in order to maximise their potential, develop their skills, improve their performance and become the person they want to be. (Parsloe and Wray, 2000: 22)

These ideals are all very positive and encouraging but, in our experience, as Wright noted:

> there are mentors who still regard the teaching placement as a sort of work experience (2010: 1)

This may mean placing the training teacher into the classroom and seeing if they 'sink or swim', with a critical eye on the process as to whether they are 'up to it' or not. Having given little or no support, the mentor has their suspicions confirmed when the training teacher 'sinks' and so cannot lose with this way of thinking. On your teaching placement, you will notice mentors who are assessors and others who are guides. Assessors will look at what you do and inform you – through body language, tone of voice/email, what they say to you, what they do not say to you or what you hear they have said through others – whether they think you are or are not fit to be a teacher. We have been told by mentors many times that a training teacher will never be a good teacher, only for them to be just that. Good mentors are guides who review where training teachers are, evaluate what they need and give them the tools to get there.

The influential study *What Makes Great Teaching?* (Coe et al., 2014), published by the EEF and, by extension, supported by the DfE, has encouraged mentoring to follow a **coaching** model, as in the United States of America. This could present a deficit model on a coaching basis, which can be seen as a 'remedy to a problem that tends to remain unexamined' (Britton, 2006: 111). It can bring practical techniques but does not always examine the underlying issue which causes a deficit. For example, a lack of confidence may mean that the training teacher's presence in the room does not convince the pupils that someone is in control. A coaching model gives practical steps to appear differently through body language, but not the emotional support for the low self-esteem that may underlie it. Clutterbuck (n.d.) widens this model from one of doing and telling, to the need to be thoughtful about the importance and nature of what happens between the coach and the coached:

> Firstly, a deep reflection on one's own experiences – the basis of wisdom .... Secondly, the skills of using personal experience to stimulate and support the client's thinking. Thirdly, understanding of a range of psychological and behavioural issues rarely emphasised in coach training – for example, the conscious and unconscious exercise of power, and the skills of being an effective role model. Fourthly, an appreciation and

acquisition of relevant knowledge and expertise in specific applications of mentoring, such as ethical mentoring (requiring an understanding of the psychology of ethicality) or diversity.

This widened view of what a coach is also concurs with Coe et al.'s understanding of coaching as needing to be provided in a kindly and sensitive manner: 'in an environment of trust and support' (Coe et al., 2014: 44). The Early Career Framework (ECF) concurs with this approach and specifies Instructional Coaching as the preferred model. Jim Knight, a leading proponent of Instructional Coaching in the US (2017), offers mentors guidance which can be 'flipped' to make the following suggestions for the training teacher:

- Try to do most of the talking
- Try to focus on one aspect of practice at a time
- Ask for clarification when you are not certain what is being said.

As the mentee, you have an opportunity to prepare yourself for coaching opportunities through **reflection** on your developing practice and an openness to coaching dialogue with your mentor. The ITT Core Content Framework 'Learn How To … ' elements can provide useful starting points for steering discussion with your mentor. Try using the language of the framework to ask for 'expert input', 'opportunities for practice' and for 'feedback' on stated aspects of teaching. It may take some time in your training to gain the confidence and understanding of your skills to be able to sustain an effective coaching dialogue, but once you and your mentor are able to develop this approach, it can be empowering and give you a sense of agency in your own development.

What happens if you get an inexperienced, negative, cruel, or insensitive mentor who seems to be more out to get you than to give you support? What happens if you have a personality clash which impacts on you as you are not in the power position? Even if you are one of the lucky ones with a mentor who is empathetic, understanding, supportive and kind, you still have to mentor a mentor. To mentor a mentor, realise that they will be very busy as the position does not come with many (if any) hours of remission from teaching and managing. Understand that your mentor is just a person trying their best, regardless of how effective they are as a teacher or a mentor. They have their view of teaching and may try to impose this on you, in which case you have to be guided by it, but the more you show them that you have a style that works, the more they will relax. A mentor wants nothing more than for you to be successful. Apart from the altruistic desire for the good of others, it looks good on them if they have a successful training teacher. This is something you can work on: aim to be someone they will be proud of, even if they have not been very successful in communicating it to you. The relationship is hierarchical and the school will always support them – a permanent member of the teaching staff – over you. At times, you will have to leave your pride at the school door and accept your position as below the mentor. If there is any other approach – combative, refusal or negative – there will only be one outcome and it will not be in your favour. No matter how they appear, they are not your 'mate'. We have witnessed training teachers who believed this initially then found out the hard way that this was very much not going to be the case. However friendly the mentor is, it is a professional relationship, not a personal one. If it becomes a positive personal one, then that is a real benefit, but first you must ensure that the professional relationship is in place, including the hierarchical awareness that you are the learner and they are the learned.

CONCLUSION

SD has opened up a route into teacher training that allows you to get the best training from those who know: practising teachers. It will also ask that you engage with the profession from a theoretical standpoint and the evidence base of what works. It is a period for you to develop with support in a place you have chosen to work in. If you are fortunate enough to get one of the salaried places, it comes with the addition of a contract and employee rights. If not, you can console yourself with the easier timetable and more free periods – at least, at first. The *Teachers' Standards* will need to be fulfilled consistently through the year. Your mentor will guide this, so a good working relationship is necessary. This means a professional relationship, one designed to improve your performance in the classroom. Knowing this and managing the mentoring process, including your feelings when you might feel that nothing you do is right, is part of the toolkit you will need to survive and thrive.

REFLECTIONS ON THE SCHOOL DIRECT TRAINING ROUTE

You have chosen the SD route and it is worthwhile thinking about why. What was it that suited you best and how ready do you feel to go 'directly' into the classroom? Part of this reflection should consider the other routes and what they offered. It is important to 'own' your training year and to be responsible for it.

What is your relationship with your mentor like? We have provided a 'strong steer' against arguing with your mentor and for, instead, realising the hierarchical nature of the relationship and accepting your position. How do you feel about being positioned as 'lower' than someone else? This is a professional and never personal 'lower', but you have to recognise that you are new (no matter how experienced in life you are) and they are established. If your relationship works well, then all well and good. If there are problems, examine your responses and position in the school. There will be other staff who coordinate your training and they will be able to advise in the event of significant problems.

ACTION

- You need to know and fulfil the *Teachers' Standards*. These may not be explicitly taught, because the government has told training providers to address the CCF rather than the Standards until the end of your course. Your training provider will provide you with their guide which is based on the CCF, and even ask you to evidence your work against this, but, in the end, the *Teachers' Standards* are the legal requirements.

REFLECTION-ON-ACTION BY A TRAINING TEACHER

All training teachers have to find their own way. Sam McDonagh explains how they had to work out an approach that matched their personality and who they were in the classroom.

I didn't want to use strategies at the start and if the pupils wanted to do something like talk from the front or write on the board, I would let them because I wanted me and the pupils to be equal partners in the classroom. Of course, that didn't work and I got told to use strategies, but I just couldn't do things like countdown to 3 because it wasn't me. Instead, I learnt to 'sweat the small stuff' – focus on pupils slouching, or with shirts out and be quick with the criticism. I was also quite direct and would tell them to 'stop talking' or 'sit down'. I told jokes and found out what the pupils liked and talked with them about this. It's always useful if you like football. I also focused on one or two pupils and worked on my relationship with them as I found if I could get the ringleaders, the others followed. I didn't give detentions and rarely had to send anyone out. I also didn't give much praise and the pupils knew this. Instead, I was quite deadpan about everything and instead of the school 'star of the week' I turned it into 'who hasn't done too badly, then?' award.

WHAT TOOLS ARE IN YOUR TOOLKIT NOW?

From this chapter, you know:

- More about the route into teaching that you chose
- The statutory requirements for you to pass the course
- How the content and format of your training course have been designed by your training providers
- How to be a good mentee.

PLACES TO GET MORE TOOLS FOR YOUR TOOLKIT

Blatchford, R. (2020) *The Teachers' Standards in the Classroom* (4th edn). London: Learning Matters.

This book gives good, honest advice on what the *Teachers' Standards* are and how to best fulfil them.

Chopra, V., Vaughn, V. and Saint, S. (2019) *The Mentoring Guide: Helping Mentors and Mentees Succeed*. Michigan, MI: Michigan Publishing.

Although not written for school, and produced from an American viewpoint, this guide gives a rare perspective on how to be a good mentee and shares some perspectives of others who have been in your position.

Glazzard, J. and Stones, S. (2022) *Evidence Based Teaching in Secondary Schools*. London: Learning Matters.

This book provides a digested guide to the key topics in the CCF. It summarises the main features in a thoughtful manner.

REFERENCES

Ball, S. (2003) The teacher's soul and the terrors of performativity. *Journal of Education Policy*. 18 (2): 215–228.

Barker, R.T. and Pitts, M.W. (1997) 'Graduate students as mentors: An approach for the undergraduate class project', *Journal of Management Education*, 21 (2): 221–31.

Bennett, T. (2018) *'Getting behaviour right from the start'*. Available from: www.ucas.com/connect/blogs/getting-behaviour-right-start-tom-bennett

Blair, T. (2001) *'Speech by Rt Hon Tony Blair. The prime minister launching Labour's education manifesto at the University of Southampton'*. Available from: www.theguardian.com/politics/2001/may/23/labour.tonyblair

Blair, T. and Adonis, A. (2021) *'Education, education, education'*. Available from: https://institute.global/policy/education-education-education-our-submission-times-commission

Britton, T. (2006) 'Mentoring in the induction system in five countries', in C. Cullingford, *Mentoring in Education: An International Perspective*. London: Routledge. Ch. 6.

Clutterbuck, D. (n.d.). *'From coach to professional mentor'*. Available from: https://davidclutterbuckpartnership.com/from-coach-to-professional-mentor

Coe, R., Aloisi, C., Higgins, S. and Elliot Major, L. (2014) *'What makes great teaching? Review of the underpinning research'*. Available from: www.suttontrust.com/wp-content/uploads/2014/10/What-Makes-Great-Teaching-REPORT.pdf

DfE (2010) *'The importance of teaching: The schools white paper 2010'*. Available from: www.gov.uk/government/publications/the-importance-of-teaching-the-schools-white-paper-2010

DfE (2011) *The Teachers' Standards*. Available from: www.gov.uk/government/publications/teachers-standards

DfE (2014) *'National curriculum in England: Framework for key stages 1 to 4'*. Available from: www.gov.uk/government/publications/national-curriculum-in-england-framework-for-key-stages-1-to-4

DfE (2018) *'Initial Teacher Training (ITT) Census for the academic year 2018 to 2019, England'*. Available from: https://assets.publishing.service.gov.uk/government/uploads/system/uploads/attachment_data/file/759716/ITT_Census_2018_to_2019_main_text.pdf

DfE (2019a) *'ITT Core Content Framework'*. Available from: https://assets.publishing.service.gov.uk/government/uploads/system/uploads/attachment_data/file/974307/ITT_core_content_framework_.pdf

DfE (2019b) *'Early Career Framework'*. Available from: www.gov.uk/government/publications/national-curriculum-in-england-framework-for-key-stages-1-to-4

DfE (2022a) *'School Direct: Guidance for schools'*. Available from: www.gov.uk/guidance/school-direct-guidance-for-lead-schools

DfE (2022b) *'Initial teacher training (ITT): Criteria and supporting advice'*. Available from: www.gov.uk/government/publications/initial-teacher-training-criteria

DfEE (1997) *'Circular number 10/97'*. Available from: www.educationengland.org.uk/documents/dfee/circular10-97.html

DfES (2002) *'Department for Education and Skills: Qualifying to teach'*. Available from: https://dera.ioe.ac.uk//4549/

EEF (2022) *'Education Endowment Fund'*. Available from: https://educationendowmentfoundation.org.uk

Furlong, J. (2005) 'New Labour and teacher education: The end of an era', *Oxford Review of Education*, 31 (1): 119–34.

Giddens, A. (2000) *The Third Way: The Renewal of Social Democracy*. Cambridge: Polity Press.

GOV.UK (2012a) *'New school-led teacher training programme announced'*. Available from: www.gov.uk/government/news/new-school-led-teacher-training-programme-announced

GOV.UK (2012b) *'£10 million literacy catch-up programme for disadvantaged pupils'*. Available from: www.gov.uk/government/news/10-million-literacy-catch-up-programme-for-disadvantaged-pupils

GOV.UK (2021) *'Initial Teacher Training Census'*. Available from: https://explore-education-statistics.service.gov.uk/find-statistics/initial-teacher-training-census

Gove, M. (2010) *'Schools White Paper. Volume 722: debated on Wednesday 24 November 2010'*. Available from: https://hansard.parliament.uk/Lords/2010-11-24/debates/10112456000455/SchoolsWhitePaper

Gove, M. (2013) *'I refuse to surrender to Marxist teachers hell bent on destroying our schools'*. Available from: www.dailymail.co.uk/debate/article-2298146/I-refuse-surrender-Marxist-teachers-hell-bent-destroying-schools-Education-Secretary-berates-new-enemies-promise-opposing-plans.html

GTP (n.d.) *'Graduate teacher programme'*. Available from: https://web.archive.org/web/20060925230410/http://www.tda.gov.uk/Recruit/thetrainingprocess/typesofcourse/gtp.aspx

Harvey, D. (2007) 'Neoliberalism as creative destruction'. *The ANNALS of the American Academy of Political and Social Science*, 610: 21–44.

Hindmoor, A. (2018) *What's Left Now? The History and Future of Social Democracy*. Oxford: Oxford University Press.

Klasen, N. and Clutterbuck, D. (2002) *Implementing Mentoring Schemes: A Practical Guide to Successful Programs*. Oxford: Butterworth Heinemann.

Knight, J. (2017) *The Impact Cycle: What Instructional Coaches Should Do to Foster Powerful Improvements in Teaching*. Thousand Oaks, CA: Corwin Press.

McNair Report (1944) *London: His Majesty's Stationery Office*. Available from: www.educationengland.org.uk/documents/mcnair/mcnair1944.html

Parsloe, E. and Wray, M. (2000) *Coaching and Mentoring: Practical Methods to Improve Learning*. London: Kogan Page.

Russell, J. and Adams, D. (1997) 'The changing nature of mentoring in organizations', *Journal of Vocational Behavior*, 51: 1–14.

Teach in Scotland (2022) *'Routes in Teaching'*. Available from: https://teachinscotland.scot/become-a-teacher/routes-into-teaching/

TNA (n.d.) *'Teacher training'*. Available at: www.nationalarchives.gov.uk/help-with-your-research/research-guides/teacher-training/

TRA (2022) *'Teacher self-service portal'*. Available from: https://teacherservices.education.gov.uk/SelfService/Login

Wright, T. (2010) *How to be a Brilliant Teacher*. Abingdon: Routledge.

Yost, P. and Plunkett, M. (2009) *Real Time Leadership Development*. Chichester: Wiley-Blackwell.

2
WELL-BEING

INTRODUCTION

Imagine a teacher training course in which the lessons went smoothly, you never had trouble with school, teachers or mentors, the pupils were compliant and there was no stage at which you were ever under any stress. What a dull, uninspiring and worthless experience it would be. You have chosen to go into a job which is stressful – in a good and bad way. The adrenaline, 'buzz', 'ego rush', need to 'think on your feet' and the sense of 'do or die' about the ever-changing days are surely what you want. It is what we wanted. Even if you are one of the very few (or possibly the first) to experience a problem-free training year, life is stressful. Taking care of your emotional and mental health is essential to your survival in teaching and we provide tools for your toolkit in this chapter to help. We advocate a process of rethinking. While you cannot control all events, you can work on your thoughts about them. It may seem like a strange idea, but our thoughts are not, necessarily, us – sometimes we have to battle with them. Our thoughts can be unhelpful and do not reflect how we want to think and feel, or who we want to be. While you cannot, individually, change the system, government, or school, you can take greater control of your thinking practice. Through **reflection** (the process of being able to think differently about a situation/experience), **refraction** (the process of mentally negotiating with the circumstances) and being reflexive (the act of awareness of the self), you can survive and thrive.

REFLECTION, REFRACTION, REFLEXIVITY

The English language is a living, breathing system of communication that can forever create new words because it reuses parts of old ones. Bound morphemes – parts of words that have meaning but cannot be used on their own, such as 'inter-' or 'pre-' or '-ing' – can be added to whatever neologism ('neo' meaning new and 'logo' meaning word) you choose to make. 'Re-' is one of these bound morphemes, found in 'repeat' and 'recycle' and, if you ever had to revise to resit an exam, there too. The following words – 'reflection', 'refraction' and 'reflexivity – all mean that something happens again. All three are necessary, we feel, as they allow us to take our thoughts and change them so that they work in our favour.

We perhaps should not be admitting that, as training teachers, we were not good at keeping reflective diaries. It was a necessary component of our course, so had to be done, but some parts of ours could have been entered into a prize for fiction, such was their tenuous grip on reality by the time they had been hurriedly invented at the end of the course. It was only when researching, ready to teach the importance of keeping reflective diaries (while simultaneously feeling somewhat hypocritical) that the work of Jenny Moon (2004) transformed (or recreated) our understanding of what this meant. On our training courses, we had written down how we thought and felt in our teacher diaries, which was why we found the process unhelpful, as we knew what we thought and felt. Reflection, for Moon, is not about this first telling of events. Instead, it is about being ready to rethink, reconstruct and repurpose the thoughts and feelings about events. Reflection asks us to think and feel in new ways by reviewing other possibilities. Further, it asks us to analyse ourselves and look deeply into our past to find reasons why we are interpreting the world in the ways we do.

We present a possible process for reflection below. Start with a moment or incident which you would like to think more about, and try CASP.

1. **C**ircumstance – include the where, when and what else was going on for you and others involved, and how this may have affected what happened.
2. **A**sk – others (anyone, friends, family, mentor) about how they think and feel about the event and ask them to be honest with you. If your event concerns a pupil, ask them what they think.

3. **S**elf-analyse – to see whether there is something in your past that may have made you react, think and feel this way.
4. **P**attern – recall whether this event is recurring and whether you have acted, felt and thought like this before.

And that's it. The process of reflection is not to come to other conclusions, but to allow the possibility of other conclusions. Importantly, you do not have to change and do not have to agree with any other viewpoints. This process opens you up to dialogic thought – a range of possible views on the same situation – which includes your analysis of how you are thinking and feeling, and why.

Here is an example. Imagine that you set homework and half of the pupils did not hand it in, leading to you telling the whole class off and looking foolish.

1. **C**ircumstance – it was a hard homework task that some did not understand. It was set in a rush at the end of the lesson and some did not write it down properly. It was a boring activity and those who had completed it probably did most of it in the lesson.
2. **A**sk – you spoke to a teacher friend and they said that they do not set any homework for some classes as it gets done badly or not at all.
3. **S**elf-analyse – the experience of collecting up half of the homework made you feel like a fool and reminds you that you are not getting through to half of the class. You cannot punish half of the class as it would be noticed on the homework record and that will trigger issues for you, so you feel hopeless. This event also links in to how you felt in school when you were the only one to do the homework and others laughed, and you felt that it was happening all over again.
4. **P**attern – you had told yourself not to tell off a whole class as it does not target the problem and you are disappointed with your actions. There is not a pattern around homework as some classes hand it in without a problem.

And that's it. What has come of this process? Possibly nothing. Possibly, only the self-analysis stage affected the way of thinking, as the situation could be reconfigured as 'If I set homework, I feel like a fool', in which case, this does not seem a good enough reason to stop doing something that helps half of the class, and it can be assessed whether the value is worth the personal pain. Reflection is a process of thinking through something and, like any cognitive skill, the more you do it, the easier it gets. It does not have to improve you or your practice, and you do not always have to 'go forward'. We change, but not always for the better. As long as we are open to change, that is the end product. Reflection is 'the component of emotional intelligence that frees us from being a prisoner of our own feelings' (Goleman, 2020: 57). It does this because we experience the event that has troubled us from different perspectives and offers new ways of feeling and thinking. It gives us a valuable lesson that our thoughts and feelings are only one way of viewing a situation and we do not have to be trapped by them.

There are many useful models of reflection beyond the one offered here, including Kolb's (1984) cycle of reflection: from experience to reflection to trying something new to new experience and round again. Tripp's (1993) work on critical incidents (events that make us rethink our practice) helps the training teacher to understand that we change according to key events. Brookfield's (1995) four lenses of the teacher – self, peer, expert and theory – are also highly useful as they give four places to go to review a situation. Brookfield gave many reasons to reflect, including the need to 'ground' yourself. This is a good way of seeing a purpose of reflection – it brings us, including our emotional state, to a level of balance that means we can start afresh in the classroom each day.

Ivor Goodson's studies found that teachers have 'motivations behind practice that appears at odds with predominant waves of reform' (Rudd and Goodson, 2016: 101). Teachers do not always support the prevailing political and ideological systems in which they work, but they remain teaching quite happily. They manage to do so by coping with unwanted expectations, through a process of altering (or refracting) what they mean. Both in the doing and in the not doing, the teacher resists aspects of the system that are not agreed with. This is not an act of wilful rebellion. Instead, the teacher has changed the unwanted policy, initiative or pedagogy in their minds and they conform to a new reading of it. To give an example: one teacher who had the role of an 'assessor' was told that they were now to be a 'coach'. They decided that the new title did not mean anything and the job remained the same. This was not true as, apart from anything else, the 'coach' role meant that no assessing was done, and there was a greater need to model and instruct the students. Nevertheless, the teacher carried on viewing it this way and did not alter their day-to-day performance. In the mind of this teacher, they were conforming to common goals with the system, while their practice was not. Refraction of light is often symbolised by a pyramid of glass which receives a single white light and transmits a rainbow of colour. This image is a good one, as it visualises how we make sense of a sometimes cold reality of government and school policy and turn it into a rainbow of individual practice.

Reflexivity is the in-the-moment awareness of ourselves. The reflexive teacher responds well to the class, because they can feel the mood shifts and adapt. A reflex is something that seems to happen involuntarily and a reflexive teacher has the ability to change something automatically rather than stick to a fixed script. Rather than having to adhere to a lesson plan's timing, for example, a teacher develops an in-the-moment responsiveness to the pace and responses of the class. Reflexivity is reflection-in-action (Schön, 1991) – the ability to rethink the lesson while it is happening. The trainee teacher who can see that a lesson is not working and start again is at an advantage to the one who cannot sense the lack of understanding or engagement of the class and ploughs on regardless. Questioning is a good example of reflexivity as it has its own built-in dialogue with responses from the pupils that have to be responded to in-the-moment. Like reflection and refraction, being reflexive is a thinking skill that needs to be exercised in order to get better. The processes of reflexive thinking are part of our mental gym, and need a regular workout.

WELL-BEING

The irony of teaching is that, although it is such a stressful profession, teachers have to teach pupils about well-being. You are the children's guide for how to balance life and make sense of the spinning universe. The comedian Jasper Carrott once made a (rather cruel) joke about the attempts of the balding musical star Sting to stop the deforestation of the Amazon rainforest by pointing out that he could not even save his own hair. It may seem the same with your monumental task: how can you help children to cope with their lives when you do not always feel able to cope with your own? You have to be a champion of Social, Emotional and Mental Health (SEMH) needs and teach about Relationship and Sex Education (RSE), even if both your partner and your dog have just packed their bags and left you that morning, and even your mum isn't returning your calls. The balance of 'being real' about yourself and your life, and performing the role of a teacher who safeguards children, is a difficult act.

In the midst of the need to protect others, you need to ensure your own well-being. In our view, some well-being advice can give you more to do (do some yoga, try mindfulness, try colouring in a picture of a bunny, manage your time better). Each time, the pressure to act is as an individual and, if you are stressed, it is because you have not done enough of it (and so your fault) and yet this overload may be what is really 'stressing you out'. Furthermore, it makes the issue your problem and not the conditions of society or the school – which is why it may be popular with policy makers, as it means they do not have to address the untenable conditions of work. At risk of doing the same, we recommend the following from our experience of seeing how training teachers cope with the year.

- Give yourself time to reflect on your practice – think and self-talk. Treat this as a necessary part of your development. This can be done whenever and wherever – on the bus, walking the dog, etc.
- Outside school, become a person again with hobbies, friends and a family. It is easy to get lost in the workload and, in teaching, this will never disappear.
- Care for yourself. There is no reason in the world not to be kind to yourself. Praise yourself and have treats and rewards. Why not? Speak to yourself in the way you would speak to a friend. Do this out loud if you like (best not to do so while in school).
- Parkinson's Law states that: 'Work expands to fill the time available'. This means that whatever task you have to do, given an hour or given three hours, that is how long it will take. Learn to focus for a short time and concentrate on the task in hand and you will be more effective.

- Finding private space to work in a school is not always easy and needs to be balanced with being around other professionals. Training teachers who remove themselves from communal areas may be seen as being anti-social and not wanting to be part of the team. Try to find a balance between being part of the team and finding a quiet space in the school where you can focus on your work.
- Remember that you are in the learning business and are supposed to make mistakes.

CONCLUSION

As teacher trainers, we are in a fascinating and privileged position. Before us come a series of individuals with their lives, views of the world, hang-ups and anxieties. Place them in the classroom and see what happens. Through reflection, refraction and being reflexive, a training teacher can keep aware of what is happening and seek help if needed. We have also encountered plenty of training teachers like the one whose mentor told us 'hasn't got a reflective bone in her body.' This training teacher worked perfectly well in the classroom, but their practice was always the same and therefore limited. When change comes to the system, such teachers may get left behind as they cannot rethink what they do and why. In this chapter, we have encouraged you to use three ways of rethinking your role and circumstances. We also believe you should prioritise your tasks, and find the headspace and physical space that will allow you to survive and be kind to yourself throughout the year. If you cannot be kind to yourself, why should anyone else?

REFLECTIONS ON WELL-BEING

Do you refract the school, the system, the 'best practice' models offered by others? Where are the spaces in which you say 'no' to ideas and those spaces in which you say 'yes'? By naming these spaces, you will be able to better realise your pedagogy, the reasons which instruct your teaching. It is hard to see refraction because you have given your own interpretation of how the school and system works and seem to be conforming to it. Look at the way other teachers operate, see, the differences, and become part of the rainbow of practice in a school.

How are your thoughts? Do you think that they give a true picture of who you are and want to be? The idea that our thoughts are not us is a big realisation and frees you up from your current state of mind and actions. Talk back to your thoughts and feelings and take them through a process of rethinking, either the CASP one we propose or Brookfield's or Kolb's, or read more about Moon's approach.

> **ACTION**
>
> - Build reflective dialogue into your routine. Think about the day and rethink about the day. The dialogue with yourself is a key to success in teaching, otherwise you are likely to find that your mind finds other ways of dealing with the stress and new situations.

REFLECTION-ON-ACTION BY A TRAINING TEACHER

Training teacher Arte Artemiou decided to reflect using drama or, more specifically, as it is about the performance of self-thinking or talking to the self, autoethnodrama. This highly original approach is explained in Arte's preamble.

My focus on reflective practice has arisen through my own observations of others' lessons, conversations in the department office afterwards, and watching other lessons on the same content with different students. I decided to explore autoethnodrama as a reflective tool because it allowed me to voice my concerns and experiences in a constructive way; not just 'writing about' but critically and reflexively writing about. The focus for my own reflection was behaviour as I had encountered various incidents during my teacher training in which I fundamentally disagreed with how the teacher handled the situation. This caused a tension between being the student-in-the-space and the practitioner-in-my-head, a tension that needed air to breathe, a place to run. I dove into writing my experiences as they came – from my thoughts and feelings – not drawing on any written reflections or notes of my observations. I poured these words onto the page in the hope of making sense of the incidents and how I stood in relation to them. Reflecting in a creative way not only allowed me to purge/reconcile/transform the ill feelings I was garnering towards the teachers, but also offered me a reason to express myself creatively. I was challenged by the student behaviour and the teacher management, so I started by writing down my reactions to these observations. As I wrote, I found that I didn't want to feel and think like another teacher to sympathetically understand their position, but to think and feel like them to better understand my own reactions from their position. Creating a short performance drawing on the thoughts, feelings and experiences of a teacher which may or may not include characters and text based on students, teachers, parents, governors, school inspectors, etc., is inevitably going to be a sensitive document, and one way in which I have navigated this is to include thoughts and feelings that aren't particularly gracious and are quite self-righteous. I chose to write in a self-critical and reflexive style to not let myself 'off the hook', so to speak. I'm not interested in creating something that just 'airs the dirty laundry' but something that considers my positionality within the space and that of others, something that helps me to learn how I can become kinder and more patient, more creative and confident, more understanding and generous. Autoethnodrama can allow for this process to happen because it is steeped in the desire to be reflexive and critical.

ARTE [to audience] Hey, thanks for coming, erm, so what you're about to see is what goes on in my head when I'm in the classroom. I, I often have, erm, like dialogues and sort of monologues and just like things going on in my head whenever I'm, erm, in sort of I don't know it's like teaching scenarios or sort of power dynamic scenarios, that thing where, like, someone has authority over somebody else, erm, and especially in teaching 'cause teaching's meant to be something that's beneficial to the young people right, erm, and in these situations I can't help but see the power dynamics, and I have all these like idealistic things going on inside of me about how I think and believe it should be, erm, but then there's also the very real practical considerations of how it actually is and how you, I don't like using this term but how you like survive? So yeah basically that's it, erm, I find behaviour, erm, quite an interesting thing so this this became a thing about behaviour, became about managing behaviour, erm, and when I was talking to somebody a friend of mine in Australia, erm, they sort of came up with the title of *Pedagogy on Trial* and I thought that was quite nice, erm, so I've used that, erm, but yeah, I've tried to, erm, I don't know what I do is I just write, I sort of free write, erm, and then go back and edit and stuff but yeah there's, yeah so that's basically what, what this is, erm. My name is Artemis Artemiou, or just Arte, teacher trainee, candidate number 00398651. I'll be playing OLD HAND who is a mentor who has done it all and seen it all in teaching, TRAINEE who hasn't, yet, and myself, ARTE who is looking at it all and wondering what it is all about. I'm wearing [insert clothing]. TRAINEE wears this [insert clothing] and OLD HAND wears this [insert clothing]. We are tidying up the drama room after school.

OLD HAND [to audience] So we're there in the drama room, alright. It's erm, it's a standard black box couple of, erm, lighting rigs. There's a lighting desk black curtains that sort of thing, erm, it's the end of the day on a Friday we've had a full day of teaching with, erm, one teacher going off sick, another needing immediate cover and students bouncing off the walls. Anyway, here we are, packing away the chairs looking forward to home time, dinner, maybe cheeky gin in front of the TV and new boy here, that's the trainee asks a pretty explosive question.

TRAINEE [to OLD HAND] Do the kids always behave like that last lesson on a Friday?

OLD HAND [to audience] Okay, so it hasn't exploded yet, that's, you know that's just him removing the pin but wait.

TRAINEE [to audience] I don't know about you but whenever adults insult children it strikes me as odd. I'm not entirely sure that it's the most appropriate thing to do. [to OLD HAND] Do you ever shout at them?

OLD HAND [to TRAINEE] Of course, like, you can't not sometimes the amount of pressure we've got. I mean I know it's not right but you just lose it sometimes you just explode at 'em 'cause they're, 'cause they're just bags of hormones and insecurity and they just wanna poke and prod you and so yeah 'course I shout at 'em not often it's not like what I want to do I don't wanna do it, erm, but sometimes you just think they need, like, a bit of fear putting into 'em, making 'em realise they're not the 'big bad' you know? There's this one time this kid was rude to me so I said: 'Oi! Who the hell do you think you are? You're this close to being expelled, No! Don't talk back to me! Actually, just get out! Leave!' [laughs] he'd only said something little but I'd just bellowed at him, just sent him out and then the next lesson I gave him written work, erm, but he still didn't learn, he was still rude to me but [laughing] what can you do? D'you know what I mean?

TRAINEE [to audience] Do you ever, erm, overhear a conversation and just think this has nothing to do with me, I shouldn't get involved, I shouldn't say anything, there's no need but then your heart starts pumping and your adrenaline goes round your body because you feel like you have something to say, like, there's some sort of societal pressure that you feel you need to say something. [to OLD HAND] How will he learn if you just shout at him?

OLD HAND [to audience] You know when you're just venting and like you're not really thinking about what you're saying, it's just coming out and then someone picks you up on what you're venting and you're just like, why are you being so stupid? Was there a need? [to TRAINEE] What else do you expect me to do in the situation? Like, the kid's just stressing me out and I need him out the class so I can teach.

TRAINEE [to OLD HAND] But, it's not just your classroom is it? [OLD HAND and TRAINEE look at each other.]

ARTE [to audience] Okay, so now it could explode. [ARTE holds up a sign 'Pedagogical Practice on Trial'. Staging transforms into a court room during his speech. OLD HAND is standing at one podium and TRAINEE at another.] When I wrote the first draft of this it was very much TRAINEE raging against OLD HAND, erm, and it was very one way, it was sort of like OLD HAND is the enemy, erm, and he's what's wrong with soci-, soci-, teaching, erm, but actually when erm, when I sent it to my friend in Australia, erm, he gave me some really good feedback, erm, about the teacher's right to reply and I was, like, actually fair point.

[ARTE gives a sign to OLD HAND: 'The Defendant'. ARTE gives a sign to TRAINEE: 'The Prosecutor'.]

TRAINEE [to audience] How exciting.

OLD HAND [to TRAINEE] Wooah, hold on a minute, how're you, how're you gonna make me responsible for like, a whole way of teaching? That's not fair.

TRAINEE [to OLD HAND] Well, erm, you have a certain teaching practice and I have a different teaching practice. In my eyes you represent, erm, the status quo of education in the UK and I represent something else, so just go with it don't think about it too much and let's see where it goes.

OLD HAND [to TRAINEE] Fine, alright, I'll play along. To answer your question then yes, it is my classroom and that isn't me being like, erm, dictator, a mini-Hitler or whatever or a Mussolini in the classroom, like I'm paid to be there. I'm employed by the Government. I have a responsibility to make sure that these children are safe and to make sure that, actually, they're being brought up with our values we talk about, British values. We talk about democracy that's on me to do that. If I've got some kid being rude in my class and he won't listen to reason and he won't listen to me trying to be his friend what else do you expect me to do sometimes? Enough is enough: you've earnt this shouting, deal with it. You're 13/14. How about you start acting responsible and a bit like an adult and I'll start treating you like that.

[ARTE changes the sign 'Pedagogical Practice on Trial' to 'The Cross-Examination'.]

TRAINEE [to OLD HAND] So, erm, what is it that you think you're teaching them?

OLD HAND [to TRAINEE] What are you getting at?

TRAINEE [to OLD HAND] I'm getting at your assumptions.

OLD HAND [to TRAINEE] My assumptions? Have you not for one minute thought that they could be 'presumptions'? And to answer your question I'm teaching them drama. Obviously.

TRAINEE [to OLD HAND] What type?

OLD HAND [to TRAINEE] Honestly, you're winding me up now. Just say what you need to say.

TRAINEE [to OLD HAND] Fine. You believe that if you plan your schemes of work, create your PowerPoints make your, erm, your instructions clear, manage their behaviour, mark their homework then they will learn what they are there to learn, right, the, erm, 'formal' curriculum but you are also teaching them a hidden curriculum about things like power, authority, adulthood, relationships and emotions, social status and a whole host of other things.

OLD HAND [to TRAINEE] What do you mean?

TRAINEE [to OLD HAND] Well, let's take the story of you, yelling at a student.

OLD HAND [to TRAINEE] Of course you'll pick that story.

TRAINEE [to OLD HAND] Don't be so defensive, defendant. I wasn't passing judgement. Yet.

ARTE [to audience] I'm not gonna lie, I judge teachers quite harshly when I observe them. I mean I've not really got any particular backing as to that, like, I don't have an extensive amount of experience, it's just I'm quite an idealistic man and my ideals are sometimes not tempered by reality, erm, and so what this is, I guess this script that, erm, this play that you're seeing is my idealism being tempered by realism, erm, not like the theatrical sort of realism but like the actual pragmatic, 'what can we do in this situation to achieve what we need to achieve?' type of realism, erm, erm, but I still can't not consider some actions as more or less effective, erm, but I guess that's why I'm honing in on this shouting experience, erm, that I, I witnessed 'cause it was just so ineffective, erm, but I guess it was just a display of someone's frustration maybe of their fear, erm, I don't, I don't know what, 'cause in the real world, I didn't talk to the teacher after it' cause it, 'cause I didn't know how to approach it, erm, but yeah, even teachers that shout and raise their voices a lot you hear people saying, 'Well, that's their teaching style', I'm, like, yeah but surely some teaching styles are like more conducive to learning than other teaching styles?

[ARTE replaces 'A Cross-Examination' with 'Teachers' Standard 7'. The play continues …]

> ## WHAT TOOLS ARE IN YOUR TOOLKIT NOW?
>
> - The language and process of reflection, refraction and reflexivity – ways of thinking that will act as psychological armour for the year
> - Permission to question the structures you find yourself in
> - Permission to admit to mistakes and see the human in you and your colleagues
> - Encouragement to act on your thoughts and feelings rather than be a victim of them.

PLACES TO GET MORE TOOLS FOR YOUR TOOLKIT

Bethune, A. and Kell, E. (2020) *A Little Guide for Teachers: Teacher Wellbeing and Self-care*. London: Sage.
'Look after yourself' is the message of this practical self-help book which should be a guide to keeping your head when all around are losing theirs.
Gomes, B. (2020) Teacher Workload: *How to Master it and Get Your Life Back*. Independently published.
Written by a UK-based teacher about teaching with an independent publisher and mindset. This is practical advice from someone who has been there.

REFERENCES

Brookfield, S. (1995) *Becoming a Critically Reflective Teacher*. San Francisco, CA: Jossey-Bass.

Goleman, D. (2020) *Emotional Intelligence: Why It Can Matter More Than IQ*. London: Bloomsbury.

Kolb, D. (1984) *Experiential Learning. Experience as the Source of Learning and Development*. Englewood Cliffs, NJ: Prentice Hall.

Moon, J. (2004) *A Handbook of Reflective and Experiential Learning*. London: Routledge.

Rudd, T. and Goodson, I. (2016) 'Refraction as a tool for understanding action and educational orthodoxy and transgression', *Revista Tempos e Espacos em Educacao*, 9 (18): 99–110.

Schön, D. (1991) *The Reflective Practitioner*. Aldershot: Ashgate Publishing.

Tripp, D. (1993) *Critical Incidents in Teaching: Developing Professional Judgement*. London: Routledge.

3
ROLE

WHAT THIS CHAPTER WILL COVER

- The teacher's day
- Crisis management
- Continuing Professional Development

INTRODUCTION

This chapter examines a possible day: emails, briefing, form, assembly, lesson one, duty, lesson two, lunchtime detention, lesson three, break, lesson four, bus duty, detentions, meeting, contacting parents, **extracurricular** class, marking, preparation of lessons, and the etcetera which always appears. This is the typical content of a day without emergencies; we also factor in a what-to-do in the event of crisis and a training teacher's role in these circumstances. The chapter explains and explores Continuous Professional Development, including school responsibility roles. It details the types of meetings that training teachers go to and advises on the etiquette required to survive them.

THE TEACHER'S DAY

So, you arrive in the car park at 7.30 am, knowing that if you come in any later, you will be battling the traffic and the journey will take you twice as long and, anyway, you will not find a space in the car park. Entering the building, you realise you are far from being the first one through the doors and the 'usual suspects' are beavering away at their computers, or rushing around their room, or desperately trying to finish marking that is due back today, and which they fell asleep with at 11 pm last night. You make a cup of coffee, washing the mug that 'you know who' did not wash the day before and look in vain for some milk, but the pint tucked at the back of the fridge is turning into cottage cheese and, anyway, it has someone's name on it in thick green marker. Printing out resources for the first lesson and photocopying them is a priority as the printer and the photocopier get super busy and if you do not get there first, someone will block the machine trying to copy onto something as unlikely as cling film. The printer you connect to does not work. There is another printer in the other building, so you rush over, connect your laptop and mercifully, this works. Next, to the photocopier, to wait while someone is seemingly printing 30 copies of *War and Peace*. You stand a little closer to the person photocopying in the hopes that this might speed matters up a bit; eventually, you have your resources for the first lesson. For the next lesson, you quickly decide to change your resources, as there is no way you can go back to that printer and get this photocopied in time. Into your first classroom and check the technology. In comes a colleague to ask about a pupil and another 10 minutes go by. You run through your presentations, get typos sorted and the morning, at least, is ready. You log onto the system and see 30 messages waiting for you. Most can be delayed, but some are about today's lessons and pupils in your form. You read and reply to what you can, as briefing is about to begin. None of this narrative is very edifying and hopefully speaks more about our practice in school than yours, but it gives a picture of a school day that is busy from start to finish. In this narrative, we are not even at 8.30 am.

In the absence of pupil welfare concerns, your priority has to be the lessons – planning (the major part), delivering and feedback. For each lesson, you will need to know:

- what knowledge, skills and understanding are to be taught
- what pupils are expected to know and be able to do
- what was the prior learning and how secure it is
- what the barriers to learning will be
- how you might respond to these barriers.

Beyond these lessons, the day can seem like endless happenings. Few of these happenings (hopefully none) are vital in themselves, but each is a part of what makes the teacher's day. The conversation with a form tutor about a pupil, contact with the Safeguarding Officer, arrangements for a school trip, a phone call to a parent to praise a pupil and then the interaction with hundreds of children each day. Every moment is an opportunity to work on a problem or celebrate a success, and it can be tiring. The teacher's day is tiring because of the sheer amount of different activities and because so much of what you do in a typical day is emotional labour. Hochschild (1979) wrote about this at the dawn of what Daniel Bell (1976) called *The Coming of Post-Industrial Society*. The move away from manufacturing economy – it did not disappear but was largely exported to cheaper labour markets – meant that the UK economy was to be dominated by people-to-people work or services. One person works in a café to serve the worker on the way to the insurance brokers via the gym; the worker's house is currently being decorated by a painting and decorating firm called Mr Brush. Each is in the business of serving another and no one has a physical output to speak of – except the coffee and cake drunk to fuel a session in the gym and a day's selling of insurance which earns the money to pay for the front room to be covered with flock wallpaper which was made in Taiwan.

Emotional labour is not unique to teaching, but it is particularly needed alongside emotional intelligence. It is important to understand that it is not the 'long hours' alone that make us tired. Our tiredness can sometimes be self-destructive, when we work harder to justify why we are feeling this way. Here, we can 'lean on' the ideas of Daniel Goleman (1996) whose book, *Emotional Intelligence*, opened up the idea that it was as important to be able to control, adapt and understand emotions as to be able to think or rationally respond. Emotions flood through us in an ever-changing manner, but in the professional environment of a school, and especially around children, they need to be managed and controlled.

What has to be done might be best dealt with in a list that will never be exhaustive (but may well be exhausting) but is worth a reminder to anyone teaching or managing teachers about the variety and the sheer doingness of the day. The list in Table 3.1 presumes that you do not have any 'responsibility points' – which, as a training teacher, you will not. There are many areas where you can be paid extra money for leading on an area the school needs. These include literacy specialist, head of **Key Stages**, head of subject, assistant head of subject, head of year, and more. Each time you take responsibility, you should be awarded what is known as a +1 or a +2 or more, dependent on the level of responsibility offered. The + is a move up the salary scale. Usually, you will go up one point for each year of service, so taking on responsibility points speeds up the process of being paid more.

CRISIS MANAGEMENT

The list in Table 3.1 relates to a day without incident. Schools may 'lock down' if there is a threat from outside or inside. **NASUWT** (n.d.) provided schools with advice about lockdown and safety procedures. Lockdown is a regrettable feature of modern life, but better than a lack of awareness or process which was in place before tragedies such as the 'dark, tragic time' (*The Guardian*, 2014) that tennis coach Judy Murray related. Judy Murray's sons, future tennis stars Andy and Jamie, suffered as pupils at Dunblane primary school when someone shot at a class of 5- and 6-year-olds, killing 16 children

Table 3.1 List of responsibilities

With pupils	Without pupils
Chat to pupils around the school	Attend briefings
Attend school trips	Prepare for parents' evenings
Teach lessons	Attend and take part in meetings
Mark pupil work	Have face-to-face meetings with parents
Perform bus and playground duty	Contact parents by phone, email and app
Monitor school corridors and implement school behaviour policy	Plan schemes of work
Plan school trips	Liaise with Teaching and Learning Assistants
Check that diaries have been signed and communication with parents is being received	Plan lessons
Be a teacher of Relationship and Sex Education	Print worksheets
Be a teacher of Personal, Social, Health Education and Well-being	Check emails and VLE
Take registers	Respond to absences in registers
Be a teacher of numeracy	Attend and respond to parents at parents' evening
Tidy up rooms after a lesson	Attend and respond at Continuous Professional Development meetings
Prepare rooms for lesson	Write reports for all pupils
Be a subject specialist teacher	Keep up-to-date with subject knowledge
Be a teacher of literacy	Keep up-to-date with curriculum changes
Be a form tutor	Liaise with Safeguarding Officer
Check uniforms	Liaise with form tutors
Anything we have missed	Anything we have missed

and their teacher with four handguns and 700 rounds of ammunition. Acts such as these, unthinkable even after the event has taken place, resulted in schools preparing themselves more fully for emergencies, and you must know what the school emergency policy is, how it is enacted and what it means for you and the pupils. Someone else will be responsible for the policy and communicating this to you; you need to make sure that you know the process and are ready to support the children if it occurs.

Pupil injury is another possible emergency which can take up your day. One of us once ended up taking a pupil to hospital and waiting in Accident and Emergency in one of our 'frees' and after school (to no thanks from school or parents, we rather bitterly recall). Two of the Four Horsemen of the Apocalypse may arrive. While we have so far, thankfully, seen little of the third and fourth horsemen's specialisms of famine and war on these shores, fire and flood are possible. It is hard to set fire to a school, but it happens. Fires tend to affect schools out of school time and while in England there were only 87 secondary school fires between 2015 and 2020 (Zurich, 2021), fires in both primary and secondary schools affected 389,830 hours of teaching time in this period. In 2007, when the water table was at its height in this country, in Hull alone, 95 out of 98 schools were damaged by floods (Floodflash, 2021). As a teacher, you must be reflexive to the situation and respond in the moment; your primary concern is for the welfare of the children.

CONTINUING PROFESSIONAL DEVELOPMENT (CPD)

Teachers never stop learning about their profession. The only constant in teaching, as the old cliché goes, is change. There is a need, therefore, to attend meetings that involve you in these changes. As a training teacher, you will probably have a bespoke session as your professional development is 'initial' not 'continuing'. When you have qualified, you can then join in with the other teachers. CPD mostly happens after school, but it can also happen in what used to be known as Baker days. This is a term from education history and refers to Kenneth Baker, Education Secretary, who, in 1988, insisted that teachers take part in five days of training each year. The term 'Baker day' was always a term of abuse from reluctant teachers fed up at having something else imposed on them. *The Times* (2011) relates how they also became known as B (insert rest of swear word here) days. Five days of training have remained in the teacher calendar and this training can be done in a variety of ways, but these are mostly very welcome days in which teachers can learn more, relax and wear non-school clothes, and the school building changes into a place of strange calm.

Meetings are part of CPD and are an important time to share practice and eat biscuits. Legally, meetings must be planned in advance, be on the school calendar and teachers cannot be required to attend more than one a week (NASUWT, n.d.), but for training teachers, we are afraid, no such promises exist. Meetings are usually subject-based and a great opportunity for you to contribute to the life of the school. They may not always seem relevant, but we strongly recommend that you attend all meetings and offer to do so as it is seen as being 'proactive' and mentors like this. From our experience, it will cause a lot more work for you if you try to miss meetings, as you will be more closely watched. We recommend that you are on time, prepared with whatever has been asked and be alert to opportunities to contribute, while at the same time recognising that you may not know what you do not know yet.

CONCLUSION

A school day is a busy one, fun-filled, stress-filled and never dull. There is a lot to do, and you will be doing it, and it will bring tiredness. This is a 'good tiredness' from a job well done. Sleep (which can be hard to come by) brings a new beginning. You have to start your relations with staff and pupils anew or the coastal shelf effect of accumulating problems and grudges will wear you down more than the day-to-day tasks. Our advice is to let go and start each day and each lesson afresh. CPD, meetings and eventually responsibility for whole-school concerns will add to your day and crises will come every day – some big, some small. Among all of this, look after yourself, as a priority, or you will not be able to look after others.

REFLECTIONS ON ROLE

How are you coping with the demands of the job? School can be an unforgiving environment where people often work to their maximum capacity and some people can 'look down' on those who are struggling or not seeming to do as much as they are. The danger is to enter the daily life of a teacher without thinking about yourself, your role, your capacity and where you need a break. A metaphoric 'brick wall' is never something people expect to 'hit' or they would never do so. Stop, think, assess and find the spaces where you can rest and be yourself. Forgive yourself the mistakes and do not undertake, in the words of Brookfield, 'self-laceration' (2017: 86). 'Beating yourself up' does nobody any good. Have a good voice in your head which is full of kind thoughts and places where you can rest. One of us, in our first year of teaching, had a recurrent mental image of being on a boat on the sea in the summer holidays. It ended up being a rubber dinghy off the Dorset coast, but it still felt good when we got there.

ACTIONS

- Look at the above list about the things to do in school with and without pupils and see if you can add more.

Familiarise yourself with the school's lockdown policy and find out what the fire evacuation process looks like.

REFLECTION-ON-ACTION BY A TRAINING TEACHER

In this reflective extract, Ellen Jones explores ways in which the job of teaching can, at times, feel overwhelming.

During my second placement, I witnessed classroom discomfort between Colleague A and a class that she had described as a group that she did not 'particularly gel with'. After observing the class, it became apparent that 'interpersonal relationships' (Aelterman et al., 2007, p. 286) had either not been established or had completely dissolved, which was possibly contributing to the level of stress of the teacher. In turn, this may have contributed to her negative outlook towards the school life as a whole. I also witnessed what is known as teacher 'burnout', reasons for which include, but are not limited to workload, managerial organisation (Senior Leadership), and pupil behaviour (Collie et al., 2015, p. 745). During my PGCE I have found that the intense training workload, including lesson planning, lesson preparation and delivery, assignments, and evaluating and evidencing all aspects of my practice, to be extremely stressful due to time constraints which are negatively impacting on my personal sense of well-being, which in turn drained my 'emotional resources' (Maizdi et al., 2017, p. 4) and ultimately impacted upon the professional relationships that I have created with pupils, colleagues and management. This is concerning to me, as during my practice I have been complimented numerous times on my ability to form positive relationships with pupils and it is incredibly important to me to 'connect with [my] students' (Vitto, 2003, p. 4) and maintain these relationships to facilitate a positive learning experience for all, which directly correlates with my humanistic pedagogy. However, both myself and Colleague A were beginning to feel so demoralised for different reasons that we were beginning to lose our sense of autonomy and, ultimately, 'teacher effectiveness' (Jin et al., 2014, p. 310). Recently, the school has introduced what they have called 'mindfulness interventions' which currently take place on Friday during PM registration, and it is possible that as teachers we could participate within these activities with our students to improve our personal sense of well-being and in turn, we would be able to both create and re-establish positive professional bonds with our pupils.

WHAT TOOLS ARE IN YOUR TOOLKIT NOW?

- Readiness to face the variety of activity in the school day, including moments of crisis.
- Knowledge about responsibility points and CPD.
- Better meeting etiquette.

PLACES TO GET MORE TOOLS FOR YOUR TOOLKIT

Buckler, S. (2021) *How to Challenge the System and Become a Better Teacher*. London: Sage.
Another working teacher, and one who 'tells it like it is'. Scott Buckler is a highly thoughtful practitioner who advises on which voices to listen to in teaching and how to challenge the system from within.
Mullin, S. (2019) *What They Didn't Teach Me on My PGCE: And Other Routes into Teaching*. Ontario: Word and Deed.
Each short chapter, written by a practising teacher or senior leader (including the editor, Sarah Mullin) gives a first-hand account of what it is like to be working in the profession, alongside invaluable advice for new teachers.

REFERENCES

Bell, D. (1976) *The Coming of Post-industrial Society*. London: Penguin.
Brookfield, S. (2017) *Becoming a Critically Reflective Teacher*. San Francisco, CA: Jossey-Bass.
Floodflash (2021) Available from: https://floodflash.co/england-flood-risk-which-areas-have-it-worst/
Goleman, D. (1996) *Emotional Intelligence: Why It Can Matter More Than IQ*. London: Bloomsbury.
Guardian, The (2014) Judy Murray on the Dunblane massacre: 'I just left the car and ran'. Available from: www.theguardian.com/sport/2014/jun/17/judy-murray-dunblane-massacre-just-left-car-and-ran
Hochschild, A. (1979) 'Emotion work, feeling rules, and social support.' *American Journal of Sociology*, 85: 551–75.
NASUWT (n.d.) *School Lockdown Procedures*. Available from: www.nasuwt.org.uk/advice/health-safety/school-lockdown-procedures.html
Times, The (2011) 'Baker Days'. Available from: www.thetimes.co.uk/article/baker-days-5526ltjw66z
Zurich (2021) Available from: www.zurich.co.uk/media-centre/more-than-1100-classrooms-gutted-by-school-blazes

4
LAW

WHAT THIS CHAPTER WILL COVER

Review of the main laws which affect teachers:

- Education law
- Child protection law and safeguarding
- The Equality Act
- Knives Act/Offensive Weapons Act
- Sexual Offences Act
- Copyright law
- Laws that protect teacher training teachers

INTRODUCTION

In *Bleak House*, Charles Dickens describes a legal case between Jarndyce and Jarndyce which has dragged on for so long that it is like being 'roasted at a slow fire ... stung to death by single bees ... drowned by drops' (2001: 48). As a former attorney's apprentice and a court reporter, Dickens had plenty of first-hand experience of the machinations of the Victorian legal system – enough to conclude (albeit through the dubious character Mr Bumble) that it is an ass.

Step into the regulatory system in which schools and education are encased, and you are likely to discover that the complexity and confusion that Dickens expressed in 1853 is still relevant today. There are so many 'shoulds' and not many 'musts'. This means that much of the regulatory framework refers to what teachers and schools 'ought to do', which keeps it nicely vague but means that a lot of interpretation is needed to ensure they do not break the musts, which can lead to prosecution. Even the musts come well-qualified by an 'unless' or 'if reasonable', which often makes the decision of whether the law has been broken a personal one to be assessed by police, then judge and jury. The vast majority of laws that constrain your actions in schools are general ones, but there are some extra ones that come with the position. Schools and their principals are ultimately responsible for actions that contravene laws in school, which is why there are such stringent guidelines for all matters from photocopying to safeguarding. Alongside the saying about the law being an ass is the one that states: 'ignorance of the law is no excuse'.

EDUCATION LAW

The Education Act is the law that directly governs schools and teachers. It is constantly being updated in response to the concerns of the government of the day. The first Education Act of 1870 (known as the Forster Act) made education compulsory for children from 5 to 13 years old (British Library, n.d.), which was subsequently updated to 18 years old (Education and Skills Act, 2008). Any changes to school requirements will result in an amendment to this Act; the last four significant updates were in 1996, 2002, 2011 and 2018. Sometimes, the changes are seen to be so significant that they produce a new Act of Parliament, such as the Education Reform Act (1988) and the Education and Inspections Act (2006).

The Education Act informs teachers and schools about the limits of what can be done in a classroom when a child is unruly. For example, the Education Act (1996) stipulates that a head teacher can search a pupil or delegate this role to staff, but the search must be by someone of the same gender and in the presence of another member of staff who is the same gender (unless it is urgent). The head teacher or delegated member of staff must not remove clothes (except a hat and coat). There are shades of Charles Dickens in all of this 'may', 'maybe' and 'should' language, which could either protect or convict. What if, for example, you are female and suspect a male has a knife and have heard that they are about to use it? Could you search them in this instance? Without being the same gender and having the permission of the head teacher, the answer is 'no'. There is a caveat (in law there usually is) to this, as 'reasonable force' is allowed regardless of gender and permission. The DfE also advises on such matters but this advice is not always clear. For example, having updated prior advice which had effectively outlawed touching a pupil, they stated that it can be done when physical contact with a pupil is 'proper and necessary' (DfE, 2013: 8). With such complexity, it is best to rely on the school's instructions and always err on the side of caution.

To give you a flavour of the laws a school must operate within, we have isolated one section from the Education and Inspections Act (2006). This comes from Section 90 and gives legal power to discipline a child. First, it defines the issue:

'disciplinary penalty' means a penalty imposed on a pupil, by any school at which education is provided for him, where his conduct falls below the standard which could reasonably be expected of him (whether because he fails to follow a rule in force at any such school or an instruction given to him by a member of its staff or for any other reason).

So, it is the 'standard which could be reasonably respected of him' that can allow discipline, but whose expectation would 'he' be up against and what if the standards were unfair? What if the pupil had been falsely accused? Then, the Act defines the right of the school to enforce this discipline:

The imposition of the disciplinary penalty is lawful if … reasonable in all the circumstances … made … by any paid member of the staff of the school … or … by any other member of the staff of the school, in circumstances where the head teacher has authorised the member of the staff to impose the penalty on the pupil.

If you examine this wording, you will see that a non-salaried SD training teacher needs authorisation from the head teacher – which will usually be given – but this still leaves open the problems of what is 'reasonable in all the circumstances'. The law is a slippery snake and down to personal interpretation. Schools tend to rely on 'custom and practice' (repeating what they have always done by themselves and other similar schools) and government advice from non-statutory guidance such as the *Use of reasonable force in schools* (DfE, 2013) to be on the right side of this interpretation, but it is never clear-cut.

CHILD PROTECTION LAW AND SAFEGUARDING

Parents and **carers** will be concerned primarily that you keep their child safe. This was also the case over a hundred years ago when a judge, Lord Esher, concluded a case where a headmaster had been found guilty of neglect by leaving phosphorus accessible to pupils: 'The schoolmaster was bound to take such care of his boys as a careful father would' (*Williams* v. *Eady*, 1893). Initially, such responsibility was very much seen as a 'male thing', but in 1962, when an LEA was prosecuted for fitting a pane of glass which was capable of shattering in a school, the judge summing up the case said the LEA had failed to act as 'a prudent parent' should (*Lyes v. Middlesex County Council*, 1962). This phrase was repeated three times in the DfE-produced document *Health and safety: Advice on legal duties and powers for local authorities, school leaders, school staff and governing bodies* (2014). Above all the roles you have in school, and the most important bar none, the safeguarding of children is your first concern and you are, as teachers always have been, *in loco parentis*, or, in English, in the place of the parent/carer.

Keeping Children Safe in Education (KCSiE) (DfE, 2022b – this has been updated annually for some time and you should refer to the most up-to-date version) explains the legislative framework for schools regarding safeguarding. *KCSiE* runs to 177 pages and is thorough in its scope. It provides guidance about the laws that protect children, including the Sexual Offences Act, the Children Act, and so on, and aims to eliminate the awful immoral abuse of those who cannot yet protect themselves. It has 736 'should's and 118 'must's. The 'should's will be monitored when Ofsted come calling and the 'must's will result in prosecution if any are breached. School leaders have a responsibility to ensure that staff have read and are familiar with Part One of the statutory guidance document. There is plenty in this document that relates to 'all staff' and 'any staff member', and this includes you. You need to be trained, from the beginning of your time in a school, in safeguarding practice and can expect training updates as this guidance is updated regularly. Part of this training will be on spotting signs of abuse and on who the Safeguarding Lead is. Critically, you are not entitled to investigate anything yourself. You must also never promise a child confidentiality, as any worry about a child's safety must be reported to the Safeguarding Lead. As someone being trained, this reporting may be mediated by a mentor, but that does not excuse you from the role of safeguarding. You need to be vigilant for any signs of emotional, sexual and physical abuse, including neglect. Criminal exploitation, female genital mutilation and bullying (peer-on-peer) all need to be reported to the Safeguarding Lead. If the abuse is confirmed, there will be a multi-agency system, which includes the local authority. If there are safeguarding concerns about another member of staff, these should be reported to the head teacher. If there are safeguarding concerns about the head teacher, then they go to the governors. *KCSiE* (DfE, 2022b) is an invaluable guide, including whistleblowing procedures. It states that three processes must be in place in a school:

- pupil behaviour policy
- staff behaviour policy (code of conduct)
- safeguarding arrangements.

Staff training for these processes is compulsory at **induction,** which must be updated through the year. Children should be taught about safeguarding, know the processes whereby they can get support and be guided how best to protect themselves online and offline.

The Children and Young Persons Act (2008) is concerned with the **looked-after child** and supplies details to the school about provision and the need to give responsility to a designated teacher. This was updated in the Children and Families Act (2014) where a 'virtual school head' was included as someone to monitor the provision.

'Looked-after child' is the term for those in local authority care, which may mean in a residential home, with foster carers or relatives. Children who are assessed as needing this extra support can access funds and a system of support. As a training teacher, you will develop knowledge of looked-after pupils and how to liaise with the designated teacher.

The Children Act (1989 and 2004) focuses on vulnerable children, gives recommendations about who should care for them and formalised the word 'safeguarding' as the key one, which covers the welfare of children with these words: 'reasonable in all circumstances for the purpose of safeguarding or promoting the welfare of the child' (Children Act, 1989). The word was taken up by Ofsted and schools and was further emphasised in guidance documents such as *Working Together to Safeguard Children* (DfE, 2018) which, importantly, gave the clear requirement that teachers should know who to report cases to, but not investigate them themselves.

THE EQUALITY ACT

The Equality Act (2010) safeguards everyone (including you) against discrimination because of 'protected characteristics'. By specifying age, disability, gender reassignment, marriage and civil partnership, pregnancy and maternity, race, religion or belief, sex and sexual orientation, the Equality Act works as a legal protector that who you are, or choose to be, will not result in prejudicial action against you. If a school discriminates against you because of your faith, for example, then you have recourse to this law to prosecute the school; the law being in place means that, probably, they will not be discriminatory. We hope you would comply with the Equality Act out of common decency and humanity. If not, you could be prosecuted, and the Act makes it clear that it relates as much to teachers in school as well as out of it:

> Thus, if a teacher belittles a pupil and holds her up to ridicule in class because of a disability she has, this could lead to a court case alleging unlawful harassment. The same unacceptable treatment directed at a lesbian pupil, or based on a pupil's religion, could lead to a case claiming direct discrimination. The practical consequences for the school, and the penalties, would be no different. (The Equality Act, 2010)

KNIVES ACT/OFFENSIVE WEAPONS ACT

The Knives Act (1997) states that it is an offence to carry any sharp or bladed instrument in a public place if the blade is longer than 3 inches (or 7.62 cm). As this criminalises any freelance chef, there is the caveat that a longer one can be carried if there is 'good reason'. This is not an easy law to enforce – anyone stopped with a vicious slicer might claim to be taking it to their mother's house to carve a tough avocado. The law was created as a government response to media attention to crimes involving knives by young people – or what they often call 'get tough on knife crime'.

The Knives Act (1997) prevents children from buying knives and allows the police to search for them but tends to be used, sadly, to prosecute only after a knife attack has occurred. In school, there is no good reason to carry a knife … unless it is a scalpel in biology or a paint knife in art or a knife in food technology, or a Sikh kirpan, and so on. A child baptised into the Sikh religion may carry a kirpan (knife) because the Offensive Weapons Act was amended in 2019 to specifically allow them to carry one and the Equality Act (2010) protects their religious rights. So, despite the Knives Act (1997) and the Offensive Weapons Act (2019) – which also focuses on blades but extends legislation to corrosive substances, guns and anything else you would hope to never see used as weapons in school – knives are very much part of school life. Their use needs to be monitored and regulated by the idea that there is a common law duty of care. While not legislation, the courts have recorded many cases where a person or organisation can prosecute another because they neglected to do what is 'reasonably expected' to safeguard another person. There are cases of when someone has been prosecuted for doing nothing when action could have restored safety. For the safety of all children, the teacher must monitor the classroom, be aware of health and safety risks, and monitor behaviour closely. Leaving a maths class alone with a box of compasses, for example, would not be wise. The nature of care towards pupils is an every day, every moment concern.

SEXUAL OFFENCES ACT

Anyone who touches a child (legally, defined as a person under the age of 16) in a sexual manner is committing a legal offence which is punishable by imprisonment. Those who are in a 'position of trust' – and the Sexual Offences Act (2003) states that this includes teachers – are liable to be prosecuted if the child is under the age of 18. The same is true of sexualised photographs or what the law calls 'pseudo-photographs' (the law was written in the relatively early days of the internet). There must be no sexualised imagery of children under the age of 18. The training teacher who, on being shown a sexualised picture of a child by a pupil, used their phone to record it to show the Safeguarding Officer did so in breach of the law and was quickly dismissed from the school. There must be no sexualised contact between a teacher and a pupil.

COPYRIGHT LAW

Schools pay subscriptions to companies that grant some freedom from the Copyright, Designs and Patents Act (1988). If they did not, it would be impossible to use an image on a visual presentation or give a handout containing anything other than original material. Schools pay both the Educational Recording Agency (ERA, 2022) and the Copyright Licensing Agency (CLA, 2022) to allow 'fair dealing' (IPO, 2014) so that teachers can use pictures, text, sounds and moving images from published sources. The conditions for their use are that they must: 1) be used purposefully for education; 2) not be for commercial purposes (so beware if you are charging for an event); 3) have the source acknowledged. Use of some works is still not permitted even with this licence, such as musical texts which are not allowed to be reproduced, except for small extracts. This is a law that the school will guide you with but be careful to reproduce copyrighted work as little as possible, ensuring that it is always acknowledged and used purposefully.

LAWS THAT PROTECT YOU

The Education Act governs teachers' pay and conditions, which are outlined in the guidance document, *School Teachers' Pay and Conditions* (DfE, 2021). These apply to you if you are on the salaried route and therefore employed as an unqualified teacher. You are entitled to a 'reasonable break' (whatever that might mean; unions in the past have defined it as 40 minutes). Your working year is 190 teaching and 5 training days, leaving 170 days free from either. You have a right to a written contract within two months of starting your job, which includes a job title and the work that would be expected of you. As a full-time teacher, 10 per cent of your timetable must be planning time and not used for covering absent teachers, which should happen 'only rarely, and only in circumstances that are not foreseeable' (DfE, 2021: 51). The Employment Rights Act (1996) gives details of contracts, breaks and the information you should expect from your employer. The Health and Safety at Work Act (1974) gives legal power to the need to safeguard you from physical and mental harm while you are in the workplace. In a world of constantly changing laws, that these two laws are firmly based in the twentieth century informs us of government priorities, but in the event of any injury or abuse by an employer they are the laws to refer to, with guidance from a legal representative or union.

The DfE (2022a) document, which explains the legal framework for your course, is 'School Direct: guidance for schools'. It has only four 'must's, all of which relate to the legal requirements of the training school, and none of which to how the training teacher is protected. If you are on a salaried SD route, the school will have employed you as an unqualified teacher, so you have a contract and are protected by employment law. Those on the non-salaried route have no such legal protection. The Competitions and Markets Authority (CMA, 2022) will protect you if your course did not provide what it advertised. You may also refer your complaint to the Office of the Independent Adjudicator (OIA, 2022) who can take up your case. Any issues with a higher education organisation can be dealt with first through their internal complaint system and, if this does not satisfy, by the Office for Students (2022). You can also use unions, no matter what route you are on; joining one of these is strongly advised. The National Education Union is the largest with 465,000 members (NEU, 2022) and **NASUWT** (National Association of Schoolmasters and Union of Women Teachers) is close behind with 300,000+ members (NASUWT, 2022). As training teachers, you are allowed full union rights. The union provides you with courses, training, advice and support. It is also your point of access to legal teams who will act on your behalf in disputes.

CONCLUSION

We began the chapter by suggesting that the law has donkey-like qualities, but this is unfair on the animal. There are so many ifs and buts in place and the word 'reasonably' underscores so many requirements that it comes down to interpretation, and what the police and then judge and jury may decide. Laws are continually changed, and ensuring that you are kept up-to-date is the school and its managers' job. Your job is to know, understand and fulfil the school's regulations. Considering the personnel involved in education, there are relatively few prosecutions of schools, and imprisonment for teachers for offences (other than sexual ones) are rarer. Schools do have to pay out millions per year (BBC, 2016) for accident claims and there are a number of 'ambulance chaser' legal firms offering 'no risk prosecution' fuelling the market, but even this is a small amount considering the amount of people involved. Focus on knowing the rules and regulations of the school and complying with them, and you will be on the right side of the law. A pedagogy of care will ensure that you do nothing to harm children and everything to ensure their safety, and this will also be a barrier between you and prosecution.

REFLECTIONS ON LAW

When is it reasonable to do the following?

1   Remove disruptive children from a classroom when they have refused to follow instruction.
2   Prevent a pupil leaving the classroom.
3   Prevent a pupil attacking staff or student.
4   Restrain a pupil from self-harming.
5   Confiscate inappropriate items.
6   Detain pupils at the end of school.

You will need to know the answers, as these are common acts in school. In this reflection, consider both what you will be doing as a teacher, but balance this with what you are able to do as an SD training teacher. To find the legal answers, you would have to negotiate the 'should's and 'must's and then the 'unless'es and 'reasonable' clauses. These are questions that that are best to ask an experienced member of staff in advance of entering the classroom, and also to learn from observation and experience.

To what extent do you consider the content of the first paragraph in the section 'Laws that protect you' to be true? Everything in this paragraph, sadly, we observe being broken on a regular basis by schools. Teachers are expected to work in their holidays, cover for absent colleagues, their 10 per cent of planning time gets taken away and a lunchtime in school is a rare treat; anyone quietly eating lunch in a leisurely manner may be regarded with suspicion. Consider a response you can give to a school if asked to do something illegal, but think of the impact it will have on how the school sees you and how they might accuse you of being 'unprofessional', even though you are acting within the law.

ACTIONS

- There are legal experts in school who oversee policy, so your main action is to read, revise and internalise school policy on all matters. Keep within this guidance and you have fulfilled your duties. Beyond this, it is useful to have a working knowledge of the main laws outlined in this chapter.
- Read the school policies, published on their website, that relate to pupil well-being, safeguarding and behaviour. The policies are required under statutory guidance (DfE, 2022c). Also, read the school's staff discipline conduct and grievance policy – just in case.

REFLECTION-ON-ACTION BY A TRAINING TEACHER

Law is complex in theory and practice. Dale Booton reflects on the legal and social powers that limit their practice in terms of what they are allowed to discuss in the classroom.

In a letter to John Adams, Thomas Jefferson (1816) said 'bigotry is the disease of ignorance, of morbid minds …. Educating and free discussion are the antidotes.' From what I have seen from my experiences in schools, I could not agree more. One of my school placements has provided training for their staff members in developing equality around LGBT issues. I recently completed an e-learning module provided by Diversity Role Models through my school, which guided me through a range of activities to develop my understanding and awareness for Homophobic, Biphobic and Transphobic (HBT) bullying. As a result, I now feel confident in knowing how to deal with HTB bullying across schools, particularly when against impeding factors such as religious beliefs and parents, which can prove particularly challenging. Although Clause 28, a law which prohibited the promotion of homosexuality was repealed in 2003, and then later the Equality Act (2010) enabled protection of all from discrimination for the purposes of equality, society is still governed what is 'deemed acceptable' to be taught in schools. Epstein, O'Flynn and Telford (2003, p. 4) suggest that 'appropriate knowledge' of what should be taught to students is formed through 'the relative power of the "moral majority"'. From my experience, I have found this to be true as if I were to want to teach homosexual literature in my classroom it would result in a backlash from parents and ultimately the school. Greenbaum (1994, p. 71) and Unks (1995, p. 5) suggested that because they are not included, homosexuals are seen as 'nonpersons' who are believed to have contributed nothing to society through the lack of coverage. This was further resonated on my first placement school as there was absolutely no trace of LGBT throughout the taught curriculum even though the texts covered had LGBT themes or subtexts. Stevenson's *The Strange Case of Dr Jekyll and Mr Hyde* contains a strong subtext of homosexuality but this has been omitted from classroom discussions. Through discussion with the head of department and my subject mentor they felt there isn't training currently provided for teachers to understand how best to bring sexuality into the classroom. It stands to reason that a crucial element in challenging heteronormativity in the curriculum is not just educating the students but also the teachers and parents in order to develop equality and combat social injustice. Furthermore, DePalma and Atkinson (2009) suggest that in the classroom, where teachers ignore or remain silent about LGBT characters, content and themes across ranges of literature, an impression of shame and negative suggestions about homosexuality is imprinted on students through their lack of comfortability in these discussions. I have experienced many examples of this from discussions with teachers.

WHAT TOOLS ARE IN YOUR TOOLKIT NOW?

- Knowledge of education law and how it defines what can be done in school.
- Understanding of the importance of safeguarding.
- Awareness of laws that are applicable in schools.
- The ability to refer to supporting bodies including unions, the CMA and the OIA.

PLACES TO GET MORE TOOLS FOR YOUR TOOLKIT

DfE (2022, updated regularly) *Keeping Children Safe in Education*. London: HMSO.

Part One gives a detailed guide to safeguarding responsibilities for staff and the best practice to support the children in your care.

National Education Union (2020) *School Direct: your rights and expectations*. London: NEU.

The **NEU** produced a very useful guide of your rights as an SD training teacher and it starts with the right to join a union from which you get 'full and equal access' (NEU, 2020). Otherwise, the guide does rather confirm that unless the training teacher is on a salaried route, the requirements are shoulds rather than musts. There is a useful reminder that what applies to teachers – such as cover only being required in exceptional circumstances – also applies to training teachers.

Newlance, A. (2021) *Becoming a Teacher: The Legal, Ethical and Moral Implications of Entering Society's Most Fundamental Profession*. Camarthen: Crown House Publishing.

Chapter 3 is on law and subtitled as 'The teacher you must be'. It gives clear, no-compromise instruction about staying on the right side of the law.

REFERENCES

BBC (2016) *'School compensation payouts include blindfold mishap and whiteboard accident'* by L. Cawley and P. Shepka, 7 April 2017. Available from: www.bbc.co.uk/news/uk-england-39351183

British Library (n.d.) *Synopsis of the Forster Education Act 1870*. Available from: www.bl.uk/collection-items/synopsis-of-the-forster-education-act-1870

Children Act (1989) London: The Stationery Office. Available from: www.legislation.gov.uk/ukpga/1989/41/contents

Children Act (2004) London: The Stationery Office. Available from: www.legislation.gov.uk/ukpga/2004/31/contents

Children and Families Act (2014) London: The Stationery Office. Available from: www.legislation.gov.uk/ukpga/2014/6/contents/enacted

Children and Young Persons Act (2008) London: The Stationery Office. Available from: www.legislation.gov.uk/ukpga/2008/23/contents

CLA (2022) *Copyright Licensing Agency*. Available from: www.cla.co.uk

CMA (2022) *Competitions and Market Authority*. Available from: www.gov.uk/government/organisations/competition-and-markets-authority

Copyright, Designs and Patents Act (1988) London: The Stationery Office. Available from: www.legislation.gov.uk/ukpga/1988/48/contents

DfE (2013) *'Use of reasonable force: Advice for headteachers, staff and governing bodies'*. Available from: https://assets.publishing.service.gov.uk/government/uploads/system/uploads/attachment_data/file/444051/Use_of_reasonable_force_advice_Reviewed_July_2015.pdf

DfE (2014) *'Health and safety: Advice on legal duties and powers for local authorities, school leaders, school staff and governing bodies'*. Available from: https://assets.publishing.service.gov.uk/government/uploads/system/uploads/attachment_data/file/279429/DfE_Health_and_Safety_Advice_06_02_14.pdf

DfE (2018) *'Working together to safeguard children'*. Available from: www.gov.uk/government/publications/working-together-to-safeguard-children-2

DfE (2021) *'School teachers' pay and conditions'*. Available from: www.gov.uk/government/publications/school-teachers-pay-and-conditions

DfE (2022a) *'School Direct: Guidance for schools'*. Available from: www.gov.uk/guidance/school-direct-guidance-for-lead-schools

DfE (2022b) *'Keeping children safe in education'*. Available from: https://assets.publishing.service.gov.uk/government/uploads/system/uploads/attachment_data/file/1101457/KCSIE_2022_Part_One.pdf

DfE (2022c) *'Statutory policies for schools and academy trusts'*. Available from: www.gov.uk/government/publications/statutory-policies-for-schools-and-academy-trusts/statutory-policies-for-schools-and-academy-trusts

Dickens, C. (2001) *Bleak House*. London: Wordsworth Classics.

Education Act (1996) London: The Stationery Office. Available from: www.legislation.gov.uk/ukpga/1996/56/section/550ZA

Education and Inspections Act (2006) London: The Stationery Office. Available from: www.legislation.gov.uk/ukpga/2006/40/contents

Education and Skills Act (2008) London: The Stationery Office. Available from: www.legislation.gov.uk/ukpga/2008/25/section/1

Employment Rights Act (1996) London: The Stationery Office. Available from: www.legislation.gov.uk/ukpga/1996/18/contents

Equality Act (2010) London: The Stationery Office. Available from: www.legislation.gov.uk/ukpga/2010/15/contents

ERA (2022) *Educational Recording Agency*. Available from: https://era.org.uk

Health and Safety at Work Act (1974) London: The Stationery Office. Available from: www.legislation.gov.uk/ukpga/1974/37/contents

IPO (2014) *'Intellectual Property Office: Exceptions to copyright'*. Available from: www.gov.uk/guidance/exceptions-to-copyright

Knives Act (1997) London: The Stationery Office. Available from: www.legislation.gov.uk/ukpga/1997/21/contents

Lyes v. *Middlesex County Council* (1962) 61 LGR 443.

NASUWT (2022) *'About us'*. Available from: www.nasuwt.org.uk/about-nasuwt.html

NEU (2020) *'School Direct: your rights and expectations'*. Available from: https://neu.org.uk/media/566/view

NEU (2022) *About the NEU*. Available from: https://neu.org.uk/about-neu

Offensive Weapons Act (2019) London: The Stationery Office. Available from: www.legislation.gov.uk/ukpga/2019/17/contents/enacted

Office for Students (2022) Available from: www.officeforstudents.org.uk

OIA (2022) *Office of the Independent Adjudicator*. Available from: www.oiahe.org.uk

Sexual Offences Act (2003) London: The Stationery Office. Available from: www.legislation.gov.uk/ukpga/2003/42/contents

Williams v. *Eady* (1893) *10 TLR 41 CA*.

5
LESSON

INTRODUCTION

In our experience, a lesson begins outside the classroom where the activities, timings, pupil support and resources are prepared. At the heart of this planning is 'learning', so this chapter examines what this might mean and how the space of a lesson takes the pupils from not being able to do something to being able to do so. What the 'do' looks like varies – it may be an emotional shift towards something, acquiring new facts, gaining skills, increasing confidence, changing thought patterns. It is learning, not teaching, that really matters, and this shift away from the acts of the teacher to the development of the pupil can revolutionise lessons. The resources available to training teachers are outlined, with advice on creating lessons.

THE NATURE OF LEARNING

'Back in the day', as they say, one of us was walking to school for a training session titled 'Improving Learning' when an experienced fellow teacher muttered, 'When I came into teaching, nobody ever said anything about learning'. Teaching is not learning: that much is true. They are two different acts, and you should never presume that what you teach is what pupils learn. You should also remember that a child will be learning something in your lesson despite what, as well as because of what, you teach. You cannot turn off the tap of learning. A child who does not attend to you or your activities is still learning by thinking, talking to others, and using all their senses to create something new. Perhaps they are worrying about how to approach an issue at home and, during your lesson, work through the best way. Viewing learning in this way stops the idea of a linear input–output model of transmission of knowledge, which is one of the many tempting models of learning you can enjoy reading about. Human beings are active seekers of stimuli of whatever is in the classroom and also inside the mind.

Not only is your lesson only one of the many sources of learning in the room, it may be the least attractive. John Holt was writing about education through the latter half of the twentieth century and his message remained consistent:

> Nobody starts off stupid ... what happens, as we get older, to this extraordinary capacity for learning and intellectual growth? What happens is that it is destroyed, and more than by any other one thing, by the process that we misname education ... We destroy this capacity above all by making them afraid, afraid of not doing what other people want, of not pleasing, of making mistakes, of failing, of being wrong. Thus we make them afraid to gamble, afraid to experiment, afraid to try the difficult and the unknown. We destroy the disinterested (I do not mean uninterested) love of learning in children, which is so strong when they are small, by encouraging and compelling them to work for petty and contemptible rewards – gold stars, or papers marked 100 and tacked to the wall, or 'A's on report cards ... We encourage them to feel that the end and aim of all they do in school is nothing more than to get a good mark on a test, or to impress someone with what they seem to know. (Holt, 1990: 273–4)

Examining this quotation, you will see that Holt thought that school prevented learning – and he was not alone. The institutionalised nature of schools, government-influenced content and the falseness of the environment in which ideas are taught 'in theory' without the individuals experiencing their real-world practice are not conducive to the process of learning. Some argue that school (if it is necessary at all) should focus on creating self-fulfilled individuals and promoting a love of learning that will continue throughout their lives.

This 'freethinking child' was at the heart of Jean-Jacques Rousseau's (1712–78) musings on education. John Dewey (1859–1952) criticised the way that mass schooling was doing the opposite:

To imposition from above is opposed expression and cultivation of individuality; to external discipline is opposed free activity; to learning from texts and teachers, learning from experience; to acquisition of isolated skills and techniques by drill, is opposed acquisition of them as a means of attaining ends which make direct vital appeal; to preparation for a more or less remote future is opposed making the most of the opportunities of present life; to static aims and materials is opposed acquaintance with a changing world. (Dewey 1938: 5–6)

Rousseau was writing from France, Dewey and Holt were voicing their concerns from America. From Italy, Maria Montessori (1870–1952) advised:

Like a sponge these children absorb. It is marvellous, this mental power of the child. Only we cannot teach directly. It is necessary that the child teach himself, and then the success is great. (Montessori, 1964: 11)

In 1904 in Germany, the social commentator Max Weber (1864–1920) worried that the urbanisation of society and capitalism had created a series of *Gehause* or 'iron cages' (Weber, 1992). Humans were processed through a series of institutions, including the factory and school, restricted in movement and force-fed instruction in rooms and buildings they were not free to move into, around and from. Originally from Brazil, Paolo Freire (2000) added to the weight of criticism of education as he believed that schools acted like banks: the teacher makes a deposit and the child is the passive recipient. Instead, Freire proposed the following:

* Start with what the students love
* Understand that they must want to learn
* The teacher learns from the students.

The problem with this 'practice of freedom' (Freire, 1976), as enlightened educational theorists across the globe have espoused, is that it is not part of the educational strategy commonly supported by UK governments. Educational thinker Dave Trotman explored this in one of his speeches:

One point of contact may be in the Nordic term *Bildung* … a term that is used in philosophy in Northern Europe, is 'the promotion of liberty and human dignity' (Prange, 2004, p. 502). You can see why this corresponds with the liberal education view of John Henry Newman; 'the inner-life of the human soul, mind and humanity' (Biesta, 2002b, p. 378), the formation of the self (Beck et al., 2015, p. 445), self-cultivation (Sorkin, 1983) and edification (Masschelein and Ricken, 2003, p. 139) … or 'the spiritual aesthetic aspects of our lives, the formation of self' (Prange, 2004, p. 503). The critics come back and say, 'Yes, this is lovely Dave. It's all very middle class, isn't it? People knocking around, pontificating. It's all lovely, lovely, lovely'. (2020: 401)

Trotman gives an outline of some ideas from thinkers who would state that schools should focus on helping children 'to become everything one is capable of becoming' (Maslow, 1987: 64). Trotman's speech also highlights the privileged position from which you may be standing if you are decrying a state education system that gives everyone, regardless of their background, a chance to achieve. At the same time, and equally, we should attend to the voices of those who believe that the school system takes naturally learning human beings and places them in buildings where teachers impose forced topics at forced times, preventing rather than aiding learning. A counterpoint is that results matter and they matter most to those whose life chances are not as open as others.

At the 'toolkit end' of learning theory, there is an undoubted need to retrieve prior learning and prepare pupils for exams. Nevertheless, not attending to the criticisms of your profession, or the accusation that you are no more than government 'lackeys' ideologically controlling the populace, would be to blindside yourself to not only long-held criticisms from outside but also, we suspect, to a nagging sense that you feel they may be true. In the words of Richard Shaull, who summed up the views in Paolo Freire's (2000) *Pedagogy of the Oppressed* in the book's Foreword:

> There is no such thing as a neutral education process. Education either functions as an instrument which is used to facilitate the integration of generations into the logic of the present system and bring about conformity to it, or it becomes the 'practice of freedom', the means by which men and women deal critically with reality and discover how to participate in the transformation of their world. (P. 34)

Such voices that criticise the state's government-prescribed curriculum, taught in a false environment, have been with us across the globe for as long as the system has been in place, and yet the system persists. There is no reason why you cannot teach in schools and become part of the 'practice of freedom', because what matters is how you use the opportunity given to you, in the classroom, with the pupils. The first step is to bring your subject around to the worlds of the pupils. Harness the passion they have for what they care about and move it to your subject.

- What do they love? Try finding out and relate your topic to their passion. Try moving your passion for your subject onto them.
- Give pupils a reason to learn, beyond an exam. A 12-year-old is unlikely to be thinking as far ahead as the weekend, let alone something that may happen in over three years' time. The immediate concerns of the day – pleasures, worries, next activities, possible actions – will be far more dominant than an exam which, anyway, may not be necessary for the superstar trajectory they may have in mind.
- Be open to a classroom in which everyone learns from each other. You are not the only holder of knowledge, skills and understanding. Celebrate what each child brings.

LEARNING THEORIES

Although Socrates (*c.* 469–399 BC) declaimed ideas which could loosely be translated as that 'I cannot teach anybody anything. I can only make them think', since his day there has been no shortage of people talking about how anybody can teach. This comes in an array of learning theories but, as Jean Baudrillard noted: 'The secret of theory is that truth does not exist' (2007: 120).

In place of 'truth' comes insight – greater understanding of the topic. Below is a short list of learning theories and an explanation of each. Each is an 'ism', which means a belief system, as no one knows how the brain acts in learning – or rather, a lot of people think they 'know', but it does not mean that it is true.

1 **Behaviourism**/social learning: pupils will respond to immediate rewards or punishments. Through the process of external control through rewards and punishments, learning becomes a norm in the classroom. Pupils learn by copying others, so if good actions towards learning are modelled, the child will develop them.

2 **Cognitivism**/constructivism: learning is a change in the brain. The brain organises knowledge in certain areas and new learning accesses this area first, then adds something new. This is reinforced by memorisation which changes the pupil's brain structure and gives new ways of thinking and understanding of the world.

3 **Humanism:** everyone creates their own sense of who they are and what the world is like. There is no one ideal way of doing this so, a pupil is free to develop at their own pace and to form their understanding of what things mean. Creativity and individualism are central to the process of becoming human.

These are some 'isms' that explain learning in different ways. We cannot be, simultaneously, both manipulable non-beings (behaviourism) and individualised developers of the self (humanism). However, dig a little deeper and each 'ism' has strengths in attempting to understand different facets of learning.

Learning acceptable social behaviours and interactions, including the 'rules' of the classroom, is an aspect of school practice where behaviourist and social learning theories such as those of John Watson (1878–1958), Burrhus Skinner (1904–90) and Albert Bandura (1925–2021) offer insights. For teachers working to support the development of new ways of thinking, cognitivism and constructivism offer insights. If the aim is to develop creativity or form a position on a controversial topic, humanism might help us to understand how to create a fruitful learning environment. Learning theories offer a set of 'tools in the toolkit' for reflecting on learning and teaching in practice, but they must be more than simply a curriculum for training teachers to demonstrate knowledge in PGCE assignments. To have value to teachers, these theoretical lenses must speak to classroom practice and experience as part of the armoury of the reflective practitioner.

It is worth highlighting the influences that some of these different learning theories have had on changing fashions in classrooms. The latter part of the last century and first decade of this one saw an increasing influence from constructivist views of learning. Perhaps the most significant influence here was a growth in research literature into 'misconceptions' – a word you will find in the research literature into 'misunderstandings' – a word you will find in the *Teachers' Standards* (DfE, 2011). There was also an influence arising from the recognition of the work of Lev Vygotsky and on the dialogic teaching approaches of Robin Alexander (2020). At the same time, there was a fashion for 'learning styles', a development of Gardner's (1984) multiple intelligence theory, with teachers being encouraged to address whether pupils preferred to learn through visual, auditory or kinaesthetic means (popularly known as VAK). This became so entrenched as a 'truth' about the ways that people learn, that it appeared in all sorts of training manuals (including the Royal Yachting Association teaching guides). It is still commonly cited in interviews with prospective SD and PGCE applicants, despite being categorised as a 'neuromyth' in the recent drive for a more scientific evidence base for learning theories. Similarly, what is known as Bloom's taxonomy (which is not by Bloom alone as it was a collaboration – see Bloom et al., 1956) enjoyed some time in fashion as a structure for differentiating learning outcomes, often in snappy acronyms such as 'IDEAL' (Identify, Describe, Explain, Analyse, Link). This, too, has now fallen from favour as a result of research suggesting that differentiating learning outcomes can negatively affect progress for some pupils, alongside a lack of evidence-base for Bloom et al's original work (multiple intelligences also had no evidence, but it was still widely adopted). As with all 'isms', a degree of caution is needed for all ideas that you are presented with because they will go in and out of fashion. The ideas that get adopted would, arguably, not exist if there was no truth in them somewhere and it is up to you to find out what this is; what works for you will be your truth.

One 'ism' that has been very much in fashion over the last few years is 'cognitivism'. When the government promotes a particular stance, as they have with cognitivism, they do not want this to be followed unthinkingly. Nothing should be parroted as, apart from anything else, to do so is the opposite of what we want from children: the ability to think freely, be creative and have the courage to explore for themselves. The 'ism' that is cognitive can be summarised as: attention – input – output. Put like this, learning seems like a machine process (and some do see learning like this!) The drive to cognitivism has been boosted by the evidence we have gained from neuroscience – the ability of computerised machines to 'read' how the brain responds. Even with developments in neuroscience and brain imaging, learning remains a far from transparent process and, thus, writers reach for metaphor to make it accessible. The metaphors of current cognitive science stem from neuroscience research that is contemporaneous with the emergence of artificial intelligence as a field of study in computer science. Language terms such as 'working memory' and 'intrinsic load' evoke a mechanistic view of learning as the formation of memory and **schema**. Steven Pinker rather dryly discounted the metaphor as only partially useful:

> Computers are serial, doing one thing at a time; brains are parallel, doing millions of things at once …. Computers have a limited number of connections; brains have trillions.

> Computers are assembled according to a blueprint; brains must assemble themselves. Yes, and computers come in putty-coloured boxes … and run screen savers with flying toasters. (Pinker, 1999: 26)

If we move away from the idea that learning is a matter of inputting data, cognitive theory adds greatly to our understanding of what works in the classroom. Attentioning, or getting pupils to listen, is the first part of the cognitive process. The writer Robert Owens Jr was once giving Jessica, aged four, an early morning lecture on manners when she said: 'Say that again. I didn't hear you. I was listening to my toast' (Owens, 2016: flyleaf).

There is no reason to think that anyone in the room is listening to you. They might be silent and even looking your way, but their minds may well be elsewhere – in fact, they are likely to be. Remember your experience of being in a class and sitting by a window looking out, or daydreaming, or worrying, or thinking about what you will eat and do for lunch. So it is with your pupils – you are teaching, but they are not listening. This does not mean they are not learning (their mental ruminations over this subject or that are making changes in their minds – even if the change is what to eat for lunch); it is just that they are not learning what you are teaching.

In order to gain pupils' attention, we can 'hook' them into a lesson. One way is to give them a cognitive jolt – something they have not thought of before or a new way of viewing a subject. Optical illusions, for example, show how the brain can process images differently. You could undermine their belief that water boils at 100 degrees with a multi-choice question that has three temperatures, none of which is the expected one. You could introduce them to the spinning cones at the bottom of the switches on pedestrian crossings that they may never have noticed, or 'stingray' them, as Socrates would have done, with a big statement such as: 'a whole kingdom is not worth a single horse'. A hook is an ideal start, but it is difficult to find very many examples and, more typically, your lesson will have a 'starter' at the beginning. This is a short activity related to the topic of the lesson and designed to begin pupils' thinking. It might be a short discussion point or card sort. It may last for 5–10 minutes – enough time for you to settle the class and take the register. If the class is unruly, then settlers – calming activities unrelated to the lesson – may be used. A good settler is free reading, which some schools employ for all lessons that support literacy, as each lesson should, regardless of subject. You might use a maths problem – each lesson should also support **numeracy**. One training teacher we observed would put the lesson title in Scrabble letters and ask the class to calculate the numbers on the letter tiles.

Once the attention of the class has been obtained and they have settled, started or are hooked, we can use the ideas of cognitivist Jean Piaget (1896–1980) to visualise how learning happens through schema development. When we are babies, objects, feelings and ideas are given labels. To give an example, a 'coat' is the outer garment worn by a child and they will be given a word for it. The word and object 'coat' looks a particular way and this will be given meanings (connotations) through use.

'Coat' could mean 'going out', but it also might mean 'security' as this is the feeling putting it on gives. 'Coat' might come to mean punishment if every time the child is naughty, the parent shoves a coat on them and sends them into the garden. The central word 'coat' is in the child's mind as a fixed set of neurons (brain cells), linked by axons (pathways for electrical signals between neurons) and activated when the word or object is mentioned or seen. This schema can change, as a child who thought of a 'coat' as punishment at two years old may have another parent who likes to wrap them up in the coat for a warm hug at three years old. The original meaning will still be there, but so will the new one; the child will see a coat, but with one parent it will mean punishment and with another it will mean love. Over time, the links to the old meaning will reduce and the new meaning will be the one that is more quickly associated with it, simply because the connection is more commonly meant. New connections will be developed and form links to a whole chain of other objects and meanings, until a single trigger from outside can activate a whole group of symbols or meanings (schemas or schemata) at the same time, along with associated feelings and bodily responses.

It is possible to create a new schema called 'What I need to know to pass my geography exam, Paper One', and by repeating this phrase enough times, the pupil may establish a whole series of objects or meanings that will need to be accessed in the exam. It is possible, but of what use would this be to the pupil in life? A colleague's son who had successfully negotiated his studies and gained a university place lamented: 'I didn't learn geography; I learned how to pass a geography exam'.

We think it is preferable to work on the child's capacity to learn naturally and simply develop their knowledge of the curriculum topic. Take the Holocaust, for example. An attempt to explain holocausts in general terms is a good starting point; then you could move on to the one which is identified as a necessary learning point in the History programmes of study in the National Curriculum. The who, where, why (if it can be fathomed), when and how need to be established, and around this central schema links will be added. So, for example, the child should have some knowledge of the Second World War. A connection will open up between this schema and the phrase 'the Holocaust' when you inform them of the dates.

To 'know' something has to mean more than just to be able to retrieve a factual memory; it also must be to understand, comprehend, make sense of. Assimilation and accommodation are words that help us to understand the way that new knowledge may be received. We learn new skills or facts and accept them as they are (assimilation). We might come across knowledge that is new and even conflicts with our understanding, and have to move our existing ways of thinking to match it (accommodation). Each time, we build or adapt our schemas. This new knowledge is partial in all of us. It is quite possible to know the mechanics of a car, a gear stick and even a carburettor, yet have no idea how they fit together. Many of us are quite happy to propel ourselves in a vehicle at quite deathly speeds without comprehending our means of so doing. These are the realities of learning: we know some; we comprehend partially. Knowledge is also something we can teach but cannot impose. The poet Kahil Gibran (1883–1931) expressed this perfectly: 'You can give them your love but not your thoughts/ For they have their own thoughts' (Gibran, 1923). There is a sense in some interpretations of cognitive theory that learning can somehow be created in a collective schema, but all we can do is access the individual's current understanding and feelings, and how what is there currently links to the sense of self – in other words, the pupil needs to know 'what it means to me'. If it does not mean anything to the pupil, then the connections to it may fall quickly into disuse, much as a pathway which is rarely trodden on is covered in weeds and plants until no one remembers that it ever existed.

MEMORY AND RETENTION

To stop this closure of the pathways of knowledge, we need to make sure that the learning is readily accessible in exam situations. Retention and memorisation are at the heart of examinations, and the theories of learning of Barak Rosenshine, Jerome Bruner and John Sweller help us to put these into practice. For Rosenshine (2010), the following four theories help memorisation:

1 Sequencing: position new learning so that it builds on prior knowledge.
2 Modelling: show how the new learning can be put into practice.
3 Questioning: assess whether the new learning is in place.
4 Reviewing: remind the pupils what the new learning is.

Having put into practice the four principles of memorisation, John Sweller's (1988) **Cognitive Load Theory** comes into play, as it suggests to the teacher that the range of sensory input in classrooms creates a cognitive 'load' on pupils. This load includes both the input, the learning objectives of the lesson (part of the 'intrinsic' load), and that which is a by-product of the complex interactions and environment of the classroom (the 'extraneous' load). Sweller argues that the extrinsic load should be minimised to avoid competition for working memory resources, which we can do by simplifying instructions, clearing away the clutter of the classroom, scaffolding tasks, etc. We also need to establish ready retrieval of long-term memory so that pupils can access complex information quickly and easily, and this can be done by regular repetition. Once a topic has been learned, the brain will naturally 'fire' a response in many places on the topic and the pupil will now be in a position to learn something more about it.

To take an example from English literature, imagine that the life of Charles Dickens has been successfully taught and now the pupil has a series of schemata connected to the central word and meanings of 'Dickens'. Pupils know the dates of his life, the context of Victorian England's urban poor alongside his impoverished (at one stage) childhood. Into these schemata comes the novel *A Christmas Carol* and the child will read about how Scrooge ill treats the poor, with the contextual knowledge that Dickens experienced life in Victorian London. The pupil is in a position to add (or assimilate) the novel to the existing schema and the load is 'light' as much of the background information is in place, so the new knowledge of the book can be added without the need to affect what is already there. It is never this easy, though. One training teacher told us about a pupil who had read about Dickens's negative views of non-white people in America and quite reasonably announced, 'Why should I want to read something by a racist?' Assimilating Dickens as a champion of the people in this circumstance would be impossible without addressing the issue blocking the initial attention point. It also informs us that we need to be where the pupils are, rather than 'steamrollering' into each topic as if we were in a neutral, amoral space.

Having made sure that the memory and retention practices of Rosenshine are in place and reduced the 'cognitive load', as Sweller advocated, you can try exercising Bruner's (1960) **spiral curriculum**. This means that you need to keep returning to the same topic, each time adding more. As teachers, we might think that if something is covered from our Scheme of Work (SoW), then it is done. Instead, Bruner advised us to keep returning to the same learning matter to build on it, reinforce it and improve retrieval. The more we revise, the quicker our mind gets at accessing the knowledge. This idea has gained support from cognitive science research that suggests that long-term memory is more likely to be secured if learning is revisited after a period of time or interleaved with other learning.

Studies of the development of knowledge have identified features that have an implication for learning, particularly in relation to the recall of learned facts. The Sequential Position Effect combines two features of recall: the 'primacy effect' that you are more likely to recall information presented at the start of a learning episode, and the 'recency effect' that information presented most recently is more likely to be recalled. This means that information presented in the middle of a sequence is recalled less well. Studies that identify these effects are typically performed under test conditions requiring subjects to recall sequences of information, but it has interesting implications for the sequencing of lessons. Other memory formation effects also have potential implications for lesson planning. The Spaced Learning Effect identifies the positive effect of repeated relearning of material after gaps of several weeks on the amount of information retrieved. With successive revisions, the proportion of material recalled and the length of time it is successfully recalled increase as stable long-term memories are formed. This effect supports the now common strategy of retrieval practice at the start of lessons. Indeed, taken to its logical conclusion, it would suggest that the idea of 'overlearning', relearning already well-recalled knowledge, would be beneficial. However, there is a complex relationship here with the dynamics of real lessons with children. Consider how some of the groups you are working with would respond to relearning information that they can already recall, albeit relatively close to the original teaching. Would they recognise the importance of forming stable long-term memory or become bored and frustrated with the repetition? More useful, perhaps, is the inclusion of activities that require the use of previously learnt knowledge to new problems and challenging tasks in lessons.

It is tempting to think that developments in neuroscience have provided, for the first time, evidence to support the biological basis of learning, but it is still not possible to 'read' the mind. At the time of his study, Kenning (2008: 47) estimated that there were around 100,000 neurons (brain cells) per square millimetre of the brain and that a pixel on a screen represented over 5 million neurons and 22 kilometres of axons (linking pathways between groups of cells). Even today, neuroscience offers us a very limited understanding of what is happening in the brain and any focus on just this organ forgets that we are also a feeling body. The educational thinker Ken Robinson criticised academics for thinking that the body is only there to take the brain to meetings. If we were to remove this single organ from the body, admittedly nothing much is possible. Yet if we were to remove the body from the brain, the same applies, just as it does if we remove the heart. Noam Chomsky saw the brain as a 'mental organ' and, like the heart, liver, glands, etc., it works as part of a whole and cannot be divorced from the 'self'. Building on Chomsky's ideas, Steven Pinker (1999) separated the organ of 'the brain' from 'the mind' – the thinking, conscious self – and it is this self that we are developing. Cognitive theory can be criticised for being too brain-obsessed and losing the sense of the whole being – the holistic. For all that, there are some important implications of the emerging views of cognitive science for teachers.

GROUPING, PEER AND SOCIAL LEARNING

If we look at the model of learning given to us by cognitivists, we can see that it is a construction of ideas. Just as when building a house, what is new is added to what is already there, and adds to, changes or makes something different. It is always not essential for another person to be involved (directly) as we can learn from books, the internet and from experience. But we also learn from each other, which is where the importance of grouping comes in. Each of us has knowledge and if we were to sit down with someone we might find that there would be something we do not know that they do, and vice versa. This process of co-learning moves the pressure of learning from the teacher to the pupils.

Here, it is traditional to give a respectful 'nod' to Lev Vygotsky (1896–1934), a lawyer-turned-philosopher, whose work was translated into English in the 1960s and since then has been a central pillar in the ideas of how we learn from each other. As with so much learning psychology, the ideas Vygotsky introduced had been instinctively known for centuries, but helped us to visualise the idea. Vygotsky gave us the image of a Zone of Proximal Development (ZPD). It links very well with the cognitive view of development being something constructed but adds the importance of not only another person who knows more (the More Knowledgeable Other – it was probably a better phrase in Russian), but also being able to 'pitch' this new learning at a pace that can be understood. It is possible that the teacher is the More Knowledgeable Other, but, equally, a pupil who has more advanced learning can do the same job. This is one reason for pairing or grouping pupils – one knowing more than the other. This can be done using a traffic light system, so you could ask the class about their level of understanding of a topic; some might be green (strong) and others red (weak), and red and green then 'buddy up'. You might also observe who has more advanced understanding in the class and put a seating plan in place so one pupil can support another. Equally, you could group pupils on tables according to their strengths and the topic could be pitched differently, as each is within the same 'zone' of learning and they can all move together. It is not a good idea, in our view, to separate groups permanently on this basis, with one table being 'high ability' and another 'low ability'. These terms are not useful, as they suggest that some are not able when surely all children are. Also, those on the tables soon figure out the label you have given and it can cause resentment. These terms do not allow for progression (unless you are going to notably move pupils from one side of the room to the next like a league table). Instead, on a lesson-by-lesson basis, groupings can be done actively, purposefully and to aid learning. The classroom may not be yours to manipulate, as the school may prohibit movement of the furniture, but the pupils can usually move, although some schools impose strange rules and even this may not be allowed.

Using the knowledge of others will take some pressure off yourself. You may have over 30 pupils in a room and cannot attend to them all, so will need to focus your attention. If you add an 'ask three before me' policy into your lesson, the pupils will not always see you as the holder of the information as they can rely more on each other. There are many ways of grouping – pairs, fours (five, in our experience results in the fifth person testing the chair's ability to stand upright on two legs, so is perhaps too many). The group can be given roles. A triad of pupils might have one as speaker, another as recorder and a third as envoy. The views of only one pupil matter here and the envoy will move to another group to share them using the notes the recorder has taken. You could jigsaw the groups by giving groups of four pupils a number each and a separate aspect of the topic to discuss. You then have mixed tables of all four numbers and each gives the perspective of their first group to the rest. Vygotsky's emphasis on the linguistic nature of learning, the formation and testing of new ideas through language in discourse with others, gives us a lens to consider how learning might be strengthened by allowing pupils to explore and examine new ideas without direct interaction with the teacher.

As with the implications of all the theoretical perspectives discussed, we would caution against too libertarian an approach to peer learning. As some of Rosenshine's research (1986, 1987, 2010) has shown, within the limits of a school curriculum and examination system, more effective teachers employ a significant proportion of classroom time in direct instruction. Direct instruction would be teacher led, including whole-class exposition and interaction through teacher-directed questions. So, you can see that in adopting a 'toolkit' approach to effective teaching, it is not about selecting a preferred learning theory, but reflecting on the implications of each for effective teaching. Even though currently unfashionable learning theories like VAK or Bloom's taxonomy are challenged on the basis of there being no evidence that consistently applying either in the classroom leads to improved outcomes, there is no evidence that some of the range of teaching approaches and strategies have done any harm – quite the contrary. This approach is in line with the founder of the approach called Cognitive Behavioural Therapy, Aaron Beck (1975), who responded to the criticism of his methods 'What can it cure?', with 'What can't it help?' We would argue that rather than seeking a 'Holy Grail' unifying theory that instructs all teachers how to act, it is more fruitful to empower new teachers to explore and reflect on how thinking about learning in different ways leads to a range of actions which can bring about learning.

LESSON PLANS

For successful lessons, preparation is all. Prepare the whole-class talk, resources, questions (what and to whom) and even the 'ad libs'. If you prepare the lesson thoroughly, you can focus on performance in the room. If you do not prepare, your mind will need to be thinking of what to say next, what to do, which resources are needed and where they are. This is too much for an experienced teacher, let alone a training one. One practice that may fool you into thinking that lessons can be planned in the room are those given by experienced teachers whose plans consist of a few words written in their Teacher's Planner. They can do this as they have enacted the lesson many times and so have their discussion and questions in their memories, and the resources are a matter of going to a folder in a filing cabinet or computer to duplicate them.

For a few decades, the school inspection agency Ofsted gave criteria for 'outstanding' lessons. Inevitably (and unfortunately), these criteria resulted in 'colour by numbers' lessons incorporating all the supposedly successful elements 'filled in' with subject details. We observed hundreds of versions of what was essentially the same lesson with only the teaching content changed. This lesson started with a learning outcome which the pupils wrote down, a starter activity, questioning, main activity, questioning, main written exercise, plenary and exit. This is a perfectly good structure, but the pupils were experiencing 'identikit' lessons four, five, six, seven or even eight times a day and were getting bored, as were we when we observed them and, possibly, as were Ofsted who gave updated advice:

> The promotion of a particular lesson methodology or teaching style claimed to be modelled on Ofsted's demands is not endorsed by Ofsted. Inspectors evaluate the quality of teaching over time by considering its impact on learning. They are most interested in the standards achieved by pupils and the progress made. The school inspection handbook states: 'Inspectors must not advocate a particular method of teaching or show preference towards a specific lesson structure … Inspectors do not expect to see any particular lesson structure'. (Ofsted, 2014: 3)

As part of this positive move from a focus on teaching to learning, lesson plans were no longer necessary. There was a time when the lesson plan was a sacrosanct document and its presence (or absence) was considered critical to success on a teacher-training course. Every aspect of the lesson had to be thoroughly documented, including the resources, seating plans, questioning schedule, timings, EAL and SEND provision, etc. Today, some schools will not even expect training teachers to create their own lessons, but merely to adapt existing plans and resources and deliver to a group. The move away from the detailed lesson plan also recognises that presentation devices such as Microsoft PowerPoint have timings, structure and resources in place. Planning through visual aids is so commonplace that it seems churlish (and hypocritical as we often do the same) to criticise the practice, but there is a limit to what they can do. We recommend a separate plan alongside the visual aids. There is an adage that a presentation slide should have no more words than a T-shirt does. T-shirt texts are designed to be read quickly from a distance and carry a single message, and your slide should do the same – providing visual support for your verbal instruction. Apart from anything else, the class ought to be looking at you, more than at a screen.

No matter what the school practice, you will need to create or adapt some lesson plans as your training institution will insist on it. Anyone who sits with a blank lesson plan in front of them is not understanding the collaborative nature of teaching. There are millions of lesson plans readily available and adaptable from others. The **Times Educational Supplement** website alone has over 900,000 resources available (TES, 2021). Your school intranet should also have a Scheme of Work, resources and lesson plans for each topic. The SoW is a plan of topics and timing, usually created by the head of subject based on the subject curriculum (which may be the National Curriculum, a school's alternative or guidance from professional bodies). At **Key Stage** 4, they will also need to map **Assessment Objectives** (AOs) which are created by government-funded subject experts who advise exam boards about how to test knowledge in each subject. At Key Stages 4 (e.g., GCSE level) and 5 (e.g., Advanced level), they are good to refer to but not, we think, at Key Stage 3, which is meant to be a place for wider exploration of the subject. Our experience in some schools of the past ten years has shown that the pressure of showing results from league tables has meant that AOs inform planning even in Year 7. We have also noticed how some SoWs are not updated and others are not accessible in schools, so it is possible that the training teacher will need to go directly to the National Curriculum or subject curriculum and AOs (if Key Stage 4 or 5) and plan from there.

CONCLUSION

Whatever you do, we urge you to do as the Chief Inspector of Schools, Amanda Spielman, encouraged – open up the pupils to wider learning in a holistic manner:

Ofsted will challenge those schools where too much time is spent on preparation for tests at the expense of teaching, where pupils' choices are narrowed or where children are pushed into less rigorous qualifications mainly to boost league table positions. (Adams and Weaver, 2018)

You are not there merely to boost the school's league table position, but to help the pupils to learn. The topic of learning is complex, but everything helps and if you engage with the theoretical ideas to improve what you and your pupils do in the classroom, that is all that can be asked of you.

REFLECTIONS ON LESSON

This is a good time to reflect on your own learning and what it has meant to you. Think of the last thing you learnt (outside of this chapter) - a few moments ago, probably. What triggered the desire to want to know? What was new about the learning? What did it do to your mind and how did you assimilate or accommodate it into your mind? Consider that how you learned may not be the same as others. We can mistakenly extrapolate our experience of learning on to all pupils but, particularly with a growing understanding of neurodiversity, it is worth reflecting on how pupils are responding to different approaches in your lessons.

ACTIONS

- Read more about the theory of learning and apply it to the classroom.
- Visualise the process of learning. You might want to try writing a mind-map diagram of it.
- Articulate a particular view of learning in a short piece of reflective writing.

REFLECTION-ON-ACTION BY FORMER TRAINING TEACHER

As with the vast majority of training teachers we come across, the reflection below shows that they knew that learning starts with engagement. They also know that some classes will not want to learn and in these circumstances the teacher has to innovate and keep trying, even when faced with a coach-load of teenagers in a theatre which they could not leave, with hours to fill before the coach returned. This is Gemma Durnford's report on what worked in their experience in and out of class.

I found engagement to be something that was very easy or impossible – there was no in-between. Students were either completely engaged and enthused to participate in the lesson or utterly disaffected and non-compliant. I found success in using shorter tasks more often than say three activities as in the starter, main task and plenary. I also used a variety of strategies in one lesson too, so that students do not get complacent in their learning. While routines are important for students, when they can predict what activity will come next in the lesson, they are more likely to stay alert, active and engage. I used Socratic questioning, class debate, drama, competition, group work, flipped learning and jigsaw activities regularly in my lessons. Ultimately, if a lesson is unsuccessful, it means that my students have not progressed. Therefore, I also make sure that I plan in Assessment for Learning opportunities in my lessons and will use the results from these to inform my future planning. Often this will determine what my starters are – either a consolidation of the previous lesson or an opportunity to resolve any misconceptions or misunderstanding. I believe that learning works best when the pupils can experience something new so in my first placement, I helped organise a field trip to Birmingham to watch *Pride and Prejudice*. Unfortunately, once we got to the theatre, we found out that the show had been cancelled, and were unable to change the pick-up time for the coach. We had only 'risk assessed' being on the coach, walking to and from the car park to the theatre, being in the theatre and back to the school so we could not leave the empty theatre! We were able to get a tour round the theatre and improvise with nuggets of information relating to the plays that were being discussed. We were able to extend learning beyond the classroom, even though at the time it was both unconventional and very challenging.

WHAT TOOLS ARE IN YOUR TOOLKIT NOW?

- An understanding that learning is a continual human action.
- An understanding of the nature of brain change and how schemas develop.
- An understanding of the importance of recall and revision to strengthen retention.
- Ways of starting your lesson to engage the class.
- Understanding of the importance of lesson variety.
- Some strategies to get the class to learn by doing.
- Ways to move the responsibility for learning and teaching to the pupils.
- Ways of grouping the pupils.

PLACES TO GET MORE TOOLS FOR YOUR TOOLKIT

Alexander, R. (2020) *A Dialogic Teaching Companion*. London: Routledge.
Robin Alexander is a champion of dialogic learning whose ideas help to vary your lesson and get the pupils to think.

Capel, S., Leask, M. and Younie, S. (2019) *Learning to Teach in the Secondary School* (8th edn). London: Routledge.
Perennial favourite of training teachers. Chapter 5, 'Helping Pupils Learn', gives clear, precise and practical advice on the subject.
Muijs, D. and Reynolds, D. (2017) *Effective Teaching Evidence and Practice* (4th edn). London: Sage.
An accessible and clear summary of the main learning theories popular in schools today.

REFERENCES

Adams, R. and Weaver, M. (2018) *'Ofsted inspectors to stop using exam results as key mark of success'*. Available from: www.theguardian.com/education/2018/oct/11/ofsted-to-ditch-using-exam-results-as-mark-of-success-amanda-spielman
Alexander, R. (2020) A Dialogic Teaching Companion. London: Routledge.
Baudrillard, J. (2007) *Forget Foucault*. Los Angeles, CA: Semiotext(e).
Beck, A. (1975) *Cognitive Therapy and the Emotional Disorders*. Madison, CT: International Universities Press.
Bloom, B., Engelhart, M., Furst, E., Hill, W. and Krathwohl, D. (1956) *Taxonomy of Educational Objectives: The Classification of Educational Goals. Handbook I: Cognitive Domain*. New York: David McKay.
Bruner, J. (1960) *The Process of Education*. Cambridge, MA: Harvard University Press.
Dewey, J. (1938) *Experience and education*. New York: Macmillan.
DfE (2011) Teachers' Standards. London: HMSO.
Freire, P. (1976) *Education: The Practice of Freedom*. London: Writers and Readers Publishing Cooperative.
Freire, P. (2000) *Pedagogy of the Oppressed*. London: Continuum.
Gardner, H. (1984) *Frames of Mind: The Theory of Multiple Intelligences*. London: Fontana.
Gibran, K. (1923) *The Prophet*. New York: Albert Knopf.
Holt, J. (1990) *How children fail*. London: Penguin.
Kenning, P. (2008) 'What advertisers can and cannot do with neuroscience', *International Journal of Advertising*, 27 (3): 472–3.
Maslow, A. (1987) Motivation and personality. New York: Harper and Row.
Montessori, M. (1964) *Reconstruction in Education*. Madras, India: Theosophical Publishing House.
Ofsted, (2014) *'Schools inspection policy: some FAQs'*. London: Ofsted.
Owens, R. (2016) *Language Development: An Introduction*. London: Pearson.
Pinker, S. (1999) *How the Mind Works*. London: Penguin.
Rosenshine, B. (1986) 'Synthesis of research on explicit teaching', *Educational Leadership*, 43 (7).
Rosenshine, B. (1987) 'Explicit teaching and teacher training', *Journal of Teacher Education*, 8 (34).
Rosenshine, B. (2010) *'Principles of instruction: Research-based strategies that all teachers should know'*. Available from: www.teachertoolkit.co.uk/wp-content/uploads/2018/10/Principles-of-Insruction-Rosenshine.pdf
Sweller, J. (1988) 'Cognitive load during problem solving: Effects on learning', *Cognitive Science*, 12: 257–85.
TES (*Times Educational Supplement*) (2021) *'About us'*. Available from: www.tes.com/about-us
Trotman, D. (2020) *Selected Papers on Education*. Birmingham: The Education Studies Press.
Weber, M. (1992) *The Protestant Ethic and the Spirit of Capitalism*. London: Routledge.

6
CLASSROOM MANAGEMENT

IN THIS CHAPTER WE WILL COVER

- Understanding classroom management
- Putting classroom management tools into practice
- Building relationships

INTRODUCTION

'We are seekers for truth but we are not its possessors', wrote philosopher Karl Popper (1979: 42). Popper, presumably, did not have to deal with 9Y on the last lesson of a wet Wednesday in October, but his point is sound and applicable to teaching – there is no one truth about classroom control; you have to seek out what works.

In this chapter, we offer some more tools for your teacher toolkit, including body language, voice control, seating plans and praise. Theories of classroom management are outlined, which give advice about rules and sanctions – how to offer pupils the choice to follow the rules or take the sanction, the importance of understanding why a rule has been broken, and how to create the expectation, and achievement, of a positive classroom environment. Your management of the classroom will be composed largely of in-the-moment acts, and we address the nature of relationships and dynamics and how 'who you are' in the classroom will help to create both. Finally, there are some points for reflection on each point in the chapter, recommendations of further study and an account by an SD training teacher showing research-in-action.

UNDERSTANDING CLASSROOM MANAGEMENT

Classrooms can definitely be managed. A teacher can organise chairs, lights, blinds, extraneous noises and resources used. Anyone who thinks that people can be managed in the same manner does not know much about people. As a new teacher, you will be working in an established school culture with policies, practices and unwritten expectations around the management of behaviour. These cultures vary, with some schools implementing authoritative approaches that emphasise rules and accountability, while others adopt restorative practices that focus on individual relationships. Within these different environments, teachers establish their own ways of using the tools available to them to establish authority within their own classrooms and to create and sustain effective relationships with the young people that they teach. You will need to navigate this intersection of school culture and your own preferred approaches and strategies.

It is possible to create an environment where a breach of rules results in an inevitable punishment. The Michaela Community School in London successfully put a non-negotiable system in place whereby a single rule-break meant punishment or 'demerit' (Michaela, n.d.) – a model copied in schools throughout the country. All schools have rules. Even Summerhill, which famously allows the pupils to run the school, has rules which they call 'laws'. They are made up by the pupils and debated constantly. Here is an extract from their website:

> We believe in freedom but not licence. This means that you are free to do as you like – but you must not interfere with somebody else's freedom. You are free to go to lessons, or stay away, because that is your own personal business, but you cannot play your drum kit at four in the morning because it would keep other people awake. Within this structure we probably have more laws than any other school in the country – usually around 250! Many laws are seasonal and are changed or abolished when not needed. Others carry on year after year. (Summerhill, 2021)

It may seem ironic that a school which calls itself 'the original free school' (Summerhill, 2021) should have so many laws. How does this inform us about institutions and restrictions? Does it inform us about children and their need to feel safe, protected against others and self-destructiveness? Freedom to do anything you like can be scary, especially when you do not know how to control your feelings or actions and are just learning to make sense of the world. In our view, a good teacher will give children, as a priority, the gift of safety. You might find a space to occupy the tensions of this range of approaches in Lemov's warm/strict approach in which teachers are encouraged to 'seek not only to be both warm and strict but often to be both at exactly the same time' (Lemov, 2015: 438).

The teacher who does not implement school rules engenders, in our experience, initial popularity, then resentment and even contempt. While observing lessons, we hear the words 'That teacher can't control us' from pupils, and this phrase informs us that children expect and even want clear boundaries. As an SD training teacher, you may have another teacher in the room who is the force of control. If so, pupils tend to keep looking at the back to see whether the 'real' teacher is watching. This teacher will be looking at you to take this responsibility off their shoulders. Some SD training teachers do not have this support, or the class teacher chooses not to intervene or may have had to leave, and the class will not be silent, nor sit down ... and there is a fight brewing in the corner.

Can we find a solution to this unruly classroom? Consider the action of disruption as X and the consequence as Y. Is the benefit of X greater than (>) or even equal to (=) Y? While this is a useful calculation and one that was posed by behaviourists such as B.F. Skinner, there is more to people than external controls on behaviour. For one matter, it relies on pupils thinking rationally when they do not always do so. When you factor in rebellion, neurodiversity, hormonal effects of being an adolescent as well as mood (the transient waves of emotion that constantly affect us), it is no wonder that the teacher is so often in a position of struggling to create a disciplined learning environment. The idea that increasing the severity of Y will stop X happening has been shown not to be the case in other parts of social life – capital punishment does not stop crime. The training teacher needs to work on other means of classroom management, starting with arranging the classroom environment. Is the lesson prepared, challenging, engaging, well-paced, and is the room set out to maximise the chances of a calm learning environment? Once these are in place, the teacher can address the issue of behaviour management. These elements being in place does not guarantee an orderly classroom, but without them, it is likely that there will be some disruption with unsettled, off-task and bored pupils.

In writing about the experience of developing the skills of behaviour management as a new teacher, there is a challenge faced in the language and metaphors that we use as professionals to discuss behaviour management. Metaphors of conflict such as 'firefighting' place the teacher in the protagonist's position with an expectation of control and victory. This can be stressful for training teachers as they take on the responsibility for 'controlling' classes. Rather than pathologising 'poor' behaviour as something that needs to be eliminated, we could view it as an effort to self-express, which could be harnessed towards the lesson's aims. We would suggest viewing the development of behaviour management skills as part of becoming a skilled influencer of positive behaviour, rather than expecting to control restless adolescents with their own motivations and agendas.

Bill Rogers's (2015) work is seminal and, as a working teacher in the past, Rogers has put this advice into practice and seen it work. Rogers is realistic about the need to negotiate rules and sanctions with pupils, the main advice being as follows:

1   Give positive instructions: 'I want you to look this way.'
2   Pause: use silence to gain the class's attention and focus them.
3   For those not following a direction, repeat it but do not name individuals who are not complying.
4   State the consequences for those not following the direction and offer it as a choice: either follow it or choose the sanction.
5   Apply the sanction.

It is hoped that there will be no sanction. The offer to allow the pupil to continue to disrupt or face the sanction allows time for them to calculate whether it is worthwhile. If, as most often happens, the pupil chooses to follow the rule rather than take the sanction, the pupil often starts to complain. Rogers advises that you do not respond to this secondary disruption. As long as the original direction gets followed, then that is all you want.

For Eddie McNamara (2012), the route to successful classroom management is as easy as ABC. A is for Antecedents, B for Behaviour and C for Consequences. To manage B, the A needs to be understood and C applied. There is a need to understand the A – the context of disruption. Asking a pupil 'why?' is a good idea, as is phoning home to understand rather than admonish. The parent/carer who receives several phone calls a week informing them about how awful their child is will soon become resentful and the act counter-productive. One of our colleagues had a teacher on the phone at the end of the first school day saying how awful her daughter had been. The teacher did not know that the daughter had Attention Deficit Hyperactive Disorder (ADHD), nor that they had spent the night in the cupboard, which was the only place they felt safe. Questions to ask include what is the child's life like out of school and which lesson has the disruptive pupil been in. A lesson after PE, or on a rainy day, for example, can be very different experiences.

Tom Bennett (2019) advises the following.

1   Be proactive: introduce rules early, show what behaviour leads to success, be 'concrete' with instruction so there is no ambiguity.
2   Language: use words that normalise good behaviour – for example, 'In this classroom, we …'
3   Establish routines: entry to and dismissal from the classroom, corridor behaviour, transition between activities, silence.
4   Sanctions, from mild to severe, consistently applied: 'Their certainty is far more important than their severity.'
5   Rewards: extrinsic (e.g., prizes) and intrinsic (e.g., praise).

Bennett stresses the need to be proactive and positive, and to create an environment that makes misbehaviour abnormal. For Bennett, the classroom should be a non-negotiable and controlled place where a dynamic of positive learning inhibits any desire to disrupt. There is a sense in Bennett's work that if the teacher does their job properly, then the class will behave. It sounds beguilingly easy, but the challenges faced in schools over decades and the experiences of all new teachers suggest otherwise.

At the heart of Rogers's, McNamara's and Bennett's ideas are 'rules' – rules, which if they are not obeyed, can be sanctioned (Bennett), investigated (McNamara) or offered as a choice whether to obey or take the punishment (Rogers). In most schools, there is a rule system that the teacher expects to enact. Masden et al.'s (1968) 'rules rules' are helpful: few in number, simple, described positively, consistent with school policy. 'Described positively' is particularly useful as it avoids what they called 'the criticism trap' – the teacher who falls into this trap gets caught delivering a series of negative comments.

PUTTING BEHAVIOUR MANAGEMENT TOOLS INTO PRACTICE

The evidence base of classroom management theory is a tool for the toolkit and the ideas of Rogers, McNamara and Bennett can all help, but what if everything is adhered to and the class still does not co-operate, or even one pupil does not? If so, you can put some other tools into practice – body language, voice control, seating plans and praise.

BODY LANGUAGE

The explicit control methods of shouting commands with threats can always be responded to with 'No! And I don't care!' The teacher who understands the importance of body language goes into a classroom armed with the means of power and control, which cannot be directly responded to. The popular theorists behind body language are Desmond Morris (2002) and Alan and Barbara Pease (2017). Desmond Morris's (1978) *Manwatching* is a classic book that popularised the pseudo-science of body language – an inborn communication system that works beyond words. Alan and Barbara Pease often glorify the hidden power of the body that is available to those 'in the know'.

Body language, as Desmond Morris stresses, is culturally defined and controlled. Many signals are misunderstood from place to place, but some seem to be universal and are seen in other animals, suggesting an evolutionary purpose to them. Chimpanzees, for example, tighten their top lips and stare when they are angry and humans do too. The teacher in the classroom can employ these evolutionary signals to great effect:

- Tight upper lip: I am angry.
- Staring into eyes: I am dominant.

Space is a major signal of how we are feeling. In lesson observations, we notice where teachers stand in the classroom. Someone nervous will employ barriers such as a desk to protect them. If we take away a desk, the arms and legs are used to protect as they fold in front or, in the case of the legs, cross over. This is a normal protective response but a teacher can over-ride it by opening up the torso. This means going into a room or a situation with the chest area unprotected by one's arms. On encountering a disruptive pupil, the training teacher, fearing the effect of this pupil, might stand well away. The training teacher could override this natural response by deliberately moving towards the person. Invading space is rude in normal circumstances, but in a classroom, it can be a necessity. The teacher signals power and control by moving into the space:

> one sign of your control … is that you always have the freedom of movement so you can adjust your distance and … invade their personal distance if you want to, whereas you often deny them freedom of movement. (Caswell and Neill, 2003: 26)

Some pupils do not need control mechanisms, but rather support and care. They may generally receive fewer positive signals such as smiles and positive eye contact, and this reinforces their feelings of low self-worth. When Babad mentions 'affect', he meant the emotional cues of acceptance – positive eye contact, smiles, body positioning – and this is read on a subconscious level by the pupil: 'teachers often have negative affect toward low-expectancy students (which is reinforced by these students' problems in learning and social conduct domains)' (Babad, 1992: 171).

Even the feet matter. Watch a group of people and look only at the feet. When a group is in harmony, the feet will be splayed out to point at each other. When someone does not want to accept another, their feet will not point to that person. If you have ever walked up to two people, at least one foot ought to move and, if it does not, you are not welcome and on a deep level you will sense it.

Body language can be used to communicate confidence and authority. The teacher who pulls at their collar, brushes down their clothes, tugs at the sleeve of a top or jacket is informing the class that they are nervous. Instead, their hands need to be purposefully used. Try the palm down gesture to calm, the palm grab (cup the hand and pull it towards you) to bring the class to attention, and learn all you can about the way to control through the body, as it is so much more effective than verbal communication alone.

VOICE

Our voices have four elements beyond words to communicate:

- pace
- pitch
- pause
- intonation.

Pace is the speed with which we speak and if there is a typical training teacher issue, it is that of speaking too fast. The words just come tumbling out of the inexperienced teacher and it takes time to find a 'whole-class voice'. As the mind can be going at a terrible speed when you are nervous in front of a group of people, consciously slowing down can be difficult, so it is a good idea to take a breath at the end of every sentence. This gives the pupils' minds time to catch up with the content.

Pitch is the loudness with which we speak. Some teachers shout their words, sometimes trying to overcome the noise in the classroom. Early in our careers, one of our mentors told us 'calm voice, calm class'. Speak quietly so pupils have to listen, especially if you are likely to say their name; directing something to them can be effective. Staying at a single level of loudness – mono-pitch – though, will allow the pupils to 'zone out', so you need to vary the loudness of key words. Your instruction could be like this: 'I want you all to *get up* out of your seats.' Equally, you could stress how many people you would want to get out of their seats like this: 'I want you *all* to get up out of your seats.'

The majestic speech by Martin Luther King with the repetitive phrase 'I have a dream' shows what can be done with stress or increased pitch on words. If any of the four words of the refrain are stressed, then meaning changes.

I have a dream – it is a personal vision.

I *have* a dream – it is something that belongs to me in the present time.

I have *a* dream – there is only one dream that matters.

I have a *dream* – the dream is something valuable.

Pause can be used to great effect in a class. If you speak continually and suddenly stop, a change signals attention. At this point, the main idea may be given – for example, if you want the class to start writing. You can say: 'I want you to start writing (pause) now.' However, there is the danger that the instruction may be missing, so you can say: 'I (pause) want you to start writing now.' Pause before the key content and play with the idea of speaking and stopping.

As well as control of the voice mechanism, we should attend to prosody. Prosody is the emotional quality in the voice which is expressed through pace, pitch, pause and intonation. If we are happy, our voice enters a sing-song mode (intonation varied, pitch high, pace fast). If we are sad, we move to slow pace, monotone, quiet pitch and many pauses. On a television programme game show, children were asked to describe something without mentioning the word. One word was 'love' and a child described this word by saying: 'You know when this happens as your name feels safe in their mouth' (cited in Lavin, 2001). When a teacher calls out the register, it might be that the name of the child who the teacher likes will have a sing-song intonation, while the name of the child who is disruptive will be delivered in a flat, stressed tone. By such means, the pupils learn what the teacher thinks of them.

SEATING PLANS

The lengths we would go to ensure an ordered class were exemplified by the act of one of us in the first year of teaching. In desperation to improve the behaviour of an unruly pupil, a self-assembly desk was bought from a DIY store, assembled at home, then brought into class with the idea of wheeling the desk around the classroom until a spot was found where that pupil would not talk with the others. They talked at the front, the back, the sides, and in the end the only place where they did not disrupt the class was in another classroom. They also destroyed the desk, which, to be fair to them, may have been easy to do due to the poor way it was assembled.

Beyond seating a pupil in another room or the corridor, classroom discipline can be aided by making sure pupils who want to chat or support each other in disruptive activities are distanced. Moving a pupil in front of the teacher's desk (it is amazing how the most disruptive gravitate to the back) is typical, but a teacher can control the room by putting a seating plan together from the start. It is also an easy way to remember names in the first instance as there is a sheet informing the teacher of each pupil's position in the classroom.

Where the pupils sit matters, as does the layout of the seats in the classroom. The classroom can be a traditional one with all the desks and seats facing the front in a line. It can be in grouped tables or a horseshoe where seats are arranged so that all the pupils are on the front row in a U-shape. Each arrangement has its benefits, so it is best to be able to move the desks if you can, although some schools do not allow the tables to be moved and laboratories cannot allow it. A teacher might start with rows for whole-class attention, then ask the pupils to move into groups for an activity. A noisy class can be calmed by the teacher moving the desks to the extremities of the room and seating everyone close to the teacher for instruction, or spaced out to discourage pupils talking to each other.

PRAISE

RPI – Rules, Praise and Ignore – was the advice from Masden et al. (1968). Those who obey the rules are praised and those who do not are ignored. This is an interesting idea to try but, in our experience, the pupil or group of pupils being ignored tends to be quite happy to carry on with their off-task conversation. One of us once spent 45 minutes of a 55-minute lesson refusing to teach a class until everyone was silent. It worked, as the class eventually got bored of its own conversations and listened, but it was a short lesson! Praise, too, has its problems. Alfie Kohn (2001) warns against praise for the following five reasons in his essay 'Five Reasons to Stop Saying "Good job!"':

1   Manipulating children: if we say 'well done' for clearing up quickly, who benefits? It is for our convenience, not for their emotional needs.
2   Creating praise junkies: rather than boosting self-esteem, praise might increase dependence on us.
3   Stealing a child's pleasure: every time we tell a child 'Good job', we are telling them how to feel. They deserve to feel pride when they want to or choose not to.
4   Losing interest: praise might get them to paint while we watch, but when we stop looking, many children stop the activity.
5   Reducing achievement: 'Good job' can undermine independence, pleasure and interest, as well as interfering with how good a job children actually do.

Nevertheless, one of the main pieces of advice a mentor will give a training teacher is to praise more. What should be praised? Behaviour? Surely that should be expected. Work rate, likewise. Achievement – against which criteria? What you will praise along-side the regulation of it are important considerations. 'Catch them being good' is a powerful phrase in the classroom. It means that those who are prone to be off-task or disruptive are not being either and praise can be given. It sends a message – and hope-fully a shot of dopamine, a chemical or neurotransmitter – that gives us pleasure. You can be a pleasure-giver in the lesson by administering praise, but this will only work in context. If a teacher becomes praise-soppy, constantly saying 'That's amazing … fantastic … wonderful', it becomes meaningless. The teacher who holds on to praise but gives it where it is needed and deserved, or to boost a pupil who is struggling, has a powerful motivator in their hands.

BUILDING RELATIONSHIPS

There are problems with viewing behaviour as something that can be controlled. One problem is that some pupils do not want to be controlled or to be 'good', and no amount of understanding, consequences, or offering choice will influence their deci-sion. Rebellion is a natural human state. We observe it in ourselves when our better self knows that something should be done, but our rebellious self refuses, as Paul Willis observed: 'the most basic, obvious and explicit dimension of counter-school culture is entrenched, generalised and personal opposition to "authority"' (1977: 11). We should always be ready for the human in the child and that includes the impulse to rebel – against us as the holders of authority and school rules. We should also be ready for the human in ourselves. Take this account by a teacher we work with:

> Some Year 9 pupils came up to me and said, 'Miss, Jake keeps getting in trouble for not doing any work but Erica doesn't do any work and doesn't get into trouble.' Erica and Jake have the same anxiety issue but Jake hides it and gets punished while Erica gets away with it and if Year 9 pupils can see this, why can't the teachers who punish Jake?'

If threatened by the action of the loud pupil who is disguising an inability to cope, the teacher may turn to sanctions when understanding may be needed. The pupils thought there was injustice as Erica was allowed not to take part in the lesson, but they could see that Jake had underlying issues which the teachers had not noticed. This is one of the many negotiables you will be faced with in the classroom, and an example of why being reflexive and responsive is so important when dealing with behaviour issues.

It is tempting to become a teacher who attempts to forestall any indiscipline by being super severe from the start. One of our training teachers made an unruly pupil write, 'I will not talk in class' 100 times, each letter in a different colour. When this was finished, they went to the pupil, observed that it had been done correctly, screwed up the paper, threw it in the bin and dismissed the pupil abruptly. On being asked why they had done this, they replied, 'Well, he won't do it again.' Iain Crichton-Smith's (1989) fictional Miss Maclean was a teacher from a different age who perpetrated her hostile view of the world on to the children in her classroom. In the story 'The Blot', a pupil wrote a creative piece about a postman which gained the scorn of Miss Maclean.

> 'I asked you to write about a postman and you write about an old woman. That is impertinence. ISN'T IT?' I knew what I was expected to answer so I said, 'Yes, miss.' She looked down at the page from an enormous height with her thin hawk-like gaze and read out a sentence in a scornful voice … I hadn't been thinking of her when I was writing the composition. But from now on I would have to think of her, I realised. Whatever I wrote I would have to think of her reading it and the thought filled me with despair. I couldn't understand why her face quivered with rage when she spoke to me, why she showed such hatred. I didn't want to be hated. Who wanted to be hated like this?'

We, too, have found ourselves shouting angrily at pupils. Did it work? Temporarily, yes. As McNamara observed about the anger-filled response:

> Thus, while there is an immediate cessation of the behaviour, in a longer time the behaviour occurs more frequently. This analysis explains why some teachers persist in using negative control techniques when they patently don't work. (2012: 13)

Some schools act *on* children and the pupils learn to expect severity. Some schools do not impose a behaviour policy, leaving the teacher as the sole source of authority.

While responding in an aggressive manner can help in the short term, it is never ideal as it gives a message to pupils that this is the way to act. It can also leave a lasting legacy of dislike for the teacher. The rock superstar Roger Daltrey's (2018) autobiography is ironically titled *Thanks a Lot, Mr Kibblewhite* in recognition of an unkind and unsupportive head teacher who spurred him on to rebel and achieve. It is unlikely that you want this to be your legacy as a teacher.

Some schools have a restorative justice programme in place. This means that instead of the usual 'act and punishment', the pupil and teacher meet and discuss the incident, and try to find a way of resolving it. Among the most incredible acts of humanity was Nelson Mandela's decision to engage with the perpetrators of evil Apartheid in South Africa with the offer of mediation. While some were 'calling for blood' from those who killed, tortured and imprisoned people based on the colour of their skin, Mandela called for a process of understanding and forgiveness. On the other hand, the teacher who gets abused by a pupil is expected to engage in a dialogue with the perpetrator and, as a victim, bear the burden of the pain. Some pupils can 'game' the system, knowing that any attack on a teacher will result in this process, by which they can be given a good hearing, a chance to further criticise the school and the teacher, and much attention.

It is here that we can think of how relationships have to become 'professional relationships' and drawing a line with our minds and feelings. 'Emotional labour' is just that. We are paid to work using our emotions and respond with happiness, sadness and even anger according to the situation. For a training teacher, feelings can be 'raw' and real, but this has to move to a managed state and feelings controlled in a professional environment. This takes time and patience. The SD training teacher in the classroom and in-the-moment with pupils will make mistakes and respond inappropriately. If this happens, in a spirit of restorative justice, we advise that you focus on understanding why and offering self-forgiveness – sometimes we have to get lost to find our path.

CONCLUSION

This chapter covers an essential part of teaching success – you and who you are in the classroom. There are 'tricks of the trade' that you can learn and this should make life easier. Beyond these, you need to find a way of being who you are in a way that the pupils will respond to. You also need to be in control of the class. It is never easy and is always an in-the-moment and dynamic act which has to be replicated several times a day. Being kind to yourself about errors, mishaps and matters out of your control is important, as things will go wrong, and something is wrong if they don't.

REFLECTIONS ON CLASSROOM MANAGEMENT

Each interaction with another person, however momentary, creates a 'dynamic' which, to go back to its Greek root, means 'force' or 'power'. Here, we seem to be straying into the realms of the metaphysical – our senses and intuition become alive to another and an energy is created from interaction. Think of an example of it in your own life, when you meet a good friend, perhaps, that you have not seen for a long time and immediately link by renewing an existing dynamic and the two of you settle into a pre-created pattern of exchange. Classes come in with a dynamic in place – they have settled into a power structure and decided who the ring-leader is, who is outside of the group majority, and so on. You interrupt this dynamic and present another force that has to be negotiated into a position. Consider how you can recognise the power forces in the room and position yourself so that you gain control.

ACTIONS

- Observe successful teachers.
- Practise positive body language.
- Practise voice control, considering pitch, pause, intonation and pace.
- Talk to pupils about their perceptions of classroom management in the school.

REFLECTION-ON-ACTION BY A TRAINING TEACHER

Aisha Ahmed used the ideas of Bill Rogers to work through a situation they later reflected was self-caused. An authoritarian approach would, they concluded, have been detrimental to all and morally wrong.

In a Year 9 mixed ability class, I encountered direct defiance from a student who refused to take part in a group presentation activity. As the class teacher I was face-to-face with outright refusal to take part; an explicit confrontation to external control (Brophy, 2003; Cowley, 2014). I leaned forward and smiled; this reaction was twofold; by leaning forward I imagined it would portray a piqued interest, followed by a smile to convey a non-threatening posture which manifests as indifference to the antagonistic behaviour and an explicit display of professionalism despite a conceited challenge to authority. Yet, I was consciously aware that she stood whilst I was seated; enforcing a reversal in hierarchy. In that moment, rising from my chair could be deemed as threatening and my primary aim was to diffuse and realign the situation as calmly as possible. Rogers (2011) identifies further the need to communicate expectant co-operation. In spite of my sincere efforts, it did not resolve the escalating conflict, rather, it antagonized the situation further; my attempt to diffuse and pacify the conflict with encouragement was met with an escalation of passive aggressive behaviour: eye rolling, shrugging, and smirking. I was aware of this power play unfolding and how this would impact the classroom and the wider sense of community. I was emotionally angry in a personal way as opposed to a professional way but to respond impulsively, without reflecting entirely led by confounded emotions would be detrimental to myself and more harmful. It would destroy the rapport I had built with the class and could potentially affect their future learning experience – a grave loss of control in one swift moment that quite possibly I may never recover from. This dialogue presents thinking strategies as 'mazes' providing structured and alternative strategies to consider different outcomes; this process disengages emotion from the conflict in favour of a professional solution (Kennedy, 1995, 1999).

In order to avoid a public power struggle and to diffuse the unfolding conflict, a professional call of judgement was made to continue the lesson in spite of the negative behaviour (both primary and secondary) whilst 'tactically ignoring' the passive aggressive behaviour (Rogers, 2011). This eliminated her attempt at control and re-engaged the class without any further attention on a negative display of behaviour (Rogers, 2011). Despite personal frustrations, maintaining composure and competence was the appropriate professional response that benefitted the class as a whole; allowing a pupil to provoke a reaction that leads to anger manifests as poor management in classrooms, pupils recognize this and in turn, respond negatively (Whitson, 2016).

The concept of the 'imaginary audience' can be applied to the classroom environment, for an adolescent to risk exposure in front of fellow peers can be considered the most humiliating social experience; this threat of humiliation instigates anxiety, negative behaviour and withdrawal resulting in a destructive self-image (Elkind, 1976). Both theories support Pupil A's hostile behaviour as a defence mechanism, strategically used as a distraction to avoid humiliation and risk of exposure through her fear of failure. This technique is calculating and provides great insight into the 'risk vs outcomes' strategies that instigate aggressive behaviour in adolescents; Pupil A was fully aware that the primary focus will be the outward hostile behaviour rather than the commitment to the collaborative task; as a result, Pupil A successfully distracted my attention to focus on the personal attack via passive–aggressive means.

I realised afterwards that Student A was blindsided with a presentation task that she was unprepared for, removed from the safety of her desk, and relocated beyond her will to the front of the class, exposing potential vulnerabilities and imposing her participation without any warning; this could be perceived as an intrusive personal attack (Shandomo, 2010). From the perspective of the learner (Brookfield, 1995; 2005), this incident can be viewed as overwhelming. As the primary-care giver I had exposed the pupil to uncertain environmental factors. Afterwards, particularly when I realised this, I was very relieved that I did not use an authoritarian approach which is demeaning and belittling.

WHAT TOOLS ARE IN YOUR TOOLKIT NOW?

- Knowing to put into place rules which are described positively.
- Giving pupils the choice between the sanction or the disruptive act.
- Understanding the antecedents to disruptive behaviour and how to mitigate them.
- Being proactive in creating an environment that expects good behaviour.
- Practising the body language of control and support.
- Using your voice purposefully.
- Managing where the pupils sit.
- Using praise as a motivator.

PLACES TO GET MORE TOOLS FOR YOUR TOOLKIT

Bennett, T. (2019) *'The trainee teacher behavioural toolkit: A summary'*. Available from: www.gov.uk/government/publications/initial-teacher-training-itt-core-content-framework.

Bennett's ideas are a staple ingredient for every school. The advice is clear and may help to put in place their no-nonsense approach to a routinised classroom.

Lemov, D. (2015) *Teach Like a Champion 2.0: 62 Techniques that Put Students on the Path to College*. Hoboken, NJ: John Wiley & Sons.

Another key text for schools today. The work on behaviour management has revolutionised some classrooms across the world.

Rogers, B. (2015) *Classroom Behaviour: A Practical Guide to Effective Teaching, Behaviour Management and Colleague Support* (4th edn). London: Sage.

Published by Sage and as sage as you will get. Wisdom from an experienced teacher and a new approach that does not match the ways of the no-compromise classroom. Rogers focuses on negotiation and mutual respect and advises ways of coping with rebellion.

REFERENCES

Babad, E. (1992) 'Teachers' nonverbal behavior and its effects on students', *Higher Education: Handbook of Theory and Research*, 219–79.

Bennett, T. (2019) *'The trainee teacher behavioural toolkit: A summary'*. Available from: www.gov.uk/government/publications/initial-teacher-training-itt-core-content-framework

Caswell, C. and Neill, S. (2003) *Body Language for Competent Teachers*. London: Routledge.

Crichton-Smith, I. (1989) *The Village*. Manchester: Carcanet Press.

Daltrey, R. (2018) *Thanks a Lot, Mr Kibblewhite: My Story*. London: Blink.

Kohn, A. (2001) *'Five Reasons to Stop Saying "Good job!"'*. Available from: www.alfiekohn.org/article/five-reasons-stop-saying-good-job/

Lavin, C. (2001) 'What is love? Out of the mouths of babes'. *Chicago Tribune*. Available from: www.chicagotribune.com/news/ct-xpm-2001-09-23-0109230461-story.html

Lemov, D. (2015) *Teach like a Champion 2.0: 62 Techniques that Put Students on the Path to College*. Hoboken, NJ: John Wiley & Sons.

Masden, C., Becker, W. and Thomas, D. (1968) 'Rules, praise and ignoring: Elements of elementary classroom control', *Journal of Applied Behavior Analysis*, 1 (2).

McNamara, E. (2012) *Positive Pupil Management: A Secondary Teacher's Guide*. Abingdon: David Fulton.

Michaela (n.d.) *'Michaela Community School Behaviour Policy'*. Available from: https://michaela.education/policies-statutory-information/

Morris, D. (1978) *Manwatching*. London: Triad.

Morris, D. (2002) *People Watching: The Desmond Morris Guide to Body Language*. London: Vintage.

Pease, A. and Pease, B. (2017) *The Definitive Book of Body Language: How to Read Others' Attitudes by their Gestures*. London: Orion.

Popper, K. (1979) *Objective Knowledge*. Oxford: Clarendon Press.

Rogers, B. (2015) *Classroom Behaviour: A Practical Guide to Effective Teaching, Behaviour Management and Colleague Support (4th edn)*. London: Sage.

Summerhill (2021) *School website*: www.summerhillschool.co.uk

Willis, P. (1977) *Learning to Labour: How Working Class Kids Get Working Class Jobs*. Farnborough: Saxon House.

7
ADAPTIVE TEACHING

WHAT THIS CHAPTER WILL COVER

- Differentiation, inclusion and adaptive teaching
- Stretch and challenge
- Scaffolding
- The Pupil Premium
- English as an Additional Language (EAL)
- Special Educational Needs and Disabilities (SEND)
- Hidden disabilities

INTRODUCTION

We are all special, as are our needs, and everyone is somebody's child. It is from this standpoint that we wish to approach the subject of adaptive teaching. The 'othering' of those with 'disabilities' can cause pain and we understand any child who avoids and rejects a label placed on them because it comes to define who they are: 'autistic', 'dyslexic', 'ADHD', and so on can be used as weapons to dismiss a child and their chances of success. Coming from an 'us' perspective would help to stop this, as would listening to the voices of those affected. While tempting to see a class as a group, it is a group of individuals. For each different pupil to be included in lessons, adaptations need to be made. This chapter begins with an outline of the 'adaptive teaching' agenda and a discussion of two prior approaches. The need for awareness of neurodiversity and specific learning needs is stressed, along with the importance of considering emotional states in the classroom, and of understanding that a lesson is not experienced in a vacuum, but as part of each pupil's day and life.

ADAPTING TEACHING

Coming across research literature on education, you might find yourself reading about 'differentiation', or **inclusion**, or 'adaptive teaching'. At a rough guess, 'differentiation' will be in a book, article or website from the 1990s–2000s, 'inclusion' from the 2010s and 'adaptive teaching' from the current point in time. George Orwell, in the novel *Nineteen Eighty-Four*, invented the control device of Newspeak, whereby language was changed and reduced until it no longer had a fixed meaning, nor could it be used for dissent against the ruling party, Ingsoc:

> The purpose of Newspeak was not only to provide a medium of expression for the world-view and mental habits proper to the devotees of Ingsoc, but to make all other modes of thought impossible. (Orwell, 2003: Appendix)

It sometimes feels like this with educational policy. A word or phrase that was being widely and quite happily used suddenly is no longer spoken and there is approbation from colleagues when it is uttered by mistake. The Newspeak becomes the new truth and woe betide anyone who errs into the space that has been abandoned. Pity us, the poor teacher trainers, at this point, with established PowerPoints, yellowing worksheets and memorised spiel about the importance of differentiation, when the word 'inclusion' took its place. No longer were schools to speak of 'differentiation' because, apparently and all of a sudden, it patently did not work. Search as you might for the word in official documents, it will not be there. Then, having pressed Control + F on our documents, changing 'differentiation' to 'inclusion', that word was then phased out and 'adaptive teaching' came in. One of our colleagues did not see this change – as in *Nineteen Eighty-Four*, a policy change is never spoken of directly – and mistakenly left 'inclusion' on planning documents for a PGCE course in 2021 and was firmly upbraided.

Each change signals a difference in meaning and pedagogy. 'Differentiation' meant that we gave each pupil a bespoke lesson and expected the outcomes to vary between individuals. It was part of a move to individualise the curriculum which could be summed up by the title of the government initiative to focus on child welfare: **Every Child Matters** (2003). Children were no longer to be taught 'en masse' but personally diagnosed, assessed and given what would have been called 'a learning journey' to suit their needs. This was the age of the Individual Learning Plan (ILP), Multiple Intelligences (MI) (see Gardner, 1999) and National Record of Achievement (NRA). Each pupil was assessed, given individualised targets in an ILP, diagnosed with an MI and their achievements brought together in an NRA folder. Carol Ann Tomlinson was the 'guru' of differentiation:

> A teacher in an effectively differentiated classroom seeks to develop increasing insight into students' readiness levels, interests, and learning profiles. In order to develop instruction that maximizes each student's opportunity for academic growth, the teacher then modifies content, process, product, and affect. (Tomlinson and Imbeau, 2010: 16)

Teachers' Standard 5 insisted that the training teachers must know 'when and how to differentiate appropriately' (DfE, 2011).

Ofsted promoted it: 'Outstanding teachers plan for differentiation which ensures progress for all learners' (Ofsted, 1999).

Teacher trainers, like us, instructed their charges with ways of doing so, including:

1 Task: different tasks based on prior attainment.
2 Outcome: common task but different expectations.
3 Pace: time allocated is based on prior skills.
4 Support: common task more/less support.
5 Resources: common task but different resources.
6 Grouping: common task but different groupings.
7 Information: common task but different information.
8 Role: common task but different roles.
9 Homework: different homework.
10 Dialogue/using questions: adapts questions and responses.

In 2015, an American teacher, James R. Delisle, echoed the thoughts of many tired and exasperated teachers:

> Although fine in theory, differentiation in practice is harder to implement in a heterogeneous classroom than it is to juggle with one arm tied behind your back. Case in point: in a winter 2011 *Education Next* article ... Michael Petrilli wrote about a University of Virginia study of differentiated instruction: Teachers were provided with extensive professional development and ongoing coaching. Three years later the researchers wanted to know if the program had an impact on student learning. But they were stumped: 'We couldn't answer the question ... because no one was actually differentiating'. (Delisle, 2015)

While we are not sure what was happening when we were not observing lessons, we were there while, for instance one pupil was asked a question and another was given a set of printed instructions. Differentiation was also achieved by altering the expectations of learning outcome, often on an 'all, most, some' basis, where a baseline of achievement was placed for all in the lesson, but some were expected to achieve more.

The word-change from 'differentiation' to 'inclusion' was a deliberate move from the DfE, guided by the United Nation's Educational, Scientific and Cultural Organisation's (UNESCO) language and policy such as *A Guide for Ensuring Inclusion and Equity in Education* (2017). This document advised national governments to ensure the provision of: 'teachers who are trained in inclusive pedagogy and view it as their role to teach all learners in a diverse classroom'.

This pressure for change is partly a response to the UK's position in the global league tables. Those who decide on policy in England and Wales are part of an international network of thought about education and practices which are seen as successful elsewhere and are then adopted at home. The measurement of what constitutes successful education systems can be found in the Programme of International Student Assessment (PISA) run by the Organisation for Economic Co-operation and Development (OECD). PISA relies on taking snapshot measures of 15-year-olds' performance in language, maths and science and reducing this to a number. Much as happens in England and Wales, whereby individual exam results are computed by algorithm into a single Progress 8 or Attainment 8 score by which the school can be measured, so it is with international ratings of the nations' comparative skill sets. We might question the concept that a complex idea (comprehension of maths, science and language among all 15-year-olds) can be registered in single figures, but these concepts can and do drive education policy and therefore what happens in your school. Roy Blatchford in the *Guardian* noted how the move to 'inclusion' in England and Wales was connected to a new approach to teaching with the headline: 'Differentiation is out. **Mastery** is the new classroom buzzword' (Blatchford, 2015). Mastery has the presumption that all can master, and will; if not at the same pace then from extra support until they catch up. The principles of developing Mastery in Mathematics from the National Centre for Excellent in the Teaching of Mathematics (NCETM, 2014) can be applied to all subjects:

- An expectation that all pupils can and will achieve.
- The large majority of pupils progress through the curriculum content at the same pace.
- Teachers identify who requires intervention so that all pupils keep up.

In this mindset where all are considered capable and there is one 'knowledge domain' which all need to 'master', the ideas of 'all, most, some' are ideologically opposed. With one eye over the shoulder of some Asian economies who perform highly on PISA tables (while ignoring the very different approaches of Scandanavian countries who also do very well), the UK echoed the practice of statistically successful education systems, and this included a no-compromise attitude to learning. The former Education Secretary, Michael Gove, summed it up as 'Unashamedly elitist' (Bloxham, 2011). This meant that it was going to aim to bring out the best of the best. It left the question, 'What about the rest?' However, in this mode of thinking, if teachers did their job properly, all would be elite – if this is not a contradiction in terms.

The Early Career Framework (DfE, 2019a) manages to avoid both 'differentiation' and 'inclusion' and replaces them with 'adaptive teaching'. 'Adaptive' teaching is, presumably, opposed to 'static' teaching whereby a teacher perhaps fires off a single lesson in a pre-prepared manner and does not deviate from the topic (and maybe even the spot in the classroom). The very influential **Educational Endowment Fund** explained it thus:

> Having a full understanding of every child is extremely important in adaptive teaching. Time needs to be diverted to identifying reasons for learning struggles, not just the struggles themselves. As such, pupils' physical, social, and emotional well-being, including their relationships with peers and trusted adults, are fundamental. Schools need systems that ensure regular communication between teachers, families and the young people themselves to understand barriers and to share effective strategies. The success of adapting teaching also lies in careful diagnostic assessment, in order to avoid prescriptive and inflexible delivery. (Mould, 2021)

Prescriptive and inflexible could be seen as a feature of mastery (at its worst), so this was the signal that the holistic pupil – diagnosed and duly supported – was at the heart of the new approach. Responsiveness to learning meant changing the pace, adapting the resources and being in conversation with the pupils about what is and is not working.

How do you fit into the changing emphasis and word set? Do you embrace the changing logic or take a 'lens' or pedagogy through which you can filter the approach of government and school? Are you to differentiate? Are you to include all? Are you to embrace 'adaptive teaching'? Imagine that you were a teacher in 2003, quite happily ensuring that every child mattered, their multiple learning styles had been catered for, each given an ILP and an NRA, only to be told that this was no longer good practice. What would you do? You have no choice but to use the new language and approach but have to do it in a way that still fits in with what you believe about individualising the curriculum. This is not to advocate rebellion – because you will not last long in a school if you do, certainly not in your training years – but to advise finding a pathway through the changing language, pedagogy and practice which both conforms to the ideas of the day and fits in with who you are and who you want to be in the classroom.

STRETCH AND CHALLENGE

When the language of schools was about 'differentiation', there was a platform for those who were 'most able' to be singled out and catered for. **Gifted and Talented** (G&T) schemes were government-promoted and funded, and schools were expected to identify the 'best' to ensure that the 'learning elite' were promoted. In 2010, funding was phased out as the Young, Gifted and Talented programme of financial support to schools closed, as did the National Academy for Gifted and Talented Youth (2002–7), a scheme for high-achieving secondary students. There was an unstated presumption of genetic superiority (a gift from whom?), which is such a dangerous concept. Hans Eysenck was a firm believer in such genetic intelligence. Until his death, he was the most cited living academic author. His central thesis was that some naturally can and others naturally cannot. His Intelligence Quotient (IQ) was a measure of brain power that sorted out such individuals. In a fascinating account of interaction with Eysenck, Andrew Colman documented the change in a man who started out questioning his idea and ended with certainty.

> What starts out as a 'not unreasonable hypothesis', cautiously advanced by a writer who does not claim to know all the answers, is progressively transmogrified into a simple 'fact' of 'genetic inferiority' backed up by 'all the evidence to date'. (2016: 12)

Eysenck's certainty for a system that was widely suspect – as, apart from anything, you could improve your IQ score – should warn us all about theory. No matter how convincing the argument or widely quoted the author, it is always to be questioned.

There is also a much more egalitarian approach to the idea of 'stretch and challenge'. It sounds painful and, mentally or physically, it should be. The phrase means that we need to take each pupil beyond the standard level they will need and always move them to a higher level of cognitive or skill practice. Sue Cowley (NACE, 2019) always has good, measured advice about such matters, and advises the following:

1   Check learning first. This is essential for all, but for those who have an interest in the subject, they will do some extra research and it is highly frustrating for them to be in a class learning something they already know. Having established those with advanced knowledge, they can be set some additional tasks and activities or be released from the lesson (if there is a safe mechanism to do so) to continue their investigations which are working so well.
2   Encourage and equip for wider learning. Lend some books to the pupil, share your passion and 'feed the fire' of enthusiasm.
3   Depth, lateralisation and abstraction are ways of working on cognition. Every subject has levels of learning which go up from the scaled qualifications so move your pupils to the next level. Encourage 'lateral thinking' whereby the problems of the subject are presented to the pupils, and they are challenged to solve them in a new and creative manner. Move from the 'concrete' of factual recall to being able to generalise from examples and hypothesise new approaches. Your subject will provide much 'food for thought' – questions about which a person can ponder the possibilities and make creative but evidence-based solutions.
4   Give roles. Those who know can lead and teach others; the empathy and communication skills needed for these roles also develop them.

SCAFFOLDING

As with much educational theory, we move to metaphor to explain the workings of the mind. The physical 'scaffold' which allows a person to climb up high buildings safely, stage by stage, was an image often attributed to Jerome Bruner who built on (appropriately) the ideas of Lev Vygotsky. The scaffold is a useful image as it is a temporary installation – there only for as long as it is needed. Having supported the pupil up to the next level of learning, it is removed. It is here that the metaphor 'falls down', which the removal of scaffolding from beneath the pupil's feet would cause for the poor individual. The idea, we suppose, is that the scaffolding is replaced by the 'bricks' of learning and is no longer needed. Like the metaphor, the attribution of an idea to Bruner (it usually happens to a man) is simplistic. A little (to use another metaphor) 'digging' and we see that Bruner worked alongside others to develop ideas and that he was not only discussing 'scaffolding'. He was, along with Wood and Ross, for example, quite happy to support the idea of 'serendipity' – a random and sudden moment of learning:

> children do in fact gain a sense of possible outcomes as well as of means for achieving outcomes by a process of what on the surface looks like rather 'blind' (though hardly random) trying-out behaviour. (Wood et al., 1976: 90)

Bruner (who mostly studied language, not education) deserves more attention to his wider ideas than the simplified (often through the use of internet sites, which has been called Wikipedia-isation) idea that we read time and again in essays – he invented 'scaffolding'. The concept of supporting those who need extra help has been with us as long as people have been educated and he merely provided a useful image to explain it. As Robert Hook wrote to Isaac Newton, quoting twelfth-century philosopher Barnard of Chartres, when we learn 'we stand on the shoulders of giants'. If this idea was around in the twelfth century, you can be sure it came from someone before then.

Scaffolding is an easy act: you can do any and all of the following, and more.

1 'Chunk' learning into mini-lessons so that each step can be taught and learning checked. Work backwards from the outcome you want from your lesson and think of it in separate stages. Teach a stage and check the learning. If it is okay, move to the next stage; if it is not, stop and try again.
2 Model answers. Show the pupils what a good answer might look like.
3 Describe difficult concepts in different ways. Try to exemplify them. Use a range of definitions that are accessible, especially ones that the pupils might relate to.
4 Give a checklist of steps to follow.
5 Slow down. Watch an experienced teacher and you will find that they can modify voice and pace.

6   Give sentence starters to begin pupils' writing for them. There is a fine line between a 'scaffold' and 'crutch'; some rely on the latter to make life easy for themselves when they do not need it.
7   Teach academic language before using it. Have a glossary, preferably one that the pupils have made themselves.

PUPIL PREMIUM

In 2010, the UK government was a Conservative–Liberal coalition and one policy the smaller of the two parties saw realised was extra funding for children from low-income families in 2011 – the **Pupil Premium** (PP). At the same time as schools received the extra money for PP children, there was a 9 per cent cut in funding over the decade from 2010 to 2020 (Institute for Fiscal Studies, 2021). In the UK, 15,000 school staff were lost between 2014/15 and 2016/17 alone (despite an increase of 4,500 pupils to teach in this year). If the figures are correct (and being from a union and a government, on both sides there is reason to question them as they have political motives), in 2019 the funding for PP was £2.4 billion (DfE, 2019b), but the cuts were £2.8 billion (NEU, 2018). Many causes that could formerly rely on financial support for extra education costs from the Local Education Authority were denied it, as PP was a catch-all mechanism for extra support. Nevertheless, the scheme was expanded in 2014 to Pupil Premium Plus (PP+) which gives more money to the school for children in care or 'looked-after' children. The extra money (in theory, at least) being given to support those from economically disadvantaged backgrounds means that the results of PP children will be scrutinised. You must take particular care (as no doubt you would be concerned to do in any case) that they are keeping up with their peers from more wealthy families, and take active steps in lessons to ensure all children learn, regardless of their economic circumstances.

ENGLISH AS AN ADDITIONAL LANGUAGE (EAL)

What would you do if two pupils who could not speak anything but very basic English were put into your classroom at the start of the lesson with no notice or support, on a lesson you are being observed in? We have been there, observing in such scenarios – which, fortunately, are few and far between. EAL is specifically mentioned as a learning need in the *Teachers' Standards* (Standard 5), as well as the more general skills needed for planning such as 'higher order planning'. Part Two of the *Teachers' Standards* states that teachers must specifically cater for 'pupils whose first language is not English' (DfE, 2011).

A problem with EAL, as is the case with so many topics of education, is definitions. A pupil with EAL has been identified as: 'one who was exposed to a language other than English during their early years' (DfE, 2017), which is not helpful as there is no reason to presume that a child brought up by a parent or parents with another language would have been greatly affected by the experience beyond the benefits of bilingualism. Being exposed to another language, especially when young, brings many cognitive and cultural benefits, so it is hardly synonymous with the experience of a refugee child who has never spoken a word of English.

Everyday language that needs to be mastered for the child to be able to function in a school will come relatively quickly, but cultural and contextual expectations take much longer. One of our training teachers from Somalia recalled in a session how there was no cultural expectation to say 'please' and 'thank you'. On coming to England, they could not fathom why people thought this to be rude. The EAL pupil not only has to learn the language and cultural expectations, but also the academic language of each subject. Jim Cummins (1979, 1986) usefully separates the process of learning a second (or third or fourth in some cases) language into two stages – Basic Interpersonal Communicative Skills (BICS) and Cognitive and Academic Language Proficiency (CALP). BICS, Cummins suggests, will take up to two years to learn. Two years is a long time for a child, but then they will only have been able to function around the school. CALP can take 5 to 7 years to master and this takes them beyond their experience with the school. To understand CALP, we have to know something of the hypothesis, generalising and evaluating the processes that Cummins outlines. This is a trial-and-error process by which language can be learned through making a guess at which words, order and style of speech is appropriate. Each time, there is an evaluation of how successful it was, or not, and it is adapted until it gets the hoped-for response. When we are to enter any communication situation, we have to assess where we are – the context. Each word has several connotations – i.e., many meanings. We see this process most clearly in advertising and brands that try to fix positive meanings (connotations) to names and logos. Goldman and Papson (2000) document how Nike's 'swoosh' logo was 'an empty sign' in 1971, but through the advertising company Wieden and Kennedy became connected to American athletes who had 'cool' status among global youth. Global advertising and media have meant that some connotations will be shared by the pupils who newly arrive, but they will also need to learn other meanings associated with words. 'Cultural capital' is a phrase which recognises that you can be rich or poor in knowledge about the country you live in and what it values. Teaching pupils with EAL about the culture of the country they are living in – both as it is experienced and its expressions in art forms, music, dress, food, architecture and literature – will help to equip them for successful lives in the UK. The CALP stage is about learning the culture in language, and this takes time.

Various governments over the years have tried to support pupils with EAL with initiatives and funding. Each of the following reports has picked up what they see as a problem and tried to offer a new solution: Bullock Report (1975), Swann Report (1985), Kingman Report (1988). Each tried to 'fix' what it perceived the last one had not. Since the report 'Unseen Children', the government has focused support on 'our poorest children' (Wilshaw, 2013). Because of this move to PP, there has been a reduction in financial support for schools with EAL pupils, although limited funding can still be gained from the local authority. Schools can use PP funding that may come with EAL pupils for the purposes of language instruction. The amount of money will probably not stretch to teaching assistants, but there are easy steps to help EAL pupils and, as with all methods of catering for children's needs, the practice for some is good for all. First, value the child's background and home culture. Cummins warns against those who do not include it or consider them to be 'starting from scratch', which they are not:

> when students' languages, cultures, and experiences are ignored or excluded in classroom interactions, these students are at a disadvantage. Everything they have previously learned about life and the world is dismissed as irrelevant to school learning. (2000: 166)

Other methods that might help include:

- use gestures to illustrate actions and activities (pointing, miming)
- use visual cues (photographs, posters, pictures) to support the development of oral interactions
- display printed phrases on cards that are commonly used by teachers and children
- write and speak words and phrases the child can use to look for clarification – for example, 'Can you explain that again, please?'
- simplify texts
- create bilingual books
- record sessions and allow and encourage them to do the same
- put up displays in the child's first language
- encourage group work
- arrange or provide one-to-one workshops.

Any act of support for a pupil with EAL and any move towards the home culture and language will make a difference to how the pupil feels, thinks and learns. The meta-message of care, concern, support and genuine interest in their life will do more than anything else.

SPECIAL EDUCATIONAL NEEDS AND DISABILITIES (SEND)

The way you treat people will be fundamental to your success or otherwise in the classroom. With this in mind, it is most important that this section is about 'us', not them. We are born neuro diverse (thankfully) and each of us is 'disabled' in some way. Your 'disability' may actually be something like mild arachnophobia which prevents you cleaning out that cupboard under the stairs, but it is still a limitation on your behaviour. The language you will hear about will be SEN or, as it is more commonly used these days, SEND (**Special Educational Needs and Disabilities**). You will also hear about Specific Learning Difficulties (SpLD), which are neurological and result in identifiable symptoms affecting learning which can be responded to. Three of the most commonly encountered SENDs are outlined below: ASD, ADHD and **dyslexia**.

AUTISTIC SPECTRUM DISORDER (ASD)

For children with ASD, the brain is not set up to process experience in the manner of the majority of people. Of course, if the majority of people were set up in this way, it would not be a 'disorder' at all. The use of this word is unfortunate and unhelpful, and 'difference' is, quite rightly, but also quite slowly, replacing it. The parts of the brain that are affected include the processing links in the amygdala which regulate emotions, the cerebellum which regulates coordination and speech muscles, and the cortex which regulates reaction and perception. These parts of the brain are typically active for social interaction – understanding, relating, communication and creative thinking.

It is estimated that 1 per cent of the population of the UK has ASD. Of these, 700,000 – at least 4 boys to every 1 girl – are diagnosed (Department for Health and Social Care, 2021). People with ASD may find it harder to: a) understand and interpret other people's thoughts, feelings and actions; b) predict what will or could happen next; c) understand the concept of danger; d) engage in imaginative play; e) prepare for change and plan for the future; and f) cope in new or unfamiliar situations. On the other hand, they may not. There can also be a need for the security of routines and sensory over sensitivity. Then again, there may not be. The capacity of humans to overcome differences means that it can be hard to spot the symptoms because there has been compensatory activity. For example, the socialised expectations of emotional intelligence in females has compensated for the biological difference. The brain can compensate for what are seen as social deficits, and strategies are learned to replicate the responses that are not in place naturally. We have trained many teachers with ASD and seen their capacity to manage complex social interactions.

Avoid sympathy (because nobody needs that) and try empathy. There is a very good phrase, 'nothing about us, without us' which should govern those who write about matters by which they are not directly affected. Jim Sinclair (1993), writing about **autism** in the *Autism Network* magazine, wrote 'don't mourn for us':

> Autism isn't something a person has, or a 'shell' that a person is trapped inside … Autism is a way of being. It is pervasive. It colours every experience, every sensation, perception, thought, emotion and encounter, every aspect of existence. It is not possible to separate the autism from the person – and if it were possible, the person you'd have left would not be the same person you started with.

In *Pretending to be Normal*, Lianne Holliday Wiley (1999) described how she some-times experienced her environment:

> Together, the sharp sounds and the bright lights were more than enough to overload my senses. My head would feel tight, my stomach would churn, and my pulse would run my heart ragged until I found a safety zone.

The senses can mix up experience:

> my mouth tasted like I had eaten a bunch of sickly smelling flowers. (Williams, 1994)

Such sensations are not exclusive to those with ASD. The novelist Joanne Harris (n.d.) has a form of synaesthesia which causes her to smell colours. Her sensitivity to the sen-sation of smell comes through in her sensual (in a non-racy way) novel, *Chocolat*. We are neuro diverse and those who need the extra support should be given it to equalise the experience of education.

It may be that your subject has a specialised skill that may be enhanced by the condition. Music, art and mathematics are three areas where an ability to specialise in a single topic or skill may enhance performance. Where the condition causes a chal-lenge for your subject, you are a teacher. You can work to help children with ASD to develop a feelings diary or journal. Use social stories to talk through a situation and to identify feelings that may expand the cognition of such subjects. One way of support-ing pupils with ASD is to help the problem of communication.

- Speaking and listening: teach the child to learn 'conversational maxims', using and recognising paralinguistic features (the way we communicate beyond words), prosodic features (the emotional qualities of voice) and registers (different styles of speaking and writing according to the audience and other contextual factors).
- Reading: understanding inference, decoding unfamiliar words from prior use, learning idioms or figurative language, reading for meaning and being explicit about possible connotations of words, as well as how these can be 'anchored' by other words in the sentence.
- Writing: practise re-presenting information, understanding how text genre can provide the ingredients for a piece and learning about phonically irregular spelling.

These literacy skills should be part of a package for all pupils in a cross-curricular way. The school should provide the literacy framework for you; if not, it is worth fol-lowing up, if and where you can, and certainly doing all you are able to do in your lesson. Routines for children with ASD can be helpful. Dominque Dumortier (2004) noted:

Many of my problems can be sidestepped by pre-planning. Schedules are very important to me. I need to know well in advance what is going to happen, how, who is involved and so on. Everything is always planned … Any change of plan leads to frustration, powerlessness, anger and anxiety …. Being late causes difficulties, but so does being early, and people who leave earlier or later than planned also make me feel uncomfortable.

Routine seems ideal for school. Any aspect of your curriculum that demands creativity, abstract thought and communication may need extra support, but there is every reason to promote and celebrate the strengths which may come with the condition – the learning of facts, the evidence-based rationality so appreciated and rewarded in examination.

Children identified with ASD or as autistic should not be impersonalised and dismissed. Comprehension of the condition, understanding and empathy are the start points for teachers with pupils who have ASD. Children with ASD are quite rightly protected by law. The Equality Act (2010) ensures that there is legal redress for any acts against them – something worth reminding ASD pupils about. The *SEN Code of Practice* (DfE, 2013) specifically targets the needs of children with ASD. When the children become adults, they will be protected by the Autism Act (GOV.UK, 2009) but before then, we should be the ones with the care to ensure those with ASD are not dis-abled for being atypical.

ATTENTION DEFICIT HYPERACTIVE DISORDER (ADHD)

Simon Bailey's thoughtful examination of ADHD notes two aspects: first, the child becomes an 'it' and a problem because of ADHD (which they did not choose to be) and second, they are given a platform for performance as their disruption is most feared:

is the child the lowest common denominator, the powerless one at the bottom of the pile? Certainly it seems that others have authority over them …. Yet they are also 'the centre of the game' … simple changes in a child's behaviour forces these authorities to mobilise resources: time, energy, money, labour, in an attempt not just to control or quash this behaviour, but to shape it, through discipline, into something more socially acceptable and economically productive. (Bailey, 2014: 6)

Bailey viewed ADHD through the lens of social control and noted how it is easy for those in power to label anyone who does not conform to the system they created as different (at best; at worst, deviant, delinquent, 'You're ruining it for everyone else').

Changing the system is unlikely to be something you can do, but you can change your lesson. The tools below offer some approaches that may help pupils with ADHD and, indeed, all pupils.

1   Attention:
  • Stand close to an inattentive child.
  • Provide attention and recognition.
  • Incorporate a child's hobby or interest into the lesson content.
  • Give clear timings.
  • Remove unneeded stimulation from the classroom environment.
  • Use names regularly.

2   Voice:
  • Pause speech to gain attention.
  • Use a calming tone of voice.

3   Questioning:
  • Inform a child that a question will be asked in advance.
  • Ask simple questions to inattentive children.

4   Activity:
  • Shorten the length of activities and written work where you can.
  • Alternate between physical and mental activity.
  • Increase the variety of activity in lessons.
  • Reinforce instructions.
  • Repeat and clarify social rules and demands of the classroom.
  • Ask pupils to repeat your instructions.

5   Teach skills:
  • Play attention and listening games.
  • Praise accuracy over speed.
  • Teach children how to regulate emotions through self-talk.
  • Encourage planning by lists, calendars and charts.

DYSLEXIA

Dyslexia can affect children in many different ways, to the extent that Doyle believed:

> It is illogical for a person to say, 'My child cannot read because he is dyslexic' … It tells us no more than saying a person is bleeding badly because he has a haemorrhage or that someone has a high temperature because they are feverish. (1996: 69)

Pumfrey and Reason (1998) identified 11 types of dyslexia which Rice and Brooks (2004) expanded to 40 (cited in Mortimore, 2008: 50). The several processing conditions that we call dyslexia include the following:

- Auditory: difficulty processing sounds and making them into words.
- Dyseidetic (or surface): difficulty processing words that have spellings that do not correspond to letter sounds.
- Semantic processor: delayed access to the meanings of words.
- Strephosymbolia: the brain reverses the shape of letters.

Training teachers should not expect a one-cure situation for a variety of causes. Often, pupils with dyslexia are given coloured filters to read through, but this will only help those who have a visual processing issue and, even then, the colour that would help varies. As with EAL, ASD and ADHD, good practice for those with dyslexia is good practice for all, so we recommend that you ensure that your lessons include the following:

- Write down the main points.
- Use pictures, flow-charts, mind-maps.
- Colour all crucial information displayed on the walls.
- Include practical/kinaesthetic work.
- Interact one-to-one.
- Signpost topics and key points.
- Allow students time to absorb information.
- Use recording equipment.
- Always give out homework instructions ready printed.
- Use a font without serifs (squiggly bits on the ends of letters) such as Arial.
- Print copies of slides and worksheets on blue and cream (or another colour that helps) paper.

HIDDEN DISABILITIES

We both have hidden disabilities and have, at times, thought (or known) that to admit to our inability to do something would affect us negatively. One of us, for example, is scared of lifts and for years, rather than admit it, avoided any situations that involved them. A job interview generated, not fear of the act of performance or even rejection, but dread that it would involve a lift. In retrospect, applying for a job in a college that was ten storeys high had not been a good idea. Another job, based in an office on the fourteenth floor, meant a long walk up many flights of stairs for an interview, whilst realising that the job would not be performable, even if successful. The alternative to hiding the disability is to face sympathetic, non-plussed and deflated faces, or being forced to have a conversation about it and be told how someone they know was unable do the same or how they sometimes feel claustrophobic in their own bedrooms. It is wearying carrying a disability and, if it can be hidden, it does not have to define us. On the other hand, if it is not acknowledged, it cannot be helped and the more we hide disabilities, the less they will be recognised and understood. There is not much to write in this section, because how can we work with something that is hidden? It is worth closing this part of the chapter with it, though, as a reminder of how it started. We are all disabled, all special, all children, and we need to take care of each other.

CONCLUSION

You have a duty of care to equalise the learning process and need to do it in stages. It is, typically, the Teachers' Standard in which training teachers do least well, as it is hard to adapt a lesson so that it meets the learning needs of 30 or so pupils. There are, though, simple steps that will improve your lessons and meet the needs of pupils with SENDs. Once you get into the pattern of good lesson practice using these methods, all your pupils will benefit.

REFLECTIONS ON ADAPTIVE TEACHING

In the safe space of your thoughts, examine what disables you. Have you always been able to manage the problem? Could anyone have supported you better? How might your experience help you to understand others?

ACTIONS

- Read more about strategies to allow lesson adaptations for all and put them into practice.
- Look at the data the school provides and consider what you can put into practice for each identified learning issue.

REFLECTION-ON-ACTION BY A TRAINING TEACHER

Luke Amos's reflection gives an example of how each school creates its own levels of difference.

Pupils in core subjects (English, Maths and Science) were set according to attainment and they were also streamed into two 'halves' of each year group: an X and a Y band. Depending on each year group, the band indicated whether the one 'half' of the year group was the 'brighter half' or the 'less bright half'. I did find this particularly peculiar to begin with and still do, especially as it was known by the students what these groupings meant. In one class, a handful of pupils were Pupil Premium (PP), there was one EAL pupil, one pupil with SEN needs, two pupils with Free School Meals and a large proportion of the class who have specific medical needs. However, I found that the PP pupils were not 'disadvantaged' academically as is the popular idea, but were higher attainers in the class. Assessment and attainment data used from the school's Aspire system identified the trajectory of pupils and their current progress from Autumn Term. I was able to 'stretch upwards' and consider thinking and discussion at greater depth. However, what I was struggling more with was catering to my SEND and what were termed by the school, LA or 'Lower Ability' learners across both groups. With one group of mainly 'LA' learners, I had a Teaching Assistant (TA) in class and could pre-plan the activities in the classroom so that she could focus developing writing skills in breaking down a question. However, my TA was sporadic due to other commitments and so 'live marking' was another option and also bringing my mentor in to focus on each half of the group.

WHAT TOOLS ARE IN YOUR TOOLKIT NOW?

- Understanding of the words 'differentiation', 'inclusion' and 'adaptive teaching', and the pedagogies behind them.
- Ways to 'stretch and challenge' pupils.
- Ways to scaffold learning.
- Strategies to support pupils with EAL.
- Strategies to support those with ASD.
- Strategies to support those with ADHD.
- Strategies to support those with dyslexia.

PLACES TO GET MORE TOOLS FOR YOUR TOOLKIT

Peer, L. and Reid, G. (eds) (2021) *Special Education Needs* (3rd edn). London: Sage.
Each chapter is written by a specialist and will build up your knowledge and therefore confidence in giving all a fair education.
Westwood, P. (2018) *Inclusive and Adaptive Teaching: Meeting the Challenge of Diversity in the Classroom*. London: Routledge.
A comprehensive volume looking at how you can alter your practice to cater for children with a range of learning needs.

REFERENCES

Bailey, P. (2014) *Exploring ADHD: An Ethnography of Disorder in Early Childhood.* Abingdon: Routledge.

Blatchford, R. (2015) *'Differentiation is out. Mastery is the new classroom buzzword'.* Available from: www.theguardian.com/teacher-network/2015/oct/01/mastery-differentiation-new-classroom-buzzword

Bloxham, A. (2011) 'Michael Gove promises to push unashamedly elitist approach in state sector', *Daily Telegraph*, 24 November. Available from: www.telegraph.co.uk/education/educationnews/8914499/Michael-Gove-promises-to-push-unashamedly-elitist-approach-in-state-sector.html

Bullock Report (1975) Available from: www.educationengland.org.uk/documents/bullock/bullock1975.html

Colman, A. (2016) 'Race differences in IQ: Hans Eysenck's contribution to the debate in the light of subsequent research', *Personality and Individual Differences*, 103: 182–9.

Cummins, J. (1979) 'Cognitive/academic language proficiency, linguistic interdependence, the optimum age question and some other matters', *Working Papers on Bilingualism*, 19: 121–9.

Cummins, J. (1986) 'Empowering minority students: A framework for intervention', *Harvard Educational Review*, 56: 18–36.

Cummins, J. (2000) 'Negotiating intercultural identities in the multilingual classroom', *The CATESOL Journal*, 12 (1): 163–78.

Delisle, J. (2015) 'Differentiation doesn't work', *Education Week*. Available from: www.edweek.org/teaching-learning/opinion-differentiation-doesnt-work/2015/01

Department for Health and Social Care (2021) *The National Strategy for Autistic Children, Young People and Adults: 2021 to 2026.* Available from: https://assets.publishing.service.gov.uk/government/uploads/system/uploads/attachment_data/file/1004528/the-national-strategy-for-autistic-children-young-people-and-adults-2021-to-2026.pdf

DfE (2011) *Teachers' Standards.* London: HMSO.

DfE (2013) *SEN Code of Practice.* Available from: www.gov.uk/government/publications/send-code-of-practice-0-to-25

DfE (2017) *'School census 2017–18 guide, version 1.3'.* London: HMSO

DfE (2019a) *'Early career framework'.* Available from: www.gov.uk/government/publications/early-career-framework

DfE (2019b) *The Education Hub.* 'Ensuring a good education for all children. Attainment gap. Reception Baseline Assessment'. Available from: https://educationhub.blog.gov.uk/2019/09/26/ensuring-a-good-education-for-all-children/

Doyle, J. (1996) *Dyslexia: An Introductory Guide.* London: Whurr Publishers.

Dumortier, D. (2004) *From Another Planet: Autism from Within.* London: Lucky Duck/Sage.

Every Child Matters (2003) London: HMSO. Available from: https://assets.publishing.service.gov.uk/government/uploads/system/uploads/attachment_data/file/272064/5860.pdf

Gardner, H. (1999) *Intelligence Reframed: Multiple Intelligences for the 21st Century.* New York: Basic Books.

Goldman, R. and Papson, S. (2000) *Nike Culture: The Sign of the Swoosh.* London: Sage Publications.

GOV.UK (2009) *Autism Act.* Available from: www.legislation.gov.uk/ukpga/2009/15/contents

Harris, J. (n.d.) *'Scent illustrations'.* Available from: www.joanne-harris.co.uk/scent-illustrations/

Institute for Fiscal Studies (2021) *'Larger funding cuts for schools in poor areas leave them badly placed to deal with COVID-19 challenges'*. Available from: https://ifs.org.uk/publications/15026

Kingman Report (1988) Available from: www.educationengland.org.uk/documents/kingman/kingman1988.html

Lehrer, J. (2010) *The Decisive Moment: How the Brain Makes up its Mind*. Edinburgh: Canongate.

Mortimore, T. (2008) *Dyslexia and Learning Styles*. Chichester: John Wiley & Sons.

Mould, K. (2021) *'Assess, adjust, adapt – what does adaptive teaching mean to you?'* Available from: https://educationendowmentfoundation.org.uk/news/eef-blog-assess-adjust-adapt-what-does-adaptive-teaching-mean-to-you

NACE (2019) *'Curriculum, teaching and support'*. Available from: www.nace.co.uk/blogpost/1761881/334589/5-key-strategies-for-stretch-and-challenge

NCETM (2014) Mastery Explained. Available from: https://www.ncetm.org.uk/teaching-for-mastery/mastery-explained/.

NEU (2018) *'Schools forced to cut teachers and teaching assistants posts to make ends meet'*. Available from: https://neu.org.uk/schools-forced-cut-teachers-and-teaching-assistants-posts-make-ends-meet

Ofsted (1999) *'Raising the attainment of minority ethnic pupils'*. London: Ofsted. Available from: https://dera.ioe.ac.uk/4386/2/Raising_the_attainment_of_minority_ethnic_pupils_school_and_LEA_responses.pdf

Orwell, G. (2003) *Nineteen Eighty-Four*. London: Penguin.

Pumfrey, P. and Reason, R. (1998). *Specific Learning Difficulties (Dyslexia): Challenges and responses*. London: Routledge.

Sinclair, J. (1993) 'Don't mourn for us'. *Autism Network International newsletter, Our Voice*. 1 (3).

Swann Report (1985) *Education for All*. Available from: www.educationengland.org.uk/documents/swann/swann1985.html

Tomlinson, C. and Imbeau, M. (2010) *Leading and Managing a Differentiated Classroom*. Alexandria, VA: ASCD.

UNESCO (2017) *A Guide for Ensuring Inclusion and Equity in Education*. Available from: http://unesdoc.unesco.org/images/0024/002482/248254e.pdf

Wiley, L (1999) *Pretending to be Normal: Living with Asperger Syndrome*. London: Jessica Kingsley.

Williams, D. (1994) *Nobody Nowhere: The Remarkable Story of an Autistic Girl*. London: Jessica Kingsley.

Wilshaw, M. (2013) *'Unseen children'*. Available from: www.gov.uk/government/speeches/unseen-children

Wood, D., Bruner, J. and Ross, G. (1976) 'The role of tutoring in problem solving', *Journal of Child Psychiatry and Psychology*, 17 (2): 89–100.

8
ASSESSMENT

INTRODUCTION

Pitching – knowing what to teach and when – is a stage of assessment where a diagnostic judgement is made about pupil knowledge and skills so that the lesson can be tailored to be neither too difficult nor too easy. Assessment for Learning (AfL) follows this process through the lesson as you keep an ongoing check about what to teach and when. When the marking comes in (Assessment of Learning), it is necessary to understand the criteria used to assess alongside the sensitivity to reveal grades individually, positively and with the understanding of its emotional and cognitive effects. Examining the nature of assessment, this chapter advises you about questioning and about using data proactively to support learning.

REASONS FOR ASSESSMENT

One of our favourite Gary Larson *Far Side* cartoons has a person tentatively knocking on a door with the sign stating 'Assertiveness Course', and a voice behind saying, ' Go away! You've failed.'

Assessment is always to be done sensitively. Sue Cowley (2011) recalled an event in a school in which a child had drawn a picture of a sad girl and written; 'The girl is sad. She has no friends'. The teacher opened this up to the class to comment on her work and some said that she could have written more, others that she could have chosen a better word than 'sad', and one classmate said: 'I'll be your friend'. They had looked beyond the content and responded to the writer, which is what McCormick Calkins (1989: 120) reminds us of when assessing work: 'It is not my piece of writing. It belongs to someone else.' When we respond to someone's work, remember that there is a person behind it, and it is not yours to scrawl over and change. You are there to guide the next steps of their learning through feedback – some call it, more precisely, feedforward, as it is all about helping to ensure improvement in the next piece.

Assessment is not a necessity. Learning is not assessment and we are in the learning business. It is the externalisation of internal processes, and the teacher and pupil use it to discover whether teaching and learning have been successful or not. There are reasons not to assess pupils, including the stress of high-stake assessments (the ones where the results impact on their lives, for example by deciding which set they will be in), alongside the negative effect they can have on self-efficacy and self-esteem. On the other hand, assessment stimulates recall, is necessary to decipher the pupils' understanding, challenges pupils to learn more and informs the pupil about likely success or otherwise given the current work rate. If assessment is necessary, it is worth asking who should do it:

- self
- peer
- teacher.

Each has its benefits and a mix of all three not only shares the burden of marking, but it opens up the pupils up to the important act of meta-learning by guiding them to reflect on not only what has been learned, but how.

If you were in the state school system from 2010 to 2014, you would have known whether you were a 4a, 6b or 7c in maths, English, science and ICT, as a scheme was in place called **Assessing Pupils' Progress** (APP). APP used grids with very specific learning topics and stages, and the pupil was graded according to whether they had reached it: just about (a), partially (b), or fully (c). In a rare show of unity, all the major teaching unions, the Qualifications and Curriculum Authority and the Qualifications and Development Agency agreed that it was a good thing, and 'has been shown to improve learners' progress' (QCDA, 2010: 10). Despite this, it was firmly scrapped four years later: 'the current system of "levels" used to report children's attainment and progress will be removed from September 2014 and will not be replaced' (DfE, 2014). Today, APP illuminates a common feature of policy: it arrives in a blaze of glory to transform education and then leaves quietly by the back door. Teacher John Dabell (2018) gave it a firm kick as it left:

> There are fads and there are super-fads. I cannot think of any initiative as mind-numbing, well-being sapping and pointless as Assessing Pupil Progress (APP). This was a workload nightmare and literally drowned us in useless data. This was a freakish fad from the land of spreadsheets with built-in madness.

During the APP years, one of us asked a group of training teachers how they started the lesson-planning process. Expecting the answer to be the National Curriculum, it was a shock to hear a training teacher say that they used the APP grid – and then it turned out that all of them were. The grid was meant to be used to assess work against, but instead, teachers were identifying a place on the grid, teaching it and, if it was achieved, stamping the pupil's work with a number and letter. It took a while for schools to get away from the specific assessment culture of numbers and letters when 'Assessment without Levels' (GOV.UK, 2015) replaced it and schools had to inform pupils only whether they were meeting or exceeding expectations. APP now acts as a warning to schools not to let assessment guide learning. Assessment is what happens after learning, a process which ought to be rich with new content, active and imbued with the joy of the subject.

DIAGNOSTIC ASSESSMENT AND PITCHING

Diagnostic happens prior to teaching. It checks where the pupils are with their knowledge and skills. Just as a surgeon should not plunge in blindly with the knife, there should be no launch into learning before what is already known is diagnosed. This will be done by the department in school, but you should also start each lesson with a check of prior learning before proceeding as, apart from anything else, it is a waste of everyone's time if you are trying to teach what they already know.

Once prior learning has been assessed, the teacher is ready to pitch or present the lesson content, knowing that the pupils are ready to receive it. Pitchers pitch in baseball, but they do not do so on their own. They wait for a signal from the catcher and throw a curveball, a hesitation pitch, a cutter, a change-up, a knuckleball or any number of combinations. When you pitch your lesson, you could do the same – throw them a problem that changes their views (curveball), makes them think about something (hesitation), saws through their current understanding of a topic (cutter), moves them to a new level of understanding (change-up) or gives them a no-nonsense 'sit down and do the work' (knuckleball). Really knowing how to pitch a lesson is something possibly only experience can bring so, for now, be guided by the signals you get from other pupils, teachers and mentors, and read about teaching at different levels. One less preferable way is to experience your own poorly pitched lessons and be forced to change next time. In the days when training teachers were left alone in the classroom to sink or swim, one of us sank pretty badly in our first ever lesson in which the word 'totalitarianism' was put on the board (there was no PowerPoint in those days) in order to trigger a 30-minute classroom discussion. A half-hour of silence later, the bell mercifully went, leaving only a rictus grin on the face of this training teacher, but at least that experience meant that the next lesson was going to be pitched properly.

Each class will be in a year group – 7 to 13 – where there are expectations about levels of knowledge, skills and understanding in your subject. These expectations can be found in the curriculum, schemes of work, lesson plans of colleagues and example work. There are, though, a range of expectations for each year group, as we all learn at different stages. Usually, these are reflected by setting the pupils, but at Years 7–9, mixed-ability classes are very common. Just as socialites learn to 'read rooms' when they go in – quickly computing who to talk to and when – you will have to do the same.

Pitching starts with your knowledge of the subject and curriculum. You should read as much as you can from guidebooks about content so that you can take the material beyond the subject's curriculum, which always gives the minimum requirement. Observe other teachers of your subject at the different levels, and take note of the lesson content and the responses of the pupils. Never miss an opportunity to observe your class with someone else, even when you are used to teaching them. Pitching is like marking – you internalise the levels after a while and it becomes second nature to know which level a Year 7 pupil is likely to need because experience of their responses teaches you what to expect. Finally, be brave and talk to the pupils about the content. Was it too easy? Too hard? Had they already done it? Pupils will not see it as a weakness if you enter into an honest dialogue with them.

ASSESSMENT FOR LEARNING

Assessment for Learning (AfL) can be defined as:

> The process of seeking and interpreting evidence for use by learners and their teachers to decide where the learners are in their learning, where they need to go, and how best to get there. (Broadfoot et al., 2002: 2–3)

The AfL Toolkit compiled by Mike Gershon (n.d.) contains graphics, including Microsoft Word's Clipart stick people, which tells you how long it has been supporting teachers. We will supply some here and guide you to the AfL Toolkit for the rest:

- Two stars and a wish: assess their own or another's work with two good points and one not-so-good.
- One-sentence summary: all they learned in a lesson in a sentence. Can be used as a 'pass out' from the lesson (necessary to get out of the door) and assessed in time for the next one.
- All you know: stream-of-consciousness, timed writing about a topic.
- Post-it notes: popular tool to assess and gives an opportunity to move in the classroom as they get stuck either on a board at the front or in a particular place in the room.
- Show and tell: pupils get up, stand up and present a topic to the class.

The AfL Toolkit was inspired by the work of Black and Wiliam whose 'Assessment and classroom learning' (1998a) summarises results from quantitative studies published in eight different pieces of research, which conclude that AfL is important. Of course, teachers knew this anyway, but it did so in the language of science and gave numbers, which those who create policy like to have. To give one section of this paper: 'a total of 681 publications ... 250 ... a total of 47 different labels ... an average of 2.4 labels per reference.' You get the picture, perhaps. Black and Wiliam's research had a positive impact on the classroom, as it has been pivotal in government thinking about learning as a process. They had the greatest impact with their journal article 'Inside the black box: Raising standards through classroom assessment' (1998b) with its focus on inter-active learning and informed pupil self-assessment. A 'black box' is an electrical circuit in which the workings are not understood. So widely used was Black and Wiliam's paper that, by 2014, this image was repeated through Coe et al.'s *What Makes Great Teaching*, as if it had become a common-sense phrase.

ASSESSMENT OF LEARNING

Should your summative assessment be ipsative, value added, norm-referenced or criterion-referenced, and will the moderation and standardisation process work? If these terms make you feel nonplussed, step this way.

- Summative assessment is what you do at the end of a period of learning, finishing the topic and revealing success or failure, usually with a letter or number.
- Ipsative assessment is when you rate the performance against the pupil's usual standard. It is what athletes do to themselves when they aim for a 'PB', or Personal Best. In the end, they may be on the track trying desperately to see through all the dust their competitors are kicking up in front of them, but if they stay true to the PB philosophy, they only need to be disappointed if they are not near to their own targets. Translate that into a school setting, and each pupil is allowed to learn at their own pace, and we can praise individual success. This is not a popular approach in the current system which expects everyone to achieve a certain level.

- 'Value added' seems more like a phrase you would see in a supermarket than a school. It has the same sort of meaning – 'more bang for your buck'. The success of pupils is not always measured equally. Those who came into the school with low marks in their Key Stage 2 exams might be worth more to the school than those who did not, as the final marks they get in exams will be compared to the grades they got previously. Value added can even be applied to those for whom expectations are different because of factors such as gender and parental income. If one grouping, on average, typically achieves at a lower level than another, then a higher-than-expected result for a pupil from this grouping has greater value. The value might translate into an improved ranking on school league tables and/or future funding and/or praise from Ofsted. While schools may be credited for adding value to some pupils' results, this credit is not transferred on to those pupils. The pupil who gets a 1, say, still has a 1 and no one puts an asterisk on this grade linking to: '*they went to a rotten school'.

- Criterion-referenced assessment means there is a set of explicit expectations for the answer and it is just a matter of finding them in the answer. This makes marking, particularly at exam level, a relatively easy task, especially when the answers are right or wrong.

- Norm-referenced assessment is what takes over from criterion-referenced marking in an official examination. Every year, results come in and they are put through an algorithm to make sure they follow the expected pattern of grades. If, for example, in this year 90 per cent of the pupils got below a 4 at GCSE, then the marks are changed to reflect the difficulty of the exam. In 2017, on a particularly tricky mathematics GCSE exam, 8300H, 15 per cent would have got you a 4 (C-grade equivalent) (AQA, 2019). There is the presumption that a cohort of exam takers are equally able and that the exam is to blame if the results do not follow the expected pattern.

- Standardisation happens before marking and is a check, usually with sample scripts, that everyone is grading in the same way. You will be given something to mark and a mark scheme. This should be done separately, then either send it to a central adjudicator who will check that the grades are similar or get together and discuss them.

- Moderation happens after marking and is a check that there is agreement about grading. Teachers share their marked work with others and re-mark it. If there is disagreement about a mark, there is discussion first and, if no agreement can be made, a third marker is involved. Often, from our experience, this results in a verbal 'punch-up' as no one wants their grades to be lowered. It is important to learn from this process in school and the disagreements of markers show that it is never an easy process. Even with criterion marking, there will always be differences in the way that more complex answers are graded.

CHARACTER EDUCATION

Traditionally, we assess levels of skill and knowledge but, according to Carol Dweck and other advocates of what might be called 'character education', it should be attitude. It is not uncommon for exasperated teachers and parents to rail at a child because they are capable of more if only they tried harder. In a **growth mindset** way of thinking, they are not capable (regardless of results) because they do not try. Carol Dweck and the Character Education movement turn assessment on its head:

> It is becoming common practice in much of our society to praise students for their performance on easy tasks, to tell them they are smart when they do something quickly and perfectly. When we do this we are not teaching them to welcome challenge and learn from errors. We are teaching them that easy success means they are intelligent and, by implication, that errors and effort mean they are not ... What should we do if students have had an easy success and come to us expecting praise? We can apologise for wasting their time and direct them to something more challenging. In this way, we may begin to teach them that a meaningful success requires effort. (Dweck, 2000: 43)

One of us visited a Character Education school and found it exhausting, as around 75 pupils went past us, each saying, 'Good morning, Sir! How are you?' In this school, the Year 8 pupils serve the Year 7 pupils their meals at lunchtimes, having a positive attitude was paramount, and was modelled by the teachers. Character Education schools can do wonders to transform the atmosphere of an educational establishment. The attitude of staff and pupils is a model for other schools. There is no panacea to education, though. It comes with a package of issues, along with benefits, yet for some areas, some staff and some pupils, it is perfect ... and we mean this with the most positive mindset we can muster.

QUESTIONING

Here are some answers. What is the question?

1   43.6
2   1.5–2 million
3   > 1 second

The questions (answers!) will be at the end of this section (you can peek if you like). Giving an answer but not a question is one innovative way of eliciting learning from the pupils. There are lots of ways of doing this, so there is no need to YAVA (You Ask, Volunteers Answer). Not relying on YAVA is a central piece of advice to training teachers in the book *How to be a Brilliant Teacher* by Trevor Wright (2009). To their and our bewilderment, there are few lessons that do not have YAVA and, to this day, despite our continued advice to the contrary, it thrives. Instead of YAVA, use questioning purposefully. This takes planning, which is why so many teachers may resort to YAVA which does not, but the results will be more ordered, interesting and purposeful, and worth every minute spent.

Robin Alexander's (2017) work on classroom talk opened a generation of teachers to the benefits of a dialogic classroom with the following advice that it must be:

1   Collective: teachers and pupils learn together.
2   Reciprocal: teachers and pupils listen to each other, share ideas and consider alternative viewpoints.
3   Supportive: pupils express ideas freely without fear of being 'wrong' and help each other to common understandings.
4   Cumulative: teachers and pupils build on their and each other's ideas and connect them into a coherent response which answers a question.
5   Purposeful: teachers plan and facilitate dialogic teaching with particular educational goals in view.

Plan questioning in advance. Consider the following:

• Who is to be asked a question? Plan whether you are going to target a pupil or ask all of them to respond. Be aware of 'blind spots' where you might be choosing the pupil who you know has the answer.
• What is the question achieving? Is it checking knowledge or opening up debate and alternative ways of thinking?
• How will they respond – on whiteboards, for example, or verbally?

The questions to the answers, if true, and still applicable to today's classroom, inform us that we have some way to go before questioning is used productively.

1   Average number of questions a teacher asks in a lesson (Kerry, 2002).
2   Average number of questions a teacher will, therefore, ask in a teaching lifetime (Kerry, 2002).
3   The average wait time for an answer to a question (Rowe, 1986).

CONCLUSION

Assessment through pitching and marking comes with experience. You can make sure you keep learning about your subject and the curriculum, and take as many opportunities as possible to encounter pupils and practise marking. Think about what you can control, which includes your ability to vary AfL and questioning, and the various ways of assessment, including through attitude, an ipsative approach and understanding the factors that are likely to affect attainment and how to mitigate them.

REFLECTIONS ON ASSESSMENT

Consider what is not assessed in your subject because it is difficult to do so. Are creativity, originality, personal growth and the feeling aspects of your subject ignored in favour of more simplistic knowledge?

How can you enliven lessons through a range of AfL, including questioning techniques?

Consider who you are asking questions, why and how they are expected to respond.

ACTIONS

- Observe as many lessons as you can and note the way the subject is pitched at different year groups and classes.
- Take part in standardisation and moderation processes to help you gauge the expected levels of work.
- Talk to pupils about the lessons and assessment and keep them informed about what is happening.
- Encourage pupils to self- and peer assess.

REFLECTION-ON-ACTION BY A TRAINING TEACHER

During their training year, Flick Ellis reflected on the development of formative and summative assessment processes. Flick welcomed the way this development meant that teachers can be judged on performance, but saw some negative effects on pupils.

When starting my placement, I never fully understood the importance of assessment. By the end, I realised assessment is a great way to provide accountability for teachers and schools as well as advancing student learning (Ryser and Rambo-Hernandes, 2016). I noticed, though, how the use of high stakes assessment in particular can cause a negative effect on students (Harlen and Crick, 2003) which would then lead to a fixed mindset of 'I can't do this' (Dweck, 2011). Instead, I used formative assessment more. I printed the coloured cards for the students and would assess at the end of every lesson how the students' understanding related to the provided lesson outcomes (James et al., 2006). I would ask the students to be honest in their response so we could revisit lessons if needed and explained it was important for them so I could help them. Surprisingly, the class were very honest and some students were not afraid to hold up the red card at all.

I found this rewarding myself as I felt I had gained their trust. When I first started marking the books of this Year 8 class, I merely used ticks and crosses, corrected spelling and wrote simplistic comments such as 'good work'. This provided students with no interest in the feedback I was supplying, as I didn't render them with anything of importance for them to develop (Price et al., 2010). From then on, I was certain to ensure the quality of feedback (Price et al., 2010) was specific and informative as well as providing targets and questions (Tanner and Jones, 2005) to enable the students to enhance their knowledge and stretch them.

WHAT TOOLS ARE IN YOUR TOOLKIT NOW?

- Reasons for assessment.
- Strategies for AfL.
- Ways of creating a dialogic classroom.
- The vocabulary of assessment: ipsative, value-added, criterion-referenced, norm-referenced.

PLACES TO GET MORE TOOLS FOR YOUR TOOLKIT

Black, P. and Wiliam, D. (1998) 'Inside the black box: Raising standards through classroom assessment, *Phi Delta Kappan*, 80 (2): 139–48.
An example of a piece of academic study changing the way schools operate. Black and Wiliam provide reasons for, and an impassioned plea to use, formative assessment to check and enhance learning.
Petty, G. (2014) *Teaching Today* (5th edn). Oxford: Oxford University Press.
The most measured advice from an experienced and wise professional. Excellent throughout on the nature of learning and assessment.

REFERENCES

Alexander, R. (2017) *Towards Dialogic Teaching: Rethinking Classroom Talk*. Thirsk: Dialogos.
AQA (2017) *'Grade boundaries – June 2017 exams'*. Available from: https://filestore.aqa.org .uk/over/stat_pdf/AQA-GCSE-RF-GDE-BDY-JUN-2017.PDF
AQA (2019) *'Grade boundaries – June 2019 exams'*. Available from: https://filestore.aqa. org.uk/over/stat_pdf/AQA-GCSE-GDE-BDY-JUN-2019.PDF
Black, P. and Wiliam, D. (1998a) 'Assessment and classroom learning', *Assessment in Education: Principles, Policy & Practice*, 5 (1): 7–74.
Black, P. and Wiliam, D. (1998b) 'Inside the black box: Raising standards through classroom assessment, *Phi Delta Kappan*, 80 (2): 139–48.
Broadfoot, P., Dougherty, R., Gardner, J, Harlen, W., James, M. and Stobart, G. (2002) *Assessment for Learning: 10 Principles*. Available from: www.stir.ac.uk/research/hub/publication/640252

Coe, R., Aloisi, C., Higgins, S. and Major, L. (2014) What Makes Great Teaching: Review of the underpinning research. London: The Sutton Trust. Available from: https://www.suttontrust.com/our-research/great-teaching/

Cowley, S. (2011) *Getting the Buggers to Write*. London: Bloomsbury.

Dabell., J. (2018) *'Educational super-fad: Assessing pupil progress'*. Available from: www.teachertoolkit.co.uk/2018/04/22/educational-fad-2/

DfE (2014) *'National curriculum and assessment from September 2014: Information for schools'*. Available from: https://assets.publishing.service.gov.uk/government/uploads/system/uploads/attachment_data/file/358070/NC_assessment_quals_factsheet_Sept_update.pdf

Dweck, C. (2000) *Self-theories: Their Role in Motivation, Personality, and Development*. London: Routledge.

Gershon, M. (n.d.) *'AfL toolkit'*. Available from: https://mikegershon.com/download/assessment-for-learning-toolkit/

GOV.UK (2015) *Final Report of the Commission on Assessment without Levels*. Available from: https://assets.publishing.service.gov.uk/government/uploads/system/uploads/attachment_data/file/483058/Commission_on_Assessment_Without_Levels_-_report.pdf

Kerry, T. (2002) *Explaining and Questioning*. Cheltenham: Nelson Thornes.

McCormick Calkins, L. (1989) *The Art of Teaching Writing*. London: Heinemann.

QCDA (2010) *'Assessing pupils' progress: Learners at the heart of assessment'*. Available from: https://dera.ioe.ac.uk/10945/7/Assess_pupils_progress_webo_Redacted.pdf

Rowe, B. (1986) 'Wait time: Slowing down may be a way of speeding up!' *Journal of Teacher Education*, 37: 43–50.

Wright, T. (2009) *How to be a Brilliant Teacher*. Abingdon: Routledge.

9
LITERACY AND NUMERACY

WHAT THIS CHAPTER WILL COVER

- Literacy in the classroom
- Numeracy in the classroom

INTRODUCTION

The *Teachers' Standards*, against which you will be judged at the end of your training, state that:

> Teaching includes clear development of pupils' literacy and numeracy skills within the subject. (DfE, 2011)

Part Two of the Professional Standards includes the need to:

> Address the mathematics and English needs of learners and work creatively to overcome individual barriers to learning. (DfE, 2011)

There are many 'literacies' that teachers need to attend to, including digital, health, financial and visual, but the legal framework insists that you include specific teaching of English and maths in your lessons. As for the third of the 'key skills' (as they are traditionally known), **Information Technology** (IT), (sometimes called ICT or Information Communication Technology), as Lord Sutherland explained: 'The DfE policy on

ICT is there is no policy on ICT' (SecEd, 2013). Despite this, you will still have to teach the pupils how to use IT safely and to optimise their learning, and this chapter includes IT as a third key literacy that you should include in your lessons.

LITERACY IN THE CLASSROOM

This is a moral imperative to teach children the skills to explore their worlds, beautifully summed up by former Secretary-General of the United Nations, Kofi Annan.

> Literacy is a bridge from misery to hope. It is a tool for daily life in modern society. It is a bulwark against poverty, and a building block of development, an essential complement to investments in roads, dams, clinics and factories. Literacy is a platform for democratization, and a vehicle for the promotion of cultural and national identity .... Literacy is, finally, the road to human progress and the means through which every man, woman and child can realize his or her full potential. (Annan, 1997)

Unfortunately, some children in the UK do not leave school with the expected ability to read, write and communicate orally.

In the document *The Importance of Teaching* (DfE, 2010), which was the forerunner to the legislation which governs schools today, literacy was so important that it was mentioned on page 3 (and page 2 was blank). The solution to improving literacy among children, as posed in this document, was to copy the styles of teaching in countries they called the 'Far East':

> The only way we can catch up, and have the world-class schools our children deserve, is by learning the lessons of other countries' success. (DfE, 2010)

It would have hurt to recognise the success of other countries had it not been that this Conservative–Liberal Coalition government was replacing New Labour who had been in power and were therefore seen as responsible for any 'decline'. By 2015, the DfE was reporting that around 42 per cent of employers needed to organise additional training for young people joining them from school or college. It is as if the message is a stuck record which went something like this: 'pupils' literacy standards are not good enough and here is what we are going to do about it'. In 2016, the then Education Secretary Justine Greening (2016–18), suggested that we: 'Don't let young people hit a brick wall in English and maths' (*TES*, 2016). This painful fate was to be remedied, once again, by government plans. Such plans have a history of not solving the problem. Of course, it was deemed the schools' fault that literacy levels are not good enough and, by extension, the teachers' fault:

> Too few schools currently develop reading skills effectively across the curriculum .... In subjects other than English ... teachers are less aware of approaches that might help pupils to read effectively and make sense of what they are reading. (Ofsted, 2012: 30)

One initiative which had an effect on what schools did was the 'whole-school' approach to literacy, launched – or relaunched, as it had been posed many times in the past – in 2012. Notwithstanding, this one would work:

> All teachers should have a better understanding of the role literacy plays in their subject ... and ... [this will] enable them to understand how improved reading, writing and speaking and listening skills would help them make more progress in their own subject. (Ofsted, 2012: 54)

And so it is that all teachers are English teachers and maths teachers. In order to 'move English forward' as Ofsted (2012) so ineloquently put it, all teachers need to embed the following literacy skills into their lessons:

- skimming
- scanning
- reading for detail
- using an index
- using a glossary.

Table 9.1   Literacy skills

Adapting language for different purposes	Paragraphing
Appropriate language use	Proofreading
Comprehension	Presenting assignments appropriately
Constructing an argument	Referencing and avoiding plagiarism
Creativity of expression	Revising
Debate	Selecting appropriate evidence
Developing critical analytical skills	Spoken Standard English
Discussion	Syntax
Embedding quotations	Understanding assessment criteria
Genre	Using Standard English to explain, explore and justify ideas
Grammar	Use of linking and signposting words
Handwriting legibility	Punctuation
Improving reading comprehension	Using reading lists and the library
Identifying key points of an argument	Using evidence to support points
Making effective notes	Subject-specific terminology
Making presentations	Scanning, skimming, speed reading
Planning and structuring work	Vocabulary

Beyond these expectations from Ofsted, there are other literacy skills you must embed into your lessons.

The literacy that you are expected to teach is not English as it is used in an everyday fashion. English is a language constantly reimagined by people in a stunning display of human creativity: in slang, subcultural words and phrases, dialect (regional ways of speaking) and idiolect (the individual's style of speech). Nevertheless, such matters are not usually seen as the concern of the school. Things are not 'bostin' (Black Country for 'good') for dialects in schools, as spoken and written Standard English are expected of teachers and pupils alike. If you are fortunate enough to stand on the upper floor of St Michael's CE School in Rowley Regis, you will view a stunning scene of the Black Country with a landscape of hills, and a fascinating variety of houses, pillars and posts. Add to this, snow, fog, darkness and sunset, and not a day will go by without some visual wonder. The view spans at least three areas which have differing versions of Black Country dialect. This dialect, or 'spake' as it is known in the region, still includes 'thee', 'thy' and 'thou' as pronouns. Far from being a vulgarised form of English, it is closer to the original Middle English than the Standard version and the last of the Mercian region (Conduit, 2007). Those in the Black Country hold on to their way of speaking as a matter of geographic pride and identity: 'Language ... is not simply a means of communicating messages. It is also very important as a symbol of identity' (Trudgill, 1983: 74). Nevertheless, Standard English is the only type advocated by the National Curriculum and all examinations require pupils to be able to read and write it. It is just a dialect – a version of English – but it has power status and this is the one to use in the classroom. While we wish more respect was given to the English of everyday use in official reports and instructions to teachers, we agree that you need to equip pupils with the power of the power dialect.

NUMERACY IN THE CLASSROOM

Whoever is running your course is responsible for 'assuring' schools that you have the required level of numeracy to be able to guide pupils and be – as you must all be – teachers of maths. The word 'assure' is an interesting one to use, as it seems very comforting and is often used in the word 'reassure', which always makes us feel better. Assurance is a guarantee that the trainee is good enough, mathematically speaking, to teach the pupils. This means that you can guide pupils up to Key Stage 4 to:

1   use data
2   complete mathematical calculations
3   solve mathematical problems.

Quite a lot, in other words, so we will take each separately.

USE DATA

How good are you at extracting numbers from graphs and interpreting the information? Can you identify patterns and trends, and draw appropriate conclusions? Can you interpret pupil data and understand statistics and graphs in the news, academic reports and relevant papers? Cast your mind over the following points and ask whether you know how to interpret and create them:

- Tables, including two-way tables
- Bar charts, including composite bar charts
- Box-and-whisker diagrams
- Cumulative frequency graphs
- Line graphs
- Pie charts
- Scatter graphs.

Do you know the difference between the charts, why they are used and how to make sense of them? We suspect you have often used the most commonplace ones of pie, line and bar charts, but what about the more complex forms of these charts, and the others on the list?

COMPLETE MATHEMATICAL CALCULATIONS

You can all add up, take away and multiply, or you would not be teachers. You are probably (as you need to be) fluent with whole numbers, but what about your use of fractions, decimals and percentages? You can use a variety of methods and approaches to:

- estimate and round up (and down) numbers to make sense of them
- break down problems into simpler steps
- explain and justify answers using appropriate mathematical language.

SOLVE MATHEMATICAL PROBLEMS

You will need to be able to use mathematics and mathematical formulae to find ways of solving a problem using numbers including:

- Time (the nature and calculation of it)
- Money (how to calculate its use)
- Ratios
- Measurement, including distance and area

- Conversion between currencies, fractions, decimals and measures
- Averages: mean, median and mode
- Range
- Estimation and rounding.

Look for opportunities in your subject teaching to reinforce the numeracy skills you have developed. Pupils need to be able to transfer skills between subjects and maths is an ideal interdisciplinary way of thinking. Maths is a language as well as a process of thinking and, through your training year, one of your many tasks is to make sure that you are fluent in both. There should not be a perverse pride in not being good at maths, so do not communicate this to pupils: you are their maths teacher. Of course you may be a real maths teacher, in which case you are unlikely to have needed this section, but please do help your colleagues and then they will be able to support you more effectively in your job.

CONCLUSION

If everyone teaches numeracy and literacy, pupils will be able to access knowledge and skills more easily, which will improve their performance in your lesson and beyond. These are life skills. To teach them, you will need to ensure that your skills in all areas are strong enough to make you a role model for children, so this is an ongoing training need.

REFLECTIONS ON LITERACY AND NUMERACY

Consider what your strengths and weaknesses are in these core areas and what practices would be most useful to help you to develop your skills. Think about what training needs you have and how you can work to fulfil them.
  Think about ways of embedding literacy and numeracy into your lessons.

ACTIONS

- Strive to ensure that your standard of English and mathematics is excellent.
- Identify an opportunity to teach explicit literacy and numeracy skills in your lessons.
- Look at the table of literacy skills and choose one to form a learning moment.

REFLECTION-ON-ACTION BY A TRAINING TEACHER

Barwago Ismail explores the many processes in their academy which aim to improve the literacy standards of pupils who come from an economically deprived area.

Academies were re-established in 2010 to enhance and support 'failing' schools in order to raise the attainment of disadvantaged children (Lord Adonis, 2011; Glatter 2013). Unfortunately, some academies have not had the desired effect. They have created a two-tier system where they hold the best facilities and teaching staff, which compromises other schools in the area. Additionally, middle-class parents are drawn to academy schools, blocking access to disadvantaged families (Lord Adonis, 2011). Academies have some freedom to choose their students and sometimes 'cherry pick' their pupils, thus there has been lack of engagement with disadvantaged families, and some schools have not been able to maintain their outstanding judgements (Lord Adonis, 2011; Glatter, 2013; Sellgreen, 2013). Nonetheless, there have been significant positive changes brought by academies, schools previously judged poor or satisfactory have been judged by Ofsted as Outstanding or Good now they have become academies (Glatter, 2013). School A has turned from what was termed at the time of the last inspection 'Satisfactory' to an 'Outstanding' school. School A is in the heart of a disadvantaged area, it has close connection with the families of the students, there are representatives of Asian, Arab and particularly Somali background that work closely with parents and pupils. These representatives embody the ethnic make of the students and families within the area.

The school day starts at 8:20am and finishes at 4pm; there are 6 lessons during the day. Students receive up to 5 hours of English per week, students in years 7 and 8 get an additional thirty minutes of targeted literacy provision at the start of each day. Whilst 2 classes out of 5 in years 7 and year 8 get 5 hours a week of a phonics-based reading instruction programme. One class in year 9 gets 3 hours a week of specialist literacy teaching. Teachers have claimed that this is by far the highest immersion of literacy and reading compared with any other Birmingham schools. Statistics show 'one in four children in Birmingham are leaving primary school unable to read properly' (McKinney, 2015), therefore, the school is immersing and providing reading opportunities to raise reading attainment, as well as getting students interested in reading (Dean, 2003). A year 7 class I observed were given this opportunity; the class was split into 3 groups, and 2 groups were with teaching assistants in separate classrooms.

The school feels this was the best foundation for their pupil's future career aspirations. 'English will teach pupils to speak and write fluently so that they can communicate their ideas and emotions to others and through their reading and listening, others can communicate with them' (Department for Education, 2015). The school uses summative assessment to check literacy skills based against the guidelines of the National Curriculum levels for year 7 and year 8 and GCSE grades for year 9, 10 and 11, these take place every half-term (6 weeks). There are other summative assessment such as Cognitive Ability

Tests (CATs). These are used to assess students in year 7 and new students, where appropriate, to be used to identify Special Education Needs students. In addition, reading tests are embedded in the assessment policy to align with the literacy support the school gives. The tests will be used to asses all year groups, three times a year, in order to close the gap between current and chronological reading ages. These forms of summative assessments are to maintain standards where judgements are made by authorised examiners and teachers (Blanchard, 2009).

WHAT TOOLS ARE IN YOUR TOOLKIT NOW?

- An understanding that you are a teacher of literacy and numeracy as well as your subject.
- Details of the practical literacy skills you need to teach.
- Details of the practical numeracy skills you need to teach.

PLACES TO GET MORE TOOLS FOR YOUR TOOLKIT

Babtie, P. and Dillon, S. (2019) *100 Ideas for Secondary Teachers: Supporting Students with Numeracy Difficulties*. London: Bloomsbury.
Part 2 of this book gives practical ideas for putting numeracy tasks into your lessons.
Tyrer, G. (2018) *100 Ideas for Secondary Teachers: Literacy Across the Curriculum*. London: Bloomsbury.
Super-skilled English teacher Graham Tyrer gives the 'low-down' on what literacy is and how to implement it in your lessons.

REFERENCES

Annan, K. (1997) *'Secretary-General stresses need for political will and resources to meet challenge of fight against illiteracy'*. Available from: www.un.org/press/en/1997/19970904. SGSM6316.html
Conduit, E. (2007) *The Black Country Dialect: A Modern Linguistic Analysis*. Stourbridge: Laghamon Publishing.
DfE (2010) *The Importance of Teaching*. Available from: https://assets.publishing.service.gov.uk/government/uploads/system/uploads/attachment_data/file/175429/CM-7980.pdf
DfE (2011) *Teachers' Standards*. Available from: www.gov.uk/government/publications/teachers-standards
DfE (2015) *2010 to 2015 Government Policy: School and College Qualifications and Curriculum*. Available from: www.gov.uk/government/publications/2010-to-2015-government-policy-school-and-college-qualifications-and-curriculum/2010-to-2015-government-policy-school-and-college-qualifications-and-curriculum

Ofsted (2012) *Moving English Forward*. Available from: https://assets.publishing.service.gov.uk/government/uploads/system/uploads/attachment_data/file/181204/110118.pdf

SecEd (2013) *'The DfE policy on ICT is there is no policy on ICT'*. Available from: https://www.sec-ed.co.uk/news/the-dfe-policy-on-ict-is-there-is-no-policy-on-ict

TES (2016) *'Justine Greening: Don't let young people "hit a brick wall" in English and maths'*. Available from: www.tes.com/news/further-education/breaking-news/justine-greening-dont-let-young-people-hit-a-brick-wall-english

Trudgill, P. (1983) *Sociolinguistics: An Introduction to Language and Society*. London: Penguin.

10
PARENTS, CARERS AND COMMUNITY

WHAT THIS CHAPTER WILL COVER

- How to communicate with parents
- How to be sensitive to the communities in which you teach

INTRODUCTION

As teachers, we feel ourselves responsible for the pupils' education. As parents, we feel ourselves to be responsible for our children's education. There is a contradiction here that we try to bridge in this chapter. We look at the role of the teacher in school as a surrogate parent to the pupils and, conversely, the importance of the actual mum and dad, or just mum, or just dad, or mum and mum, or dad and dad, or carer (the official term given to anyone who is not a direct parent), or step-mum or … it's complicated, like families.

Meeting parents and carers is an important opportunity. It should never be seen as additional to what you do in school, but part of the triangle of support of pupil–teacher–parent/carer. The partnership with parents and carers is something that Tom Bennett encourages:

> If you say, 'We both want the best for Daniel,' then you tacitly create rapport between you and the parents because it's something they can't disagree with. You do want the best for Daniel, right?' (Bennett, 2011: 177–8)

Gaining this rapport is very important, but it must be carefully managed. Imagine that a parent or carer has been summoned to school because their child has been disruptive and you sit there with the following attitude about you and the school:

- we're right
- we're kind
- we're thoughtful
- we're reasonable
- we have thought everything through
- we know what's best for your child.

What does this mean for the parent or carer? That they are the opposite of this? The teacher can sit behind a desk and speak at parents and carers or sit beside them, listen and communicate. The one who has the stance that 'I know best and your child needs to do this' is, we think, not going to get far. Parents and carers do not want to be processed like sausages. Instead, they 'want to be treated with respect and as equals when communicating with educators' (Graham-Clay, n.d.).

As with other aspects of teaching, skilled body language and meaningful content is crucial. To communicate the partnership nature of your relationship, you might try PARENT (Bright Futures, 2019), which gives general advice about meeting parents and carers, from experienced practitioners.

- **P**repare: make sure you have records about the child and it is a good idea to have photos of the pupils by their names
- **A**ttainment: let the parent/carer know where their child is in relation to expectations and the class. It would be worth asking the parent/carer how they think their child is doing first.
- **R**espect: see the parent/carer as an equal.
- **E**ngage: this is about listening as much as talking. Link to the parent/carer and do not launch into a speech. The other person is there in a con (con means 'with') versation.
- **N**oise level: be aware of the noise and distractions in the room, and try to minimise them so you can have a calm conversation.
- **T**iming: keep aware of the time you have for each parent/carer and try to stick to it. This is never easy and needs to be balanced between what the parent/carer needs and your schedule. Some parents/carers do not want to hang around too long and have had long, hard days themselves.

To add to PARENT, we would like to add WPGALFF (it will never catch on).

- **W**elcome.
- **P**ositive body language: open body, nod and mirror. Mirroring is when you copy the pose of the parent/carer. Try it, as it gives an immediate bond if you are sitting in the same way as they are. Of course, if they are waving their fists at you, it does not work.
- '**G**ood news sandwich': start with the positive, give something negative, give something positive.
- **A**sk: how are they? How do they think their child is doing? Have they any concerns?
- **L**isten: to the answers and respond.
- **F**ollow up: this meeting is the start of the links and the conversation. This is an invaluable point of contact to improve the way your pupil can achieve.
- **F**inish positively: if only to promise more contact.

In the real world of meetings with parents and carers, there is not usually much time, so we suggest, as a quick-list of possible content, the following: APEAT (we tried a bit harder with the acronym this time):

- **A**sk the parent how they think the pupil is doing
- **P**rogress details
- **E**xample of successful work
- **A**ttitude to learning
- **T**argets and how to achieve them.

You should prepare for how you might deal with different parents/carers.

- Deeply engaged: arrange a separate time to meet and discuss concerns privately and when there is more time. Sending home family activities/projects that go with a lesson is also a good way to keep parents/carers involved in student learning. They may not be responded to, but might satisfy them; alternatively, you may have formed a link to support the pupil that is worth its weight in gold.
- Bossy: do not respond in the same manner. You may need to refer them to the Senior Leadership Team if they want further action.
- Chatty: best to schedule a meeting by phone or online, as the school policy dictates.
- Concerned you are pushing the child too hard: listen carefully to what the parent/carer wants and respond. They could be right and they know their child much better than you do.
- Angry: have data available. Remind the parent/carer that you care. Empathy is a valuable teacher trait, not only with the disruptive child but with their parents/carers. Try the 'look, repeat, acknowledge, understand' method where you engage

the eyes, repeat their concern, make an emotional link to the concerns and show that you realise why they are angry. Then, you can consider further action, which may involve the Senior Leadership Team.

The short time you get with a parent or carer is never going to be enough and should only be part of the home communication process, which includes email, apps, website, blog, phone calls, letters, merits, homework book, newsletters, report cards. Try to keep the lines of communication open because you have an ally at home (if you make them an ally) who wants the same outcome as you.

COMMUNITY

The chances are that the school you are assigned to will not be in your geographical location or among people from the community you grew up in. Therefore, you may be an outsider, and the pupils and parents, insiders. One of us worked for Teach First where the culture difference was marked because, in short, at the time Teach First wanted 'top' students from 'top' universities; by the very nature of the connection between family income and academic success, they were often from the upper echelons of society. These training teachers were placed in the most deprived areas of the country. One Teach First English training teacher recalled a creative writing lesson in which they told the class: 'Let's imagine ourselves in a beautiful desert island where the sand is clean, and the sea is clear. Look away from those dismal, grey flats out of the window and ...' A pupil, understandably indignant, said: 'That's my home!'

Sometimes, a community comes to the school, such as Gypsy, Roma and Traveller (GRT) people. These people have been grouped together due to the commonality of a travelling lifestyle (and are popularly initialised to GRT), but there are differences. Scottish Travellers, for example, may identify themselves as Cant, while Irish Travellers may be Gammon, and there are generations of circus and fairground families as well. GRT communities have been a protected Minority Ethnic Group since the creation of what is known as the Mandla Criteria, named after Mr Singh Mandla, an orthodox Sikh. The headmaster, Dowell Lee, refused to educate Mandla's son, Gurinder, unless (in a 'did I roll my eyes out loud?' moment at the religious insensitivity) he cut his hair and removed his turban. The case was taken up by the Commission for Racial Equality (CRE); amazingly, they lost the case when Lord Denning ruled that:

> You can discriminate for or against Roman Catholics as much as you like without being in breach of the law. You can discriminate for or against Communists as much as you please, without being in breach of the law. You can discriminate for or against the 'hippies' as much as you like, without being in breach of the law. (Denning, 1982)

With all this perfectly legal discrimination going on, it was fortunate that the House of Lords upheld the appeal, with Lord Fraser reframing the legal definition of race:

> The conditions which appear to me to be essential are these: (1) a long shared history, of which the group is conscious as distinguishing it from other groups, and the memory of which it keeps alive; (2) a cultural tradition of its own, including family and social customs and manners, often but not necessarily associated with religious observance. (Fraser, 1983)

Going on to list other desirable criteria for inclusion as a racial group, the interpretation also protected GRT children from discrimination, first under the Race Relations Acts and then under the Equality Act (2010). This change in the law, in 1983, came too late for Gurinder who had already gone to another – and better – school.

GRT children are, then, protected alongside other Minority Ethnic Groups by the Equality Act (2010), although the nature of a nomadic way of life leads to absences from school, with Gypsy Roma pupils being absent for around 50 per cent of the time and Irish Traveller pupils over 60 per cent (parliament.uk, n.d.). The issue is compounded by schools having target data for attendance that could trigger investigation and so possibly having an extra unwillingness to accommodate GRT pupils. In 1967, the Plowden Report on children from GRT families was damning about the situation: 'the children's educational needs are … extreme and largely unmet' (Plowden Report, 1967).

In 1975, the Bullock Report (1975) concluded that schools should accommodate the child's home culture rather than be expected to conform to the mainstream one:

> No child should be expected to cast off the language and culture of the home as he crosses the school threshold … and the curriculum should reflect those aspects of his life.

In 1985, the Swann Report (1985) thought the situation was appalling:

> The situation of Travellers' children in Britain today throws into stark relief many of the factors which influence the children from other ethnic minority groups – racism & discrimination, myths, stereotyping and misinformation, the inappropriateness and inflexibility of the education system and the need for better links between homes and schools and teachers and parents.

Ofsted likes the word 'risk' and applied it to GRT pupils in 1999:

> Gypsy Traveller pupils are the group most at risk in the education system …. Teacher expectations of Gypsy Traveller pupils are generally unreasonably low … the level of hostility faced by Gypsy Traveller children is probably greater than for any other minority ethnic group.

In 2019, a report entitled *Tackling Inequalities Faced by Gypsy, Roma and Traveller Communities* (Women's and Equalities Committee) gave the government two months to respond, and as far as we can ascertain, we are still waiting.

Alongside such reports which highlight the problems, practical steps are needed in schools and by teachers to include all communities. This means that the home and the home culture should be involved. The reports *Moving Forward Together: Raising Gypsy, Roma and Traveller Achievement* (**Department for Children, Schools and Families**, 2009a) and *Building Futures: Developing Trust* (Department for Children, Schools and Families, 2009b) did more than give the 'somebody should do something' message, but gave schools practical advice as to how schools can ensure that GRT communities are welcomed:

- Enter into partnership with families by listening to what they have to say and have appropriate systems in place for information gathering and sharing.
- Encourage positive role models from the GRT community to be involved in school decision making.
- Invite parents/carers into school to share and celebrate their children's milestones and successes informally and formally as often as possible.
- Have a regular dialogue with parents/carers.
- Challenge negative perceptions of minority ethnic groups.

There is more that schools can do, but listening is an important start to any relationship. Whoever 'they' may be, they are 'us'. Any difference is to be recognised, acknowledged, celebrated and never used as an excuse to label them 'other' and sideline 'them'; it is we who are different. The advice given to schools about how to involve GRT communities can be generalised to all cultures, ethnicities, lifestyles and communities that make the lives of the children you teach.

CONCLUSION

There is a lot to do in school, and reaching out to parents and carers when you have had a day of their children does not always seem appetising, but it is just the sort of act that makes a difference. It is equally important to be inclusive of everyone. We are all different and from differing communities, and it is a mistake to presume that the school can act in its own microcosm as if it is possible to be a neutral space. Instead, the school will most probably be reflective of mainstream society governed by the norms and values of the time. This does not reflect those whose culture, collective past and sense of belonging gives them an enriched sense of how life is to be lived. Bringing the worlds of the pupils into school and your teaching will make an enormous difference. You should make an effort with all parents and carers and a special effort with parents and carers of minority ethnic groups to which you do not belong. This starts by reaching out, formally and informally, and bridging the worlds of the child and your classroom.

REFLECTIONS ON PARENTS, CARERS AND COMMUNITY

Think about what the following statistics from the Office for National Statistics mean for communication with parents/carers:

- Between 68 and 71 per cent of single parents/carers are at work, 9–5 pm every day (ONS, 2017).
- 28 per cent of parents/carers believe that their children's education is mainly or wholly their responsibility (Peters et al., 2007)
- 22 per cent of parents/carers are unable to help children with homework because they don't understand the topic being learned in class (Goodall and Vorhaus, 2011).
- 81 per cent of parents/carers would welcome support and guidance on how best to support their child's learning at home (Education Scotland, 2018).
- 79 per cent of children reported that they would like their parents to know more about what they are learning in class so they can provide more support outside the classroom (Education Scotland, 2018).
- 84 per cent of parents/carers reported that their child's school provided them with little or no resources to help support their child's learning at home (Education Scotland, 2018).
- 38 per cent of parents/carers do not understand their children's school work (Goodall and Vorhaus, 2011).
- 80,850 pupils in England are Looked-after Children (GOV.UK, 2021), which means that they will not be with their parents but in the care of the local authority, in a foster home, residential children's home, wider family or a secure unit.

ACTIONS

- Identify ways to celebrate difference in the community.
- Discover more about the minority ethnic groups the pupils belong to.
- Reach out to parents/carers in a way that opens dialogue, with positive communication that supports the child and informs them about progress and success.
- Talk to a staff governor about the parent-governor role.

REFLECTION-ON-ACTION BY A TRAINING TEACHER

In the reflection below, Joel Collins shares their diverse experience training to teach in two multicultural schools, with a particular focus on the support provided for children with English as an Additional Language.

My time during my first placement was spent at a non-selective member of a large academy in the top 10 per cent of deprived wards in the country. It was a multicultural school with children coming from a variety of religious, ethnic, and linguistic backgrounds. Within my Year 7 class, there were three EAL students: Jafeena, and Dawud (names are changed for the children's privacy) who had very high attendance at school but tended to suffer from a lack of motivation; and Mahdi, who would rarely attend; when he did, he would often be excluded from classes by other teachers for poor behaviour. I employed Rosenshine's method of increasing the difficulty of things to recall with the aim of improving a pupil's working memory. All of the students gained a lot of motivation through being able to remember key sections of the story or studied vocabulary. Dawud was especially motivated by this, as his working English vocabulary was normally very poor. When he received a grade on his mock GCSE paper that was lower than expected, he said, 'Sir, I'm going to fail anyway. We don't speak English at home.'

The situation with these three pupils was in stark contrast to my Year 8 mixed-ability class. The difference in abilities between the EAL students in this class was very surprising to me. Among the three students there were starkly different abilities: Bilal was entirely fluent in written and spoken English and frequently volunteered answers; Maderu was rapidly gaining confidence with giving answers but often made grammatical mistakes which suggested that he was translating parts of his work from his mother tongue and Cameron spoke English fluently yet could barely read or write. Cameron, along with three other peers, was assisted by a teaching assistant who acted as a motivator and a scribe. I was able to have several meetings with the teaching assistant about Cameron's abilities and how we could enable him further.

My second placement showed an obvious dissimilarity to Placement School 1. It was located in the town which has a 56 per cent black, Asian and minority ethnic population – 53 per cent of pupils are from Romania, Italy, and India, and do not have English as a first language (Sandwell Trends, 2022). In Placement School 2's last Ofsted inspection, it was noted that more than two-thirds of pupils have EAL needs. This population is supported by the school's ability to maintain an EAL department for its Key Stage Three pupils. I strongly assume that the school is able to direct its, presumably, higher than average EAL funding allocation towards an entire department which is something that schools with fewer EAL pupils, such as Placement School 1, were unable to do.

> ## WHAT TOOLS ARE IN YOUR TOOLKIT NOW?
>
> - Knowledge of the importance of parent/carer communication.
> - Some good techniques to improve face-to-face communication with parents/carer.
> - Awareness of the importance of bringing pupils' home life and culture into your classroom.
> - Greater understanding of GRT pupils.

PLACES TO GET MORE TOOLS FOR YOUR TOOLKIT

Morgan, N. (2016) *Engaging Families in Schools: Practical Strategies to Improve Parental Involvement*. London: Routledge.

As the title suggests, this book has practical steps to bring families into the life of the schools; some of it has an institutional basis, but there is plenty that involves the classroom teacher and comes with an impassioned plea for the benefits of parent/carer involvement.

Whitaker, T. and Fiore, D. (2016) *Dealing with Difficult Parents*. London: Routledge.

It is not all positive out there; some parents/carers will want to be in contact with the school, sometimes reasonably, sometimes unreasonably. This book gives advice on how these situations can be managed.

REFERENCES

Bennett, T. (2011) *Not Quite a Teacher*. London: Continuum

Bright Futures (2019) *Blog: 'Parents evening'*. Available from: www.allianceforlearning.co.uk/blog-parents-evening.

Bullock Report (1975) *A Language for Life*. Available from: www.educationengland.org.uk/documents/bullock/bullock1975.html

Denning, Lord (1982) *Mandla v. Dowell-Lee* [1982] UKHL 7.

Department for Children, Schools and Families (2009a) *Moving Forward Together: Raising Gypsy, Roma and Traveller Achievement*. Available from: https://dera.ioe.ac.uk/746/7/mving_fwd_tgthr_bkt1_0066009_Redacted.pdf

Department for Children, Schools and Families (2009b) *Building Futures: Developing Trust*. Available from: https://dera.ioe.ac.uk/10537/7/00741-2009BKT-EN_Redacted.pdf

Education Scotland (2018) *Review of Learning at Home*. Available from: https://education.gov.scot/media/zk2mbwlt/par19-learning-at-home.pdf

Fraser, Lord (1983) *Commission for Racial Equality, (CRE) ICR 385*, House of Lords.

Goodall, J. and Vorhaus, J. (2011) *Review of Best Practice in Parental Engagement*. Available from: https://assets.publishing.service.gov.uk/government/uploads/system/uploads/attachment_data/file/182508/DFE-RR156.pdf

GOV.UK (2021) *Children Looked After in England Including Adoptions*. Available from: https://explore-education-statistics.service.gov.uk/find-statistics/children-looked-after-in-england-including-adoptions/2021

Graham-Clay, S. (n.d.) *'Communicating with parents: Strategies for teachers'*. Available from: www.adi.org/journal/ss05/graham-clay.pdf

Ofsted (1999) *Raising the Attainment of Minority Ethnic Pupils*. Available from: https://dera.ioe.ac.uk/4386/2/Raising_the_attainment_of_minority_ethnic_pupils_school_and_LEA_responses.pdf

ONS (2017) *Families and the Labour Market, England: 2017*. Available from: www.ons.gov.uk/employmentandlabourmarket/peopleinwork/employmentandemployeetypes/datasets/workingandworklesshouseholdstablepemploymentratesofpeoplebyparentalstatus

Parliament.uk (n.d.). *Education*. Available from: https://publications.parliament.uk/pa/cm201719/cmselect/cmwomeq/360/report-files/36008.htm

Peters, M., Seeds, K., Goldstein, A. and Coleman, N. (2007) *Parental Involvement in Children's Education*. Available from: https://dera.ioe.ac.uk/8605/1/DCSF-RR034.pdf

Plowden Report (1967) *Children and their Primary Schools*. Available from: www.educationengland.org.uk/documents/plowden/plowden1967-1.html

Swann Report (1985) *Education for All*. Available from: www.educationengland.org.uk/documents/swann/swann1985.html

Women's and Equalities Committee (2019) *Tackling Inequalities Faced by Gypsy, Roma and Traveller Communities*. Available from: https://publications.parliament.uk/pa/cm201719/cmselect/cmwomeq/360/full-report.html

11
CURRICULUM

INTRODUCTION

'Curriculum' means the official content to be taught and learned, and this chapter takes you through the ways that schools are set up, how subject specialism works, the need for ongoing subject knowledge improvement, and the restrictions given to training providers as to what they are and are not supposed to promote. No-one is free to teach what they like; there are constraints at every level. Recognition of these constraints can, paradoxically, generate freedom to work within the system, to find and expand areas of creativity and expression.

SCHOOL STRUCTURES

In the UK there is a primary sector and a secondary sector; some local authorities have a straddling middle school system. There are independent schools, grammar schools, faith schools, academies, maintained schools, pupil referral units (PRUs), community schools – we could go on. Take Warwick as an example of a single town set-up. Warwick School is one of three independent schools in the town for those whose parents can afford the fees of £4,779 per term (Warwick School, 2022) or gain one of the reductions or bursaries. For those who pass the 11+ exam, there are a couple of grammar schools in nearby Stratford-upon-Avon (nearby in the sense of over 10 miles away, so transport will prevent some) with a very selective intake of 600 (GOV.UK, n.d.) for a catchment area whose radius has a 45-mile diameter. The only faith-based secondary school is the Roman Catholic Trinity School in nearby Leamington Spa, and the secondary school catchments are two mixed-sex (co-educational) academies – Myton and Aylesford. There is an all-round (4- to 19-year-old) special educational needs (SEN) school, Evergreen. There is a pupil reintegration (rather than the usual 'referral') unit in Leamington for anyone who has struggled in the mainstream schooling system.

In the 1960s, there was a move to make the school system comprehensive – all children getting the same experience. As it turned out, some local authorities kept their grammar schools, and faith schools were always allowed to select pupils based on the beliefs of parents. A further stratification of schools occurred when schools were encouraged to become academies and free schools in 2010. The freedom they are given is that they can set their own conditions of pay, and the school terms and days. One head teacher of a free school took this freedom a bit too far when they paid themselves double their own salary (*TES*, 2020). Ofsted, the Teacher Regulation Agency or the Independent Schools Inspectorate (whose leaders are selected by or answerable to the Secretary of State for Education), have the power to give or withdraw a teaching and school licence, so all schools are regulated by the government.

Alongside free schools, there are:

- faith schools
- academies
- city technology colleges
- state boarding schools
- private schools
- special schools
- pupil referral units.

There are subdivisions for each. For example, free schools may be called university technical colleges or studio schools. It is difficult to see how academies differ greatly from free schools or where the old-fashioned term 'comprehensive school' (which, technically, most pupils still attend) fits in. These types of schools host the vast majority of pupils, as 80 per cent of schools are academies or free schools which teach 79 per cent of all secondary school pupils (GOV.UK, 2022). The academisation and collection of schools into multi-academy trusts (MATs) was part of the government's control mechanism to reduce costs and ensure that 'failing' schools can be adopted by non-failing ones and recover with a new name, identity and board of governors. There are 1,170 MATs in England which each run between 2 and 29 schools (BESA, 2022). Initially, 'failing' schools were forced to become academies. The next round of academisation came with the Conservative–Liberal Coalition government of 2010 which wanted to make schools into businesses, independent from local authorities. This allowed schools to act as independent businesses in what is known as 'quasi-market' conditions as the government (or rather, the taxpayer) is still paying but, in theory, the school can spend as it wishes.

Within the fee-paying sector there are many types of provision, including that offered by Montessori and Steiner schools which focus on pupil autonomy, expression and creativity. Parents and carers can take their children to join up in community schools. A.S. Neil's Summerhill School stands as a famous (and sometimes when the media coverage gets negative, infamous) example of a school that allows the pupils freedom to learn or not to learn. Children do not, by law, have to attend school. If a child is withdrawn from an educational establishment, the parent has to satisfy the DfE that an educational curriculum is in place and there are many home schooling companies ready to provide (paid-for) support. The choice is out there, but the reality is constrained by funds, geography, transport and catchment areas (parents cannot choose their school, but have to apply and, if they are outside the catchment area, may not get their first choice). For all the landscape complexity, most children still tend to go to the 'local comp', as it may well be thought of.

CURRICULUM DESIGN

For some of you, the National Curriculum will frame the subject content you must teach in schools. For other subjects, local schools or organisations collaborate on an agreed framework. Exam boards (informed by the DfE) will determine subject content at Key Stage 4, anyway. Subject leads will be responsible for creating long-term, medium-term and short-term plans for their subject. Schools vary as to how much planning is offered to teachers, with some not doing it at all and others putting it on the internet somewhere you cannot find – in much the same way that, in Douglas Adams's (2009) book, *The Hitchhiker's Guide to the Galaxy*, planning permission for the demolition of Earth was placed in Alpha Centauri, 6 trillion miles away. Our training teachers sometimes respond with bemusement when we mention schemes of work and long-term plans. In these cases, the training teacher has to go back to the National Curriculum or agreed subject content and create their own plans. There is nothing wrong with this, as it develops their subject knowledge and independence. It is increasingly the case, though, that schools give the teachers (including training ones) lesson content, resources and presentations, and ask merely for adaptation and delivery.

SUBJECT KNOWLEDGE

Many training providers expect 50 per cent of the secondary teacher's undergraduate degree to be in the same subject as the one they are going to train to teach, but will accept prior teaching experience and Subject Knowledge Enhancement (SKE) courses. SKE courses were introduced in response to a shortage of teachers in key subjects such as mathematics and science, and form part of an ongoing concern about teachers' subject knowledge (DfE, 2013). Whatever your subject background, learning is lifelong and ongoing. Your ability to 'stretch and challenge' the pupils demands that you also study the topics taught and have more to teach the pupils than the lesson's learning content.

CONCLUSION

You cannot control the curriculum. You will all need to teach towards the examinations and the content and material provided by the chosen examination board. The chances are that you will be given a lesson presentation or at least access to the department's resources. Your lesson content is, to a greater or lesser extent, already in place. You are the one who takes the established knowledge, skills and expectations, and interprets and acts on them. You have agency – the ability to decide and to act – so use it.

REFLECTIONS ON CURRICULUM

Now is a good time to list your strengths and weaknesses in subject knowledge. Think about the areas you have to teach that your degree skipped – that is, if you took a degree in your subject. What do you need to know more about? Reflect on the idea of yourself as a 'lifelong learner' alongside your pupils. You have to be passionate about the subject you chose to teach in order to fire the imaginations of children.

ACTIONS

- Read, or view, books and other media about your teaching subject, starting with the ones directed at the age group of your pupils. Make every day a learning one as well as a teaching one, so that you keep developing the knowledge and skills you will share with the children you teach.
- Read around every subject you are to teach and get some 'nuggets' which you can deliver to the class on a one-to-one basis as these will enrich pupils' learning. The 'secret knowledge' you can give to an individual in passing, as it were, will often be remembered.

REFLECTION-ON-ACTION BY A TRAINING TEACHER

Leaon McDonald reflects on the curriculum they had been told about as a training teacher and views the curriculum and its examination system as being affected by the needs of 'big business'.

The Education Reform Act of 1988 gave 'a very high level of detailed control of the Curriculum to central government' (Butterfield, 1995, p. 51). This Act endows each new Secretary of State for Education 'with extensive powers ... to revise the Curriculum whenever he considers it necessary or expedient to so' (Butterfield, 1995, p. 51). Consequently, the 'Secretary of State may by order specify in relation to each of the foundation subjects: (a) such attainment targets; (b) such programmes of study; and (c) such assessment arrangements; as he considers appropriate for that subject' (quoted in Butterfield, 1995, p. 51). Over time this has allowed corporate ambition to bleed into Britain's secondary schools, as business entities impress upon governments the need for grade attainment, so that the citizens of tomorrow can prove themselves ready to compete in a global jobs market. Our governments, in my opinion, are all too ready to meet the requirements of business and replicate their structures by pitting schools against each other in a tug of war for prestige, via school league tables. Introduced in 1993 by John Major's government, school league tables publicise data that pertains to the 'best and the worst performing secondary, independent, and private schools' in England and Wales (Donnelly, 1999). The yearly publishing of results from school league tables has added competition to the education sector (Hill, 2002). 'Underperforming' schools now find it more and more difficult to recruit head teachers and teaching staff as the knock-on effect stigmatises and in turn affects the pupils, parents, and communities that these schools serve (Adams, 2019). These league tables are partly the result of GCSE results as 'schooling has become increasingly defined in terms of ... exam-scores' (Biesta and Miedema, 2002, p. 174). Yet, the question remains: how can a series of one hour and 45-minute written exams accurately measure all of a young person's intellectual growth? Also, where is the room in these highly formal examinations to measure the psychological and emotional wellbeing of a young person (Broadfoot, 2009)? Surely these aspects of human nature are just as important as subject knowledge. Obviously, assessments and examinations cannot be overlooked, but the obsessive inclination to focus solely on exam results is leading, I think, to a weariness amongst teachers and taking its toll on children, who are becoming all too aware of this fascination.

WHAT TOOLS ARE IN YOUR TOOLKIT NOW?

- Awareness of the school curriculum.
- The language of planning.
- Encouragement to see subject knowledge as a lifelong quest.

PLACES TO GET MORE TOOLS FOR YOUR TOOLKIT

DfE (2019) *ITT Core Content Framework*. Available from: https://assets.publishing.service.gov. uk/government/uploads/system/uploads/attachment_data/file/974307/ITT_core_content_ framework_.pdf

In this document, you will find the minimum content requirement for training teachers. There are links to key research literature and clear guidance about best practice from evidence-based literature.

GOV.UK (2014) National Curriculum. Available from: www.gov.uk/government/collections/ national-curriculum

The current picture is complex, with some schools having their own curriculum, but for many, this is still the defining document of subject and wider requirements.

REFERENCES

Adams, D. (2009) *The Hitchhiker's Guide to the Galaxy*. London: Macmillan.

BESA (2022) *'Key UK education statistics'*. Available from: www.besa.org.uk/key-uk-education-statistics/

DfE (2013) *Evaluation of Subject Knowledge Enhancement Courses: Annual Report – 2011–12*. Available from: https://assets.publishing.service.gov.uk/government/uploads/system/ uploads/attachment_data/file/224705/DFE-RR301A.pdf

GOV.UK (2022) *Schools, pupils and their characteristics*. Available from https://explore-education-statistics.service.gov.uk/find-statistics/school-pupils-and-their-characteristics

GOV.UK (n.d.) *Types of School*. Available at: www.gov.uk/types-of-school/free-schools

TES (2020) *Barred from Running Academies*. Available from: www.tes.com/magazine/archive/ liam-nolan-barred-running-academies

Warwick School (2022) Available from: www.warwickschool.org/fees-scholarships-bursaries

12
EXTRACURRICULAR

WHAT THIS CHAPTER WILL COVER

- School trips
- Clubs and societies

INTRODUCTION

As well as teaching your subject, you are expected to become part of the life of the school. Enter a typical secondary school after the pupils are gone and there are noises of a sometimes not very harmonious nature coming from the musicians in the hall. They may be disturbing the homework club which is keeping those children who cannot be collected immediately after school purposeful, warm and safe. Meanwhile, there is another group of children milling around, including those in their sports kits returning, with muddied boots and sore egos, from a defeat by their local rivals. As a training teacher, your involvement in this part of the school may be as an observer, but there is a time to look forward to when you can match your interests beyond the curriculum, perhaps beyond your teaching subject, and relate to pupils in new ways.

SCHOOL TRIPS

Take some time to think about the most valuable experiences you had at school. The chances are that, among them, somewhere, is a trip. Such events we remember in ways that we may not an everyday school experience. If learning can be seen as a process of change, school trips can alter how pupils see themselves, develop confidence and widen life choices. This latter point is important, as for some pupils there have been no trips abroad and no trips even outside of the town or city in which they were born. In Ken Loach's film, *The Angels' Share*, some people are taken on a trip by their probation worker. One Glaswegian, who has clearly not been outside of his home city, looks up at Edinburgh Castle and asks what it is. The bemused probation worker asks him whether he was born in a cupboard and had no shortbread at home (because tins of shortbread often had a picture of the famous castle on the front). For some children, their immediate geography is their entire world and trips give them the only release from it until they are old enough to travel or move away by themselves. Before you organise a school trip, you must realise that it is a big undertaking and not one to be done lightly. You will need to plan months in advance. It will involve consent from parents, health and safety assessments, financial considerations (including legal ones), costings and practical arrangements. At the end of it all, the coach may not come and will leave you stranded, so you will also need some contingency plans.

Most schools ask parents and carers to sign a 'blanket' consent form about trips. If you are working at an independent school or a further education college, there may be an issue about running trips that are not been advertised in advance. This is worth checking, as no additional costs can be added on to a course that were not agreed in advance. Most schools will be immune from the Consumer Rights Act (2015), but fee-paying schools are providing a paid-for service, which means that what is being offered must match what is being provided. Equally, if a trip was promised and it does not materialise, it contravenes the Act. If the parent or carer cannot afford the trip, there is usually a 'slush fund' in the school but, again, check that it is there before you plan, and remember that some parents are on a low income. Imagine telling a child that although all their friends are going on a trip, they cannot join in. This is something to consider and you should think about the cost of a trip, ways of paying for it and whether you have an alternative for those who cannot afford it.

You will need to:

- Have a clear purpose for the visit and evaluate how it will meet the learning objective for the curriculum topic. It is important that there is a reason for your chosen trip. It must link to your curriculum topic and your planned classroom activities to bring learning to life and consolidate the pupils' learning. You may be able to make it cross-curricular; for example, History and English departments may benefit from a trip to a museum. If so, it may double the coachload, but will bring in another member of staff to help with the planning.

- Research venues and select an appropriate one for your trip.
- Produce a pack of information and resources, including a timeline that contains all the details you have produced in the planning of the trip to help it run smoothly.

When you have done this initial assessment, start to anticipate the possible dangers. To get you in the mood for how much you need to be aware of risks, look at this advice for a two-mile walk along a pedestrian-only path:

> The Visit Leader has some basic knowledge of first aid and is carrying a mobile phone in an area of good reception …. Any significant injury here would involve such a time delay in accessing an ambulance as to make it necessary for there to be someone with appropriate first aid training and expertise as a member of the group, carrying a mobile first aid kit. (OEAP, 2020)

Amplify this concern for detail, in anticipation of what could go wrong with having 60 14-year-old pupils walking around London's West End. Risk assessments must be implemented for every trip. Each school should have a trained Educational Visits Co-ordinator who will support you when completing the risk assessment. The following points require consideration:

- Transport: what would happen in case of an emergency or breakdown?
- Contact phone numbers should be available in case of an emergency.
- If a child is poorly or injured, where could they be taken in case of emergency?
- Adult–pupil ratio: do you need volunteers? What safeguarding issues are there?
- Availability of toilet areas.
- Lunch: is this available for those who get free school meals and packed lunches? What allergies need to be considered? What dry seating areas are there?
- What barriers might there be for those with health issues? Is disabled access available for anyone who might need it?
- Health and safety: what is the dress code and what are the potential hazards or dangers around the site?
- Medical: first aid, medication needs and travel sickness must be accounted for.

The government – DfE (2018) and GOV.UK (2014) – published advice on health and safety. It is the main responsibility of the school leaders as they create their policies, but it is also worthwhile reading to get a sense of what you can and cannot do. Ofsted (2008) also reported on the many benefits of taking learning outside the classroom.

It is highly unlikely that you will be planning a trip as a training teacher, but it is a good idea to observe others who do. Someone at school will be responsible for overseeing school trips and this is the first person you should see to discuss the matter, after you have checked with your mentor. The school will not let you arrange a trip without proper staffing and support in place, but it is a very good idea for you to think ahead and anticipate issues and have a sense of what needs to be considered. While it brings extra work for you, a trip will enhance everything you do in the classroom, and will bring a stronger bond between you and the pupils as you will have shared something with them. You may not get many thanks from the pupils, but they will look back on the day or week they had on a school trip and one day be grateful. If you are not sure about that, think back to a school trip you went on and try to remember who went with you and what effect it had on the way you saw them.

CLUBS AND SOCIETIES

We recommend our training teachers to ask the question, at job interviews, of whether it would be possible to start an after-school club. It offers the school that something extra they may need, shows a commitment to the school beyond the classroom and demonstrates humility, as you are asking for the chance to help them. We have run school newspapers, film clubs (a great one because you can sit in the dark and enjoy the film), a caving club (a great one if you just want to sit in the dark), the Duke of Edinburgh's Award, science club, and a club which offered a space for pupils to sit and use our classroom computers. Clubs are places that allow the school to demonstrate it is there for the pupils beyond their subject needs, and to support parents and carers who have to work and cannot pick up their children directly after school; they also give you a chance to know the pupils better. Working with challenging pupils outside the classroom can also be a great way to break negative behaviour cycles and create more positive relationships.

CONCLUSION

Teaching means commitment to the pupils and one of the most rewarding ways of linking with them is outside the classroom. This can be chatting in the corridors about a mutual interest, taking them outside the school on a school trip or seeing them at an after-school club to engage in something you are both interested in. In these ways, you become part of the school, form relationships with pupils and enrich your experience of teaching. You also make memories. We cannot recall many lessons from schooldays, but the memories from school trips are still vivid. The children you take on trips and engage with outside lessons will remember you and what you did for decades to come. You will not know about it, of course, unless they come up to you and tell you years later – but they will.

REFLECTIONS ON EXTRACURRICULAR

Consider what are you offering the school and pupils beyond classroom teaching. If you have a passion or a skill that you can share, it is something to offer, even in your training year. It helps on many levels, because your mentor will see your value, the school management will be alerted that something new is being offered to the children and you can link with pupils in a way that the lesson does not allow. Think of what you can manage and how this might be best implemented, but always do so in consultation with your mentor.

ACTIONS

- Consider supporting or contributing to an after-school club.
- Offer a one-off session at lunchtime to enrich the pupils' experience. It will also allow you to exercise a passion or skill.
- Observe and shadow someone who is planning a school trip and go along on the trip, if you are permitted to do so.

REFLECTION-ON-ACTION BY A TRAINING TEACHER

There is so much to do in school as a training teacher, as Sidra Bi shows in this list of some of the activities performed outside the classroom.

I carried out break duties twice a week, was a Year 11 form tutor, attended CPD and training days, took my form to Year 11 assemblies every Friday, attended all Safeguarding meetings on Mondays and Headteacher Meetings on Wednesdays and Fridays. I talked to parents and carers at parents' evening, planned lessons for cover, and volunteered to go on a Year 7 school trip to Harry Potter World where I supervised students and supported other staff members. I helped in the preparation for the annual school Spelling Bee by making gift boxes for the attendees and contestants and helped the Teaching Assistants prepare an Eid lunch for all the colleagues in the school. I informally supervised students at lunch and break-times. From attendance at training sessions, I have learnt the different legislation and policies surrounding safeguarding children, such as *Keeping Children Safe in Education* (2020) and so know how to work with adolescents who are vulnerable to exploitation and I learnt to be proactive with partner agencies and have open communication to ensure effective safeguarding.

WHAT TOOLS ARE IN YOUR TOOLKIT NOW?

- Basic knowledge of what is involved in planning trips.
- Understanding the importance of risk assessments.
- Greater comprehension of the place, benefits and importance of clubs, societies and all extracurricular work

PLACES TO GET MORE TOOLS FOR YOUR TOOLKIT

DfE (2018) *Health and Safety on Educational Visits*. London: HMSO.

Don't ever start planning a school trip without reading this document. It is what protects the schools and teachers, and it gives clear advice about keeping children safe.

OEAP (2022) Outdoor Education Advisers' Panel.

More essential advice about where to go, and how to go there safely.

REFERENCES

Consumer Rights Act (2015) Available from: www.legislation.gov.uk/ukpga/2015/15/contents/enacted

DfE (2018) *'Health and safety on educational visits'*. Available from: www.gov.uk/government/publications/health-and-safety-on-educational-visits/health-and-safety-on-educational-visits

GOV.UK (2014) *'Consent for school trips'*. Available from: www.gov.uk/government/publications/consent-for-school-trips-and-other-off-site-activities

OEAP (2020) *'First Aid'*. Available from: https://oeapng.info/wp-content/uploads/dlm_uploads/2020/04/4.4b-First-aid.pdf

OEAP (2022) *Outdoor Education Advisers' Panel*. Available from: https://oeapng.info/

Ofsted (2008) *'Learning outside the classroom: How far should you go?'* Available from: www.lotc.org.uk/wp-content/uploads/2010/12/Ofsted-Report-Oct-2008.pdf

13
PRINCIPLED PRACTICE

WHAT THIS CHAPTER WILL COVER

- Government pedagogy
- Your pedagogy

INTRODUCTION

When we consider principled practice, we mean the fundamental drives behind your decision to teach. There are many ways of looking at this. The drive can be an altruistic one – for the benefit of others – or self-fulfilment, or both. Such drives, or pedagogies, may be in conflict with the ones imposed on you by the government and the school. This becomes a battleground of purpose. This chapter aims to arm you for the battle.

GOVERNMENT PEDAGOGY

Oddly, it can be a comfort that we are not wholly in control of our ability to act. As the German author von Goethe (1749–1832) wrote: 'No-one is more enslaved than the man who believes himself to be free' (1994: 151). We are kidding ourselves, in other words, if we think that we can act with freedom of thought or action. The culture (or cultures) into which we are born gives us social, economic and political norms; our parents generally reinforce these and add a few more of their own. Paraphrasing Karl Marx, Zygmunt Bauman said that people are 'not under conditions of their choice' (Bauman, 2000). Some teachers hide behind the structures in place and blame them for the failings of the school and their teaching. It is an easy response to note poor behaviour in classes, negative attitudes among pupils and disappointing exam results, and shrug the shoulders and ask, 'What could I do?' The answer is in the start of the Bauman quotation: 'People make history but … '.

You can make a difference within, and despite, the system. Conditions are the circumstances in which we work and in terms of the industry, teaching has just gone through the same processes that have affected others:

1   postindustrial/postmodern;
2   neoliberal.

Daniel Bell (1976) was among the first to identify the way that the economic system in Western countries was turning into a service or 'post-industrial' one. It had ceased being reliant on making things and moved to information and personal services (which includes teaching). In the same period, Alvin Toffler (1970) warned about the effects of this process in *Futureshock*, declaring that there was too much change in too little time, meaning psychological consequences, including 'information overload'. Alongside such social commentators, there was no shortage of employment for French-based philosophers in the latter part of the twentieth century, with Jean Baudrillard (1976), Jean-François Lyotard (1984) and Frederick Jameson (1991) warning of the effects of a social change that was affecting society – postmodernism. Postmodernism is a theory that Western society rejected fixed roles and morals, and lost a common sense of purpose. The rules on family – for example, about fixed gender roles, divorce and the inclusion of extended family members – were left to the individual; everything was acceptable on a cultural level. While Bauman was using the quite pleasant-sounding 'liquid' metaphor to describe unfixed cultural expectations, Ulrich Beck (1992) used the word 'zombie' to demonstrate how fractured the conditions were. The 'posts' in postindustrialism and postmodernism suggest that something changed in the way that society was run in the latter part of the twentieth century, and it is also thought that a powerful new social and economic force was then growing stronger – neoliberalism.

Neoliberalism is the New Liberal system that has dominated Western economies since the 1980s. Liberalism was the recommendation of economist and philosopher, Adam Smith (1723–90), regarding a system that would benefit everyone. From observations of economies across Europe, Smith concluded that if individuals were given the freedom to pursue profit, it would benefit all:

> As every individual, therefore, endeavours as much as he can both to employ his capital in the support of domestic industry …. He generally, indeed, neither intends to promote the public interest, nor knows how much he is promoting it. (Smith, 1827: 184)

Self-interest produces public good, in other words. Today, this system has been hyper-charged to the extent of: 'What is private is necessarily good and what is public is necessarily bad' (Apple, 2004: 59). This is not good news for teachers, who tend to be employed in the public sector. A neoliberalist way of thinking includes a suspicion of those who act in the interest of others, as if they are hiding something or are not able to survive in the cut-and-thrust of the real world. We see it in that most dreadful and inaccurate of phrases: 'Those who cannot do, teach', which some teachers have adapted to jokily insult their colleagues: 'And those who can't teach, teach [insert subject here]'.

Perhaps because of the suspicion of the idea of selflessly working for the good of others, neoliberalism has brought in measures to monitor and control public sector workers. Teachers are monitored by data and given targets to achieve. They are also given a script of behaviour, and responses and restrictions on their movement and actions. Perryman and Calvert's study (2019) linked this high-stakes accountability to excessive burnout and teacher turnover, arguing that their participants expressed:

> a discourse of disappointment, the reality of teaching being worse than expected, and the nature (rather than the quantity) of the workload, linked to notions of performativity and accountability, being a crucial factor. (2019: 2)

This idea was addressed in the essay 'The teacher's soul and the terrors of performativity' by Stephen Ball. The title gives a clue to his views on the system, as does his 2016 paper, 'Neoliberal education, confronting the slouching beast'. For Ball:

> Teachers are no longer encouraged to have a rationale for practice, account of themselves in terms of a relationship to the meaningfulness of what they do, but are required to produce measurable and 'improving' outputs and performances, what is important is what works. (2003: 222)

Teachers are controlled by being given a fixed way of working and monitored by a reward and sanction system. This is what is known as 'performativity', which

> requires individual practitioners to organize themselves as a response to targets, indicators and evaluations. To set aside personal beliefs and commitments and live an existence of calculation. The new performative worker is a promiscuous self, an enterprising self, with a passion for excellence. (Ball, 2003: 215)

Underscoring this idea is a theory of how to maximise people's output. It envisages us as selfish animals who will seek out personal reward and gain through incentives:

> Money, food calories, energy, time, and information, non scarce resources such as integrity and trust are treated as though they are costly and finite. (Amadae, 2015: 10)

The rewards and sanctions are based on numbers, so everything in schools is datafied – given a number and a target to achieve. The school has its Progress 8 score to improve, and its place on the league tables, and teachers are pressurised to ensure that certain grades are achieved by pupils. There is the incentive of 'responsibility points' (money, status, power) for those who take on roles such as Safeguarding Officer. Performance-related pay, where a pay rise is given for those who achieve their numbers, incentivises compliance and goals.

This culture of performance is not working to support teacher well-being, it seems. The teachers' union, the National Education Union (2022), surveyed over 10,000 teachers and found that 35 per cent were expecting to leave in five years. Ask many employees across the country if they intend to leave their jobs in five years and you may get a similar figure, especially if you ask on a Monday morning, but teachers do actually leave. Long and Danechi's (2022) study for the House of Commons stated that in 2019:

- 33,565 full-time posts were vacated for reasons other than retirement;
- 21.7 per cent of newly qualified entrants to the sector in 2017 were no longer teaching;
- for 2014 entrants this figure was 32.6 per cent.

Long and Denechi (2022) conclude to their parliamentary masters that:

> These declines in teacher retention over time mean that more new teachers are required to replace them.

They may have better concluded that workload (the reason given by 52 per cent of teachers thinking of quitting) and accountability (the reason given by 35 per cent) need to be reduced (National Education Union, 2022). If they were, then perhaps the need to replace teachers would not arise. A third reason for job dissatisfaction was government and media attitudes towards teachers (53 per cent). This is linked, we feel, to the neoliberal agenda that discourages public service in favour of private enterprise and affects how the job of the teacher is viewed. Over 20 per cent of teachers work part-time (SecEd, 2020), which seems to be a logical move in a profession that demands so much.

Neoliberalism can seem like a dystopian system of human control, but it need not be experienced as such. It is no more 'terror' than what preceded it (and probably triggered it) – the early and mid-twentieth century of two world wars followed by the Cold War. Fukuyama (2020) even presents neoliberalism as 'the end of history' as it works to maintain a functioning peaceful society to such an extent that there will be no more social–economic–political movements. There is healthy cynicism aplenty in the staffrooms of the UK (thank goodness!) and this alone lifts the burden of performativity. Matthew Clarke's study of Australian teachers 'Terror/enjoyment: performativity, resistance and the teacher's psyche' (Clarke, 2013) suggests that for all the 'terror' that Stephen Ball proposed, there is also an enjoyment of the performance. Michel Foucault's understanding of people as game-players of all discourses is one that we can find comfort in – there is a knowingness in the performance of the times and pleasure in resistance.

Schools sometimes act against the ruling ideology, despite the pressures from above. Faith schools are the most obvious places as the messages of capitalism and neoliberalism are counter to the 'we-culture' that religions promote. Steiner schools, for example, are a world away from an ideology that promotes the acquisition of grades and goods:

> We should think: I must certainly do everything for the culture of soul and spirit but I will wait tranquilly until, by higher powers, I shall be found worthy of definite illumination. (Steiner, 1910)

Some Sikh schools have a period of kirtan or spiritual singing included in their day for a time of quiet reflection on life and God/Waheguru. Faith schools are not the only places where capitalism and neoliberalism can be tempered. Most schools – all good schools – have an ethos or a moral underpinning, shared by the management and teaching staff, guiding pupil attitudes and behaviour.

YOUR PEDAGOGY

Regardless of the pedagogy of school or government, your own reasons for teaching will be the 'guiding light' for your career. Pedagogy is so central that the first question we ask those who want to train to be a teacher: 'Why do you want to be a teacher?'

The answer comes in three categories:

- To help children (usually affected by the way the candidate was or was not helped in school).
- Love of the subject or subjects being taught.
- To make sure pupils get good exam results, which will lead to good jobs and better standards of living. This is often linked to a social justice pedagogy to improve the lives of children who share their level of deprivation, race, ethnicity or gender.

What is missing from these answers is the satisfaction of the self which teaching gives. What other job gives you such variety, sense of life purpose, excitement and the good stress that challenges you every hour of every day? No two days are the same and the stories will build up about this pupil, this teacher, this meeting, this event. The scars will build up too, but they become medals of achievement as you went through it and came out the other side. One would-be teacher answered with this as a reason for wanting to teach: 'Because I love the buzz.' It was a memorable response and rare for a would-be teacher to recognise not only that there is an awful lot of fun to be had in the school building but also that there are self-interest reasons for wanting to be in there and take part in it. A milder version that we receive more commonly is to 'get that light bulb moment'. Here, there is recognition of the self-satisfaction of a job well done because a child has been helped to understand something they could not on their own. Having a strong sense of purpose is a major tool you can employ. You need to know what it is and track how it changes; be open to who you are, how you are thinking and feeling.

CONCLUSION

All pedagogies are principled. We may not like them, but they come from a standpoint that believes in something. Your principles may not be ours and we both may not share those of the government or your school. Understanding the prismatic nature of beliefs, ethos and standpoints is important, as is the ability to reflect on what we are being asked to do and why. The key is not so much that you have this or that pedagogy, but that you know what it is and why you have it. This is the drive that will sustain you on a day-to-day and year-to-year basis, and it may even change over time. W.H. Auden, poet and teacher in Malvern for three years (The Downs, n.d.), advised that we watch the eyes of those who are dedicated to their professions to see their drive and fire. Teaching is often all-consuming, but what a pleasure it is to be in a job that engages the whole being in a purpose.

> ## REFLECTIONS ON PRINCIPLED PRACTICE
>
> Principled practice means that you have an ethos or moral drive that runs your desire to teach. Take some time to articulate what this is to yourself. This is something that needs true reflective practice, so examine and cross-examine the idea and see if there is a central reason you can find.

> ## ACTION
>
> - Listen to teachers talk about their drives and get a sense of how passions for the profession come in many guises.

REFLECTION-ON-ACTION BY A TRAINING TEACHER

Dan Bevan reflects on an incident that happened in their lesson and how, through a process of critical reflection, they examined possible reasons for a pupil's actions.

> When I was first alerted to this disruption, I was discussing feedback one-to-one with another pupil at the other side of the classroom. When I asked Pupil A what their issue was, the response was 'I don't know what to do'. I presumed that this meant that the pupil had not understood the task and proceeded to re-explain the task. Pupil A then became

bad tempered, questioning why I had highlighted wrongly spelt words and misused punctuation, and arguing that these were not errors. In an attempt to pacify the pupil, I explained the errors to them and encouraged them to continue to make corrections and respond to the rest of the feedback. The pupil made no attempt to complete the task while I was stood by, therefore I told the pupil that I would give them some time to think it through and read back their work and I would check on them in five minutes. As soon as I had turned my back the pupil was clearly disgruntled and hardly participated. When marking Pupil A's work from this lesson the work produced was not up to their usual standard and it was clear that this incident early in the lesson had had a detrimental effect on the rest of the involvement in the lesson, both written and verbally. In a report published by Department for Education, Mark Cameron (2019, p. 2) categorises behaviour into five channels: 'Aggressive behaviour … physically disruptive behaviour … socially disruptive behaviour … authority-challenging behaviour… self-disruptive behaviour'. The behaviour of Pupil A detailed previously would be tenuously categorised as authority-challenging behaviour, what the Education Standards Analysis (2012, p. 9) report, *Pupil behaviour in schools in England* (2012) defined as 'refusing to carry out requests, exhibiting defiant verbal and non-verbal behaviour, using pejorative language'.

Being in year 7, Pupil A had only spent two full months at secondary school and would have still been experiencing the effects of the primary to secondary transition period. 'The transition from primary to secondary school in the UK, and its equivalent elsewhere, has been depicted … as one of the most difficult in pupils' educational careers' (Zeedyk, et al., 2003, p. 63). The assessment carried out by this group was the second assessment that they had completed in secondary school, meaning this way of working and delivery of feedback remained very new to them. It is possible that this is the first time Pupil A had received any detailed, written feedback that outlines successes, areas for concern and how this could be rectified. As opposed to an act of defiance, Pupil A not completing the task could have been a result of feeling overwhelmed and not knowing where to begin with making corrections.

The very nature of this assessment was different to the previous lessons delivered to this group. The idea that summative assessment has no conceivable meaning to pupils at this level is understandable and poses the question: what is at stake? In lessons prior to the assessment pupils were practising new skills and honing previously acquired skills with the motivation of producing a better plan – a plan that would be used for their assessment. Comprehensively, this means that there is a purpose to both the learning of new skills and the writing of a plan. However, the writing of the assessment itself outwardly has no purpose for pupils. As a trainee functioning in a highly data motivated system, summative assessment is vital as it provides that all-important grade. For a year 7 pupil, their final GCSE grade has no worth at present, meaning that there is little to no point justifying the reason for the assessment with a grade. Summative assessments are standalone entities which often have no link to work done previously nor work that will be done in the future; this means that a pupil may find great difficulty in understanding the purpose of summative assessment as they are unable to link the assessment to prior knowledge or recent learning.

Daisy Christodoulou, former secondary teacher, stated that feedback 'needs to be precise, so I think it needs to hone in on a specific thing that people have misunderstood … students need to understand it, they have to be able to take an action in response to it, and it has to be precise' (Hendrick & Macpherson, 2017, pp. 28-29). Had Pupil A's feedback not been a generalised comment, but a target improvement with a directed success criterion they may not have been demotivated and reluctant to participate in this and subsequent tasks. It is worth, though, considering the added time to and intensification of workload that marking of this detail and depth would generate. The feedback was delivered a week later in period one, meaning that not only was the pupil given enough time to build up their own assumption based around the feedback but the first thing that was presented to them on that day was feedback on a summative assessment. However, due to the workload of teachers, feedback is often delivered at the earliest point possible. At the time of marking this assessment I also had another group's assessment to mark meaning that the delivery of this feedback (one week later) was the fastest turnaround that I was able to achieve.

Continuing with this focus it is highly possible that Pupil A had completed the assessment itself with an air of negativity due to the purpose of the task being unclear. While this was not made common knowledge, it was clear that the reasoning behind this level of summative assessment was to assess pupils early on in a topic, record what would be a relatively low grade and then assess pupils again when they had received the full teaching of the topic in order to show progress. It has been noticed that 'in recent years there has been increasing interest in the idea that assessment might be used to improve the process of education, rather than simply evaluating its results' (Wiliam, 2014, p.1). This is in line with Wiliam's (2006, p.2) idea that 'much of the feedback that students receive has, at best, no impact on learning, and can actually be counter-productive'. Kohn adds to this: 'never grade students while they are still learning' (Kohn, 1994). Assessing pupils before they have completed the learning of a topic can be damaging to a pupil's confidence; there is no benefit in telling a pupil that they are not working at the level that they should be working at when the teaching has finished. Kohn (1994) continues to state that teachers should 'never grade on a curve. The number of good grades should not be artificially limited so that one student's success makes another's less likely'. However, during my placement I was encouraged to mark what was expected to be the highest achieving pupil's book and the lowest to set a benchmark. Pupil A was a low prior attainer and I expected his grade to be nearer to the bottom of the range, I was correct in making this prediction.

It is possible that Pupil A responded in the way they did because of a poorly timed assessment. Was the pupil ready to be assessed on the topic? Had the appropriate teaching for the assessment been delivered?

WHAT TOOLS ARE IN YOUR TOOLKIT NOW?

- Awareness that teachers move into the profession and maintain their position from the driving force of pedagogy.
- Awareness that pedagogy needs to be examined and nurtured through the year as it will keep motivation and momentum going when energy levels are low.
- Awareness that your pedagogy is not the only one and there needs to be an understanding of what drives the government's education policy and the pressures that schools are under to fulfil the given requirements.

PLACES TO GET MORE TOOLS FOR YOUR TOOLKIT

Freire, P. (1970) *Pedagogy of the Oppressed*. New York: Herder and Herder.

Old-style pedagogy from a thinker from another age, which still resonates with teachers today who want to think about what learning really is.

Holt, J. (1967) *How Children Learn*. London: Penguin.

American commentator whose pedagogy was a voice for a free-er education system. It didn't quite happen this way, but that does not mean it should not have done and perhaps one day it will.

hooks, b. (1994) *Teaching to Transgress*. London: Routledge

Radical in the best possible way, bell hooks, from their lower case and non-gendered name onwards, reminds us of the need to think about gender, race and the forces that can dominate education.

Robinson, K. (2022) *Imagine If* .... London: Penguin

Imagine if Ken Robinson had been responsible for the direction of UK education. Robinson gives a call to think about thinking skills and creativity rather than memory and repetition.

REFERENCES

Amadae, S. (2015) *Prisoners of Reason*. Cambridge: Cambridge University Press.

Apple, M. (2004) *Ideology and Curriculum* (3rd edn). London: Routledge.

Ball, S. (2003). The teacher's soul and the terrors of performativity. *Journal of Education Policy*, *18*(2), 215–228.

Bauman, Z. (2000) *Liquid Modernity*. Cambridge: Polity Press.

Baudrillard, J. (1976) *Symbolic Exchange and Death*. London: Sage.

Beck, U. (1992) *Risk Society: Towards a New Modernity*. London: Sage.

Bell, D. (1976) *The Coming of Post-industrial Society*. London: Penguin

Clarke, M. (2013) 'Terror/enjoyment: performativity, resistance and the teacher's psyche', *London Review of Education*, 11 (3): 229–38.

The Downs (n.d.) '*About the Downs: History of the School*'. Available from: www.thedownsmalvern. org.uk/about-the-downs/history-of-the-school.html

Fukuyama, F. (2020) *The End of History and the Last Man*. London: Penguin.

Jameson, F. (1991) *Postmodernism, or, the Cultural Logic of Late Capitalism*. Durham, NC: Duke University Press.

Long, R. and Danechi, S. (2022) '*Teacher recruitment and retention in England*'. Available from: https://commonslibrary.parliament.uk/research-briefings/cbp-7222/

Lyotard, J. (1984) *The Postmodern Condition*. Minneapolis, MN: University of Minnesota Press.

National Education Union (2022) '*State of education: The profession*'. Available from: https://neu.org.uk/press-releases/state-education-profession

Perryman, J. and Calvert, G. (2019). *What Motivates People to Teach, and Why Do They Leave? Accountability, performativity and teacher retention*. Available from: https://discovery.ucl.ac.uk/id/eprint/10068733/3/Perryman_Teachers%20Leaving%20revised%20final.pdf

SecEd (2020) *'Part-time working in the secondary school'*. Available from: www.sec-ed.co.uk/best-practice/part-time-working-in-the-secondary-school-flexible-working-nfer-retention-recruitment-teachers/

Smith, A. (1827) *The Wealth of Nations*. London: Thomas Nelson & Son.

Steiner, R. (1910) *The Way of Initiation*. Available from: www.gutenberg.org/files/39986/39986-h/39986-h.htm

Toffler, A. (1970) *Futureshock*. New York: Random House.

Von Goethe, J. W. (1994) *Elective Affinities*. Oxford: Oxford University Press.

CONCLUSION AND WHAT NEXT?

WHAT THIS CHAPTER WILL COVER

- Job interviews and applications
- Early career teacher
- Teacher

INTRODUCTION

Standing in a foot of water in a cellar with a screwdriver in one hand and a torch in the other, trying to fix an electric light, one of us had a timely reminder of the ancient advice to practitioners of medicine: 'First, do no harm.' In teaching, your first responsibility is to ensure the safety of children and the second is to yourself. Make sure that you are coping and doing no damage to your mental and physical health. This book has tried to give you the tools of safety. These include support, advice and positioning you in a community of training teachers through their reflections to let you know that you are not alone in your quest nor in the troubles and triumphs you have found.

John Gray's (1992) book *Men are from Mars, Women are from Venus* highlights that responding to emotional problems with solutions is rarely helpful. Gray proposes – with wild simplification – that one difference in the genders is that women want understanding, but men give solutions. A problem with solutions is that if the person receiving the advice or instruction either refuses to do it or does it badly, the initial problem becomes their fault. If you had followed my advice, goes the twisted logic, you would not have this problem. In teaching, there is much advice like this: do this and it will work. If you do not do it and encounter problems in the classroom, it is because you acted in this way and if you do it and it does not work, then you are not doing it correctly. When managing behaviour, for example, is presented as a step-by-step guide to success and you try the steps but they do not work, the person giving the steps has such faith in them that it is your practice that is questioned. Actually, the steps do not work, or do not work for you, or with this class, or they would work for you and with this class at another time and day. This book has tried to make this point clear. There are tools for your toolkit but every 'job' is different and requires a particular skill at a particular time. We recommend that you become a 'thinking user of tools' like the training teachers whose reflections are presented in this book.

This chapter takes you into the next stages of your training. Should you complete this year successfully, you will still not have finished training. If you do not finish this year successfully, it should not stop you from trying again. Sometimes the timing is not right and/or the circumstances you find yourself in might be untenable and might not allow you to fulfil all that is required of you in such an intense and demanding year. There are no easy paths to what you really want to do and if it is teaching, persevere. Regardless of everything, we conclude, be kind to yourself.

JOB APPLICATIONS AND INTERVIEWS

The process for applying for a job may be forestalled by the school you are teaching at wanting to keep you – this is an expectation of the course (DfE, 2014). Some schools take on SD training teachers with a view to this being the start of a three-year process that they want to see through. This makes sense because in this first year, the school has expended so much time and effort on getting you ready for teaching that they may as well reap the benefit. If the school is not for you or you are not for them (which might be because they have a process of taking on a new SD training teacher each year), you will need to apply for a job. This can be done at any stage in the year, but there will be a surge of vacancies after 31 May. On this date, anyone who wishes to leave their teaching job and wants to be paid until the last possible day before the new term (31 August) gives three months' notice to terminate their contract. The school is only then legally able to advertise their post. In the days when the *Times Educational Supplement* (where most teaching jobs used to be advertised) was a physical object, it was hard to lift in mid-June, so full was it of teacher vacancies. Today there are multiple sites and the government has tried to simplify the process by offering a centralised online search engine. If you see a job you like on there, you will have to go through two stages: written application and interview day.

The first stage is application and this is the main way that the school wll assess whether you are the right person for the job. For most teaching posts, you will be required to complete an application form specific to the school and provide a supporting letter of application that includes a personal statement, which is the main way in which a shortlist is determined. CVs are not typically asked for, as the application form structures the key information needed. There are 'job specifications' and 'person specifications' for every job. You have to directly tell the school that you can do the job and are the person they need by informing them how you fulfil the job specifications. If they have an 'essential' specification for the person – for example, a degree in the teaching subject – and you do not have it, do not apply. There is a 'weeding out' process based on whether you fulfil these or not. Once you are sure that you fulfil the person specification, demonstrate that you have more to offer than others. We sit with training teachers with job application forms and ask them what they have done and their expressions are as blank as their forms. We ask: 'What have you achieved?' and again, we get the same blank looks. We then ask whether they have ever won anything or got an award and find out they were gymnastics champion of Great Britain, or something else, but they did not think it counted. Everything you have ever done counts, as it demonstrates your personal and professional skills. Use these experiences as evidence that you have fulfilled the person and job specifications. If you are reliable, tell them that you did not miss a day from your placement. If you are trustworthy, tell them that you were allowed to handle the cash from your job in accounts at a supermarket. If you are a good communicator, tell them that you won the debating competition at university. We advise training teachers to write their applications as a boxer would in a ring: each point made as to why they should be chosen is like another punch. Given an award for being such a dedicated training teacher? Pow! Student representative on the PGCE? Pow! Taught in Dubai for three years before coming to train in the UK? Pow!

In the interview, do not presume that the panel members have read the form – it was used to get you there and the panel often have it printed out in front of them on the day for the first time. There will be a list of achievements on this form and these should create the basis of the answers to their questions. If they ask how to deal with an unruly pupil, for example, relate how as a manager of a shop you not only had to deal with the pupils from the local school but their parents (pow!) and as a teaching assistant this was a main role in some classes (pow!) and how you got called 'outstanding' for the way you dealt with the behaviour in a classroom by the head of your subject (knockout!). In this way, you are ready for questions because you already know what you want to include in your answers.

Another piece of advice we can give is to try to answer in threes. You will see in the example above that one point followed another, then another and by the third, it was convincing. Four or five would wear them out, but three is a magic number in rhetoric:

'Friends, Romans, countrymen' (William Shakespeare, c. 1599)

'We cannot dedicate, we cannot consecrate, we cannot hallow this ground' (Abraham Lincoln, 1863)

Prepare three-point answers for the following questions:

- What qualities can you bring to the school and department?
- What are your strengths and weaknesses as a teacher?
- Describe the worst or best lesson and state why it was or was not successful and what you would do differently.
- How do you assess or ensure the progress of pupils in your subject?
- If we visited your classroom, what could we expect to see?
- Where do you see yourself in five years?

For the question about weaknesses, rather than telling them you spend your weekends playing on computer games in your pyjamas eating crisps, take a key area of practice that you would like to develop – but don't be too self-critical. So, perhaps you need to broaden the range of the subject topics being taught or to have more opportunities to work with more challenging pupils as experience to date has been limited. The question about where you see yourself in five years' time, we have been asked many times. The first time, one of us recalls thinking: 'I haven't planned my weekend, yet.' The second time, we thought: 'Not here!' In the end, the more interviews we did, the better we got at answering questions. So, we learned not to reply that we wanted to be head of department and therefore take over the job of the person who was interviewing us, but that we would be looking to: 1) take responsibility for an aspect of the curriculum; 2) be responsible for a thriving after-school club, but above all, 3) keep improving as a teacher in the classroom.

On the interview panel, there may be a representative from Human Resources (and yes, sadly, that is all we are in employment, a resource that happens to be human). There will probably be a member of the Senior Leadership Team (SLT) and someone from your subject area – probably the head of subject. Each will have a particular question to ask related to their area of responsibility. There will also probably be someone from the Special Educational Needs and Disabilities team as well. There will almost certainly be a question relating to safeguarding of pupils, so it is worth rereading *Keeping Children Safe in Education* (DfE, 2022) to remind yourself of your responsibilities. There may be a governor who brings outside expertise and is concerned with the running and reputation of the school.

Job interviews have to be transparent and equitable, so the same questions are asked to all candidates in the same manner. If you are not the first to go in, you may even get a 'heads-up' on the questions being asked. There is often a number system to rate the answers you give (numbered in case there is a legal challenge and there is an accusation of discrimination), so make each answer detailed. On being questioned, take your time before answering. Even if you know the answer, pause, or they will know you are giving pre-prepared answers. Realise that in stressful situations, your mind goes faster, as does your voice, so you have to consciously slow down as the other person is writing down your response. It is hard to control voice speed, so consciously breathe at the end of sentences to allow the panel to catch up and write down your answer. When you get a question, pause, think, look at the questioner, answer. Look at your questioner only. One of us was at a school interview with 11 people, did not know this strategy and ended up with neck-ache as well as no job.

From our experience of being interviewers, if anyone shows reluctance to do any aspect of the job (or all of it!), it sets off 'warning bells' and these are usually attended to in the final decision. If you want the job, 'don't look down' is our advice. Always be positive about the job and communicate that you want it. One strategy is to look the panel members in the eyes when they ask if there are any more questions, and tell them how much you hope to work at the school. A clear message that this is the school for you cannot guarantee the job, but it sends a powerful signal to those who have to choose. All the candidates you are up against are as qualified as you or they would not be there; the school would employ all of you. To an extent, if there are six people for an interview, then the odds are the same as rolling a dice and hoping for a three. It is worth remembering that if you get rejection after rejection, you have to do six until the odds are with you. In the past, we have listened to feedback as to why we did not get a position and it has included that we could have made the panel laugh as we were too serious (what did they want us to do, fall off the chair?) and that we looked too young at the time (what could we do, wear a false beard?). In other words, there was no good reason, but the chosen person just had something extra that they were looking for. One question you will probably be asked is: 'If we offered you the job would you take it?' Your answer (unless you are convinced otherwise) has to be a fulsome 'yes'. Even feign surprise that you might say 'no', if you are a good actor. This is how they make sure you want the job. If you do not want the job, you can put your reservations in here – and you might as well do so. It will probably mean the end of the road, but is worth it, if you would only take the job if the salary was raised or conditions clear. One of us deliberately tried to fail an interview in this manner by telling the panel that they would accept the job on these conditions: no cover duty and no break-time supervision. To our surprise, the school acceded to these and on shaking hands, sensing our misgivings, reminded us that 'a verbal contract is binding'. As for this, there is a good saying: 'verbal contracts are not worth the paper they are not written on'.

We have sometimes been contacted by training teachers who have accepted a job and wanted to see if they could get out of it. Our advice is always to go through with the position on legal and moral grounds. The training teacher does not always heed by this, which is fair enough as we are not the ones who would have to go in and work there. The school could take legal action against the training teacher (and vice versa if a school withdraws a verbal contract), but we have not experienced them doing so. It is not good publicity if they are suing a training teacher, as it advertises that some-one does not want to work there and costs money they do not have. We have also witnessed schools threaten and withdraw job offers to training teachers. There are veiled or explicit (always delivered orally so they can be denied) threats to take away a job offer if the training teacher does not do this or that. One of our training teachers walked away from both a placement and a job as the school told them that if they did not work in the half-term holidays, they would rescind both. Realising the kind of school they would be subjecting themself to, they made the brave decision to quit and completed the course during the following year. If you find yourself in this situation, we would advise that you approach the head teacher honestly and apologetically, and state the reasons why you have doubts about accepting a job. In some cases, we have known this to provide both parties an amicable way out, but it is likely to mean that you will not be selected for any future post in the school for as long as the head teacher's memory lasts.

For all that, if there are six people at an interview, the chances are 6:1 that we are on the other side of the interview process and know that in an interview there is a 'preferred candidate', a back-up and what might be called 'an outside chance'. We write this fully realising that we have been 'an outside chance' many times in the past. In one interview one of us went to, we noticed the other candidate came out of an office next door so was already working there and going for a more permanent position; we even recall that they were wearing slippers, but this is probably the result of an uncomfortable dream, as interviews often end up seeming to be. You must persevere on the interview circuit no matter how demoralising it is. On the third interview of the same week, one of us was at a school with five other candidates. The day had started in reception at 8.30 am, there had been an interview, a lesson to teach, lunch with the staff, awkward conversations in the staffroom and a second round of interviews. At 6 pm, the head teacher said: 'We cannot decide, but you can go'. At this, point one of us had to trudge out of the room while the other 5 stayed. Next week, two jobs were offered on the same day. Hang on in there and do not take the interview process personally.

You will most likely be asked to teach a sample lesson to pupils, in which case, the criteria by Rosenshine (2012) give you a guide as to what they will be looking for:

1   Introduce topics or activities clearly.
2   Explain clearly with examples and illustrative materials.
3   Systematic and business-like organisation of lessons.
4   Variety of teaching materials and methods.
5   Use of questions, especially higher-order questions.
6   Use of praise and other reinforcement (verbal and non-verbal).
7   Encourage learner participation.
8   Make use of learners' ideas, clarifying and developing them further.
9   Warmth, rapport and enthusiasm, mainly shown non-verbally.

The pupils you teach will be involved in the decision, so be warm and friendly, and try to learn some names quickly. You might do this with name stickers at the start (although they may invent all kinds of names) so, perhaps, ask for a class list of names and then use this. If you have any details of their circumstances, focus a question based on this. For example, if you find 'Pupil Premium' next to a name, you could ask this person a question first. In the interview, the panel are likely to ask you what you did well and not so well in the lesson and you can mention such explicit acts. Teaching is a hard task and harder when you do not know the prior knowledge of the class and are being watched and judged. At the same time, a school is not going to choose a difficult class as this would put the candidate off, and there are enough teachers and managers in the room to ensure an orderly environment so you can get on and teach. Adapt a lesson you have done successfully before and, as with all teaching, try to avoid over-reliance on visual presentation or technology, which can always go wrong. Presume the technology will go wrong and have an analogue back-up plan which does not rely on computers and screens.

On dealing with interview nerves, some advice we have read about is to think of the panel as toothbrushes, naked or in underwear, but we are not quite convinced that this advice helps, especially as it may affect your facial expression when you look at them. For nerves, do not catastrophise. This school is not the only one. If you do not get the job, you had nothing to lose. Your aunty will more than likely still be able to have her hip operation if you do not get the job and everyone will still love you the same. You can walk out of that interview at any time and, if you do so politely, with no consequences. The more you build up a job to be 'the one' for you, the less likely you are to get it, as desperation is never an appealing quality. Go in, give it your best shot and if you get it, you get it. If not, act graciously and thank them for the experience and move on to your next interview. To paraphrase F. Scott Fitzgerald, the best revenge is always to live well. Go to your next school and give them the benefit of your dedication and skill. On this point, never say the 'yes' you do not mean. If you do not like the school, withdraw. It is your decision as much as theirs, and you choose them as much as they choose you. There are other jobs and other schools, and this one is just another possibility.

EARLY CAREER TEACHER

Once QTS has been awarded and you have been successful in finding a teaching job, you will become an ECT – Early Career Teacher. This title replaced the old ones of NQT (Newly Qualified Teacher in the first year of teaching) and RQT (Recently Qualified Teacher in the second year of teaching), so at least being an ECT reduces the amount of initialisms that teachers have to call themselves. The Early Career Framework (another initialism, ECF) launched in September 2021 (DfE, 2021a) made the induction, or probation, period a two-year process and formalised a training programme for new teachers in schools. This meant a mindshift in the way that early teachers were to be seen – not as a finished article by the award of QTS, but a third of the way through training. The SD course merely acts as a first year out of three and should be seen as a formative stage towards becoming a full teaching professional. You have to start as an ECT at a school which is set up to run the induction programme, undergo further training, and be judged against the *Teachers' Standards* at certain intervals. After two years, the Teaching Regulation Agency will be informed that you have successfully completed the induction period. If you do not successfully complete this, then you will no longer be able to act as a qualified teacher in local authority maintained schools. The DfE have stated that: 'Statutory induction is not a legal requirement to teach in FE or the independent sector, academies, free schools' (DfE, 2021b).

As most secondary schools are academies or free schools, in theory it makes no difference, but in practice, they are unlikely to employ you without both QTS and completion of the induction period (or in the process of so doing). You cannot fail your ECT years, you just do not satisfactorily complete the induction period. There is no time limit on when you have to do the two years and you can work in a school without starting the process. If you find yourself struggling, you can move schools during the process – be proactive in checking your progress and be ready to move and get advice from a union if it is not going well.

The ECF might be delivered by a select group of companies or in-house, or in a lead school which your employer may be affiliated to. The courses are directly funded by the DfE and cover the following topics:

- behaviour management
- pedagogy
- curriculum
- assessment
- professional behaviours.

In terms of subject content, The ECF is pretty much the same as the CCF, based on the *Teachers' Standards* and prescriptive about necessary reading and approaches to teaching. There is a consistent message between the two as the Education Endowment Foundation was behind both documents. Schools now take on first-year teachers as training teachers, effectively meaning that the process is more gradual and should be less stressful in the first year.

TEACHER

It takes a long time and a lot of work to achieve the status of 'teacher'. Two years' worth of additional training at the end of the School Direct course course and you will be equipped with the qualities of perseverance, bravery, initiative, work ethic, reliability, trustworthiness, dedication and every other positive adjective there is. Today's employment world calls on us to be: 'entrepreneurs of … self' (Foucault, 2008: 226). In this marketplace of portfolio careers (where you may be employed in a number of different jobs and can package them up by the qualities they share), we are very much our own projects and the qualities which being a teacher instils are valuable in all jobs.

You might be thinking about career progression when you have completed the ECT years. There are two main career pathways in teaching: pastoral leadership and subject leadership. Beyond these, there will also be opportunities to take on whole-school leadership work for particular areas of work, Special Educational Needs Coordinator (SENCo), coordinating enrichment activities, leading on 'stretch and challenge'. We have even known a school appoint a 'Director of Fun' to improve the well-being and morale of pupils and staff. Imagine that as your job title! We would encourage you to explore what is involved in these areas of work through staff-room conversations and work shadowing to find out the route you prefer. You can also offer to assist in these roles – on an unpaid basis of course – to gain useful experience for your next steps. You might also find it reinvigorating to move to new types of school or new education sectors. We both made the move into the university sector and found this change the best way to keep doing what we love – teaching – but in a new sector with new challenges. You can also create a fulfilling career without any formal responsibility roles, and there are currently progression options that come from demonstrating excellence in classroom teaching that access upper pay spines. Teaching remains a fulfilling career for as long as it sustains and rewards you. Seek out your niche in this world, and well done on taking this first leap.

ACTIONS

- Be kind to yourself: you are doing your best, and being a great teacher.
- Be a great teacher.
- Do your best.
- Be kind to yourself.

REFERENCES

Churchill, W. (1940) *'Speech to Cabinet'*, 10 May. Available from: https://winstonchurchill.org/resources/speeches/1940-the-finest-hour/blood-toil-tears-sweat/

DfE (2014) *National Curriculum in England: Framework for Key Stages 1 to 4*. Available from: www.gov.uk/government/publications/national-curriculum-in-england-framework-for-key-stages-1-to-4

DfE (2021a) *Early Career Framework*. Available from: www.gov.uk/government/collections/early-career-framework-reforms

DfE (2021b) *Statutory Induction Guidance*. Available from: https://assets.publishing.service.gov.uk/government/uploads/system/uploads/attachment_data/file/972316/Statutory_Induction_Guidance_2021_final__002____1___1_.pdf

DfE (2022) *Keeping Children Safe in Education*. Available from: https://assets.publishing.service.gov.uk/government/uploads/system/uploads/attachment_data/file/1101454/Keeping_children_safe_in_education_2022.pdf

Foucault, M. (2008) *The Birth of Biopolitics: Lectures at the Collège de France, 1978–79*. New York: Palgrave Macmillan.

Gray, J. (1992) *Men are from Mars, Women are from Venus*. London: Harper Thorson.

Lincoln, A. (1863) *'Gettysburg address'*. Available from: https://www.loc.gov/exhibits/gettysburg-address/ext/trans-nicolay-inscribed.html

Rosenshine, B. (2012) *'Principles of instruction'*. Available from: www.aft.org/sites/default/files/periodicals/Rosenshine.pdf

Shakespeare, W. (*c*. 1599) *Julius Caesar*. Available from: https://shakespeare.folger.edu/shakespeares-works/julius-caesar/entire-play/

GLOSSARY

Apprenticeship School-based training route to Qualified Teacher Status, also known as PGTA.

Assessment for Learning Checking the knowledge, skills and understanding of pupils in the lesson.

Assessment Objective The desired learning knowledge, skills or understanding. The government create these for each subject and they inform the content of examinations.

Assessment of Learning A test or examination that allows the monitoring of pupils' current level of understanding, knowledge and skills.

Assessment only route A way to get Qualified Teacher Status without further study for those who have worked in schools for years.

Assessing Pupils' Progress A scheme run from 2008 to 2011 which broke down the skills, knowledge and understanding in core school subjects to specific stages with numbers and letters, in order to label the pupils with their level of progress.

Autism A neurological variation that affects communication and interaction.

Behaviourism A theory that human behaviour can be controlled by external forces.

Board of Education UK national governing body for schools from 1899 to 1944.

British values Set of personal qualities essential for teachers practising in British schools, including a belief in democracy, upholding the rule of law, promotion of individual liberty, and a tolerant attitude towards those with different faiths and beliefs.

Bursary Sum of money given to support education and training.

Carer An adult who is not the biological parent of a child but responsible for their maintenance and support.

Character education Focus on moral values and a positive learning attitude towards learning and others rather than academic success.

Cognitive Load Theory Theory of learning which states that brain development is optimised by ensuring that new knowledge is made accessible to the learner.

Cognitivism The branch of psychology that studies how humans learn, remember and think.

Coaching Practical form of mentoring that works to improve actions rather than understand the reasons and feelings involved.

Core Name used for university-led teacher training.

Core Content Framework	Framework given by the government to teacher training providers, around which they can design a curriculum for training teachers.
Credits	A university value that indicates how much teaching time and work is required for a part of a course.
Department for Children, Schools and Families	The name for the Department for Education from 2007 to 2010.
Department for Education	Current name for the government branch responsible for education.
Diagnostic assessment	Method of finding out what the current level of knowledge, skills and understanding is.
Differentiation	Changing the lesson content, pace and resources for individual pupils, including those with special needs.
Dyslexia	A neurological variation that affects the processing of language by the brain.
Dyscalculia	A neurological variation that affects the processing of numbers by the brain.
Early Career Framework	The curriculum that must be followed by training teachers during their first two years.
Education Act	Laws that are often updated and give the rules for schools, teachers, pupils and parents/carers.
Education Endowment Fund	Organisation that receives funds from the Department for Education for its work to improve the educational outcomes of children from lower income groups.
Education Reform Act	1988 law which introduced a National Curriculum and moved schools away from local authority control.
English as an Additional Language	Term used to describe children in UK schools whose first language is not English.
Equality Act	2010 law which makes it illegal for anyone to act in a discriminatory manner because of age, disability, gender reassignment, marriage and civil partnership, pregnancy and maternity, race, religion or belief, sex and sexual orientation.
Every Child Matters	Government initiative in the early 2000s to ensure individualised treatment of children in the classroom and multi-agency support for those who need it.
Extracurricular	Additional activities in school that are not part of the taught subjects.
Fixed mindset	Negative way of viewing learning as something that you can or cannot do naturally.
Formative assessment	Method of checking pupil learning during the lesson.
Forster Act	First UK laws requiring provision for, and attendance at school.
Gifted and talented	A term used in schools to define those with advanced academic or physical skills.
Growth mindset	A way of thinking about learning which sees attitude rather than results as a sign of success.
Humanism	Belief that people are thinking, moral, active beings who make their own choices based on individual reasoning.
Inclusion	All children learning together and being supported to allow equal progress.
Information Technology	Computer-based systems used to communicate.

Induction	The first two years of teaching which must be successfully completed or the teacher cannot be employed in local authority-run schools.
Keeping Children Safe in Education	Regularly updated policy guidance document for schools about safeguarding children.
Key Stage	Age range that determines which subjects, knowledge, skills and understanding will be taught and learnt in schools.
Level 7	Post-graduate academic standard which may lead to a Master's degree.
Literacy	The ability to read, write and speak with developed skills.
Looked-after child	A child who is in the care of the local authority, foster home, residential care or secure unit.
Maintenance loan	Money for living expenses which will eventually have to be paid back.
Master's degree	Qualification which is above and comes after an undergraduate or Bachelor's degree
Mastery	A mode of teaching which focuses on the teacher as the holder of knowledge and who makes sure every pupil understands the topics before moving to the next development point.
McNair Report	Government study into teacher training published in 1944.
NASUWT	Second largest teachers' union in the UK, the National Association of Schoolmasters and Union of Women Teachers.
National Curriculum	A set of subjects and standards that schools run by English local authorities must abide by.
Neoliberalism	Political, economic and social belief system that human behaviour should be given the conditions that allow them to pursue individualised goals, lifestyles and economic ends without state intervention or collective organisations.
NEU	Largest teachers' union in the UK, the National Education Union.
Neurodiverse	The recognition that differences in brain make-up are natural variations in how people think and act should be part of our understanding of being human.
Non-salaried	School Direct route into teaching that comes with tuition fees which can be paid for by a student loan – also known as Training.
Numeracy	The ability to understand how numbers can be used to solve problems and create understanding.
Ofsted	Department for Education-funded organisation which checks and regulates the quality of schools, colleges and teacher training organisations.
Pedagogy	Methods and practices of teaching.
PGCE	The academic part of a teacher training course.
Pitching	Changing the content, learning materials and approach to suit the age and prior achievement of the class.
Qualified Teacher Status	Position which shows that the legal standards to teach in local authority run schools have been met.
Regulatory	Controlling powers who use rules or laws.

Reflection	A rethinking process that takes the original thoughts and feelings about a situation or event and considers alternative positions.
Reflexivity	An in-the-moment ability to consider what is being thought and done and respond to a situation.
Refraction	The way an idea, policy, document, or instruction is reinterpreted by the teacher to fit their pedagogical views.
Salaried	School Direct route which has fees paid, payment for work and the legal status of an unqualified teacher.
Scaffolding	The process of making sure that new learning is accessible to pupils and fits their current level of understanding.
Schema	A model or visualisation of the way the brain organises knowledge and skills.
Secretary of State for Education	Government minister responsible for the Department for Education.
Special Education Needs and Disabilities	Term used as a catch-all for those who need additional support to access school and curriculum activities.
Spiral curriculum	Approach to teaching which introduces the topic at any level of complexity and then keeps returning to it with the view that reinforced ideas are gradually learnt.
Statutory	Required by law.
Stretch and challenge	Term used to describe learning activities that extend pupils' knowledge and skills beyond the expected level.
Summative assessment	Examination or test that can give a grade and allow a staged check on progress
Teach First	A teacher training provider set up to provide graduates with direct access to the classrooms of schools in economically deprived areas.
Teacher Regulation Agency	Department for Education run organisation which oversees the official registration of teachers and their right to practise.
Teacher Training Agency	Governing body for teacher training providers from 1994 to 2005 when it became the Training and Development Agency for Schools.
Teacher Training Provider	Organisation which has been given the legal right to guide training teachers through their initial year and gain Qualified Teacher Status.
Teachers' Standards	Set of legal requirements that teachers must fulfil to qualify and continue to practise as a professional.
The Pupil Premium	Funding provided to schools to give extra support for those from economically disadvantaged backgrounds.
Times Educational Supplement	Newspaper and online site dedicated to school matters.
Unqualified Teacher	Someone teaching in a school who does not have Qualified Teacher Status.

INITIALISMS AND ACRONYMS

ADHD	Attention Deficit Hyperactive Disorder
AfL	Assessment for Learning
AoL	Assessment of Learning
AO	Assessment Objective
APP	Assessing Pupils' Progress
AQA	Assessment and Qualifications Alliance
ASD	Autistic Spectrum Disorder
BBC	British Broadcasting Corporation
BICS	Basic Interpersonal Communicative Skills
CCF	Core Content Framework
CMA	Competitions and Markets Authority
CALP	Cognitive and Academic Language Proficiency
CRE	Commission for Racial Equality
CPD	Continuing Professional Development
CRE	Commission for Racial Equality
DARTS	Directed Activities Related to Texts
DfE	Department for Education
DfEE	Department for Employment and Education
DfES	Department for Education and Skills
EAL	English as an Additional Language
ECF	Early Career Framework
ECT	Early Career Teacher
EEF	Education Endowment Foundation
G&T	Gifted and Talented
GCSE	General Certificate in Secondary Education
GRT	Gypsy, Romany, Traveller
GTCE	General Teaching Council for England
GTCS	General Teaching Council for Scotland
GTP	Graduate Teacher Programme
HE	Higher Education
ICT	Information Communication Technology
IQ	Intelligence Quotient

IT	Information Technology
ITT	Initial Teacher Training
KCSiE	Keeping Children Safe in Education
LGBT	Lesbian, Gay, Bisexual and Transgender
MAT	Multi-academy Trust
NASUWT	National Association of Schoolmasters and Union of Women Teachers
NCETM	National Centre for Excellence in the Teaching of Mathematics
NEU	National Education Union
NQT	Newly Qualified Teacher
OECD	Organisation for Economic Co-operation and Development
OIA	Office of the Independent Adjudicator
Ofqual	Office for Qualifications
Ofsted	The Office for Standards in Education
PGCE	Postgraduate Certificate in Education
PGDE	Postgraduate Diploma in Education
PGTA	Postgraduate Teaching Apprenticeships
PISA	Programme of International Student Assessment
PP	Pupil Premium
PP+	Pupil Premium Plus
PRU	Pupil Referral Unit
QTS	Qualified Teacher Status
RSE	Relationship and Sex Education
RPI	Rules, Praise and Ignore
SCITT	School-centred Initial Teacher Training
SD	School Direct
SEMH	Social, Emotional and Mental Health
SENCo	Special Educational Needs Coordinator
SEND	Special Educational Needs and Disabilities
SKE	Subject Knowledge Enhancement
SLT	Senior Leadership Team
SMEH	Social, Emotional and Mental Health
SoW	Scheme of Work
SpLD	Specific Learning Difficulties
TA	Teaching Assistant
TDA	Training and Development Agency
TES	Times Educational Supplement
TRA	Teacher Regulation Agency
TTA	Teacher Training Agency
UCAS	Universities and Colleges Admissions Services
UNESCO	United Nation's Educational, Scientific and Cultural Organization
VLE	Virtual Learning Environment

INDEX